Macbeth

The fatal bellman. From *Macbeth*, edited by William J. Rolfe (New York: American Book Company, 1877)

MACBETH

A Guide to the Play

H. R. COURSEN

Greenwood Guides to Shakespeare

Greenwood Press
Westport, Connecticut • London

Library of Congress Cataloging-in-Publication Data

Coursen, Herbert R.
     Macbeth : a guide to the play / H. R. Coursen.
         p.   cm.—(Greenwood guides to Shakespeare, ISSN 1387–1422)
     Includes bibliographical references and index.
     ISBN 0–313–30047–X (alk. paper)
     1. Shakespeare, William, 1564–1616. Macbeth. 2. Macbeth, King of
Scotland, 11th cent.—In literature. 3. Shakespeare, William,
1564–1616—Stage history. 4. Shakespeare, William, 1564–1616—Film
and video adaptations. 5. Tragedy. I. Title. II. Series.
PR2823.C67   1997
822.3'3—dc21   96–49733

British Library Cataloguing in Publication Data is available.

Library of Congress Catalog Card Number: 96–49733
ISBN: 0–313–30047–X
ISSN: 1387–1422

First published in 1997

Greenwood Press, 88 Post Road West, Westport, CT 06881
An imprint of Greenwood Publishing Group, Inc.

Printed in the United States of America

∞

The paper used in this book complies with the
Permanent Paper Standard issued by the National
Information Standards Organization (Z39.48–1984).

10 9 8 7 6 5 4 3 2 1

Copyright Acknowledgments

Grateful acknowledgment is given for permission to reprint excerpts from the following:

Huston Diehl, "The Visual Rhetoric of *Macbeth*," and Robert A. Kimbrough, "Macbeth as Prisoner of Gender," *Shakespeare Studies* 16 (1983).

Peter Hall, "Interview," and Robin Grove, "Multiplying Villainies of Nature," in *Focus on Macbeth*, edited by John Russell Brown. London: Routledge and Kegan Paul, 1982.

Linda Cookson and Bryan Loughney, eds., *Macbeth: Longman Critical Essays*. London: Longman. Reprinted by permission of Addison Wesley Longman Ltd.

James Bulman, ed., *Shakespeare, Theory, and Performance*. London: Methuen/Routledge.

Shakespeare and the Classroom, "Review of *Shakespeare and the Moving Image*," vol. 3, no. 1: 27–31 and "Review of *Shakespeare, Theory, and Performance*," vol. 4, no. 1: 50–60.

CONTENTS

PREFACE

The purpose of this reference book is to provide a guide to *Macbeth* for both the student and the professional. Students can introduce themselves to the issues that have grown up around the play since the early seventeenth century. For the professional, this outline encourages further study and new insights as the play approaches its four-hundredth anniversary. The Scottish play continues to lend itself to newer critical paradigms—psychological, feminist, and postmodernist criticism, for example—and continues to be produced on stage in ways that demonstrate its remarkable versatility as play-text.

No brief study of any play by Shakespeare can be exhaustive. What follows is an outline that looks at the textual issues of the script and at the sources, with more analysis of *Antony and Cleopatra* than most. How can a play be indebted to one that undoubtedly *followed* it in the canon? A scene-by-scene analysis of the script suggests the issues that a stage production must resolve. Any discussion of the themes of the play insists that the religious background of the early sixteenth century be explored, since this play, more than any other in the canon, emerges from its theological context. This material is not difficult, but it must be outlined in some detail in light of the materialist attack on "essentialism."

This play, like others in the canon, raises some perplexing questions on which the critics can disagree but which performance must address on this side of John Keats's "negative capability," which "Shakespeare possessed so enormously." Keats defined it as "where a man is capable of being in uncertainties, mysteries, doubts, without any irritable reaching after fact and reason" (1817). As critics, we must make up our minds about the options that the scripts offer, perhaps because it is our own identity that is bound up in our response. We are like actors taking on a role and bringing our own experience to the role to complete it. A director in the theater must ask (and answer) questions such as: What do the Weird Sisters look like? Does Lady Macbeth faint in the scene in which the murder is "discovered"? Who is the Third Murderer? and Does Banquo's ghost appear at the banquet?

After the summary of the play's major actions, a discussion of its themes follows. Then major critical responses to the play are discussed; however, some omissions occur in this chapter since so much has been written about *Macbeth* that several volumes would be insufficient to include them all. I have, however, included current criticisms of the plays. Furthermore, while this guide is intended to be a systematic and objective reference work, no discussion of responses to this or any Shakespeare play can be neutral. I do not apologize for debating with some of the views I summarize. I have tried to give various points of view a fair hearing, and readers of this book are encouraged, as with any reference work, to examine the works and the critical paradigms outlined here. Citations for all material I quote will permit an interested person to read further into specific areas.

Finally, I look at the play as it has appeared on stage, film, and television with an emphasis on recent productions of the play that I have seen. A selected bibliography concludes the work.

Work Cited

Keats, John. 1817. Letter to George and Tom Keats, December 1817. In *The Letters of John Keats*. Edited by Hyder E. Rollins. Cambridge, Mass.: Harvard University Press, 1958.

1

TEXTUAL HISTORY

The textual issue of *Macbeth* is straightforward. *Hamlet* has a Second Quarto widely at variance with the First Folio version and a "Bad Quarto" that has been drawing increasing attention recently. *King Lear* has Quarto and Folio versions that are often different plays. *Macbeth*, however, appears only in First Folio. The text is marred by interpolations in the Hecate scenes (3.5 and 4.1: 39–93, 125–32. New Arden numbering). These additions, which Kenneth Muir speculates (1964, xxxiii–xxxvi) were made between 1611 (the date of Simon Forman's attendance at a production of *Macbeth*) and 1623 (the date of the First Folio), are usually cut in production but are invariably included in editions of the play because of the authority of the First Folio. The Hecate speeches are in iambic, as opposed to the trochaic which Shakespeare usually assigns to his supernatural creatures. An occasional production, like that at the National Theatre in 1978 with Albert Finney and Dorothy Tutin or the ACTER (A Center for Theater Research) version of 1996, retains the Hecate scenes.

The Folio text is so short that some scholars, notably John Dover Wilson (1947), have suggested that scenes were cut from the inherited version—for example, Macbeth's coronation, Banquo's unequivocal declaration that he does not acquiesce in Macbeth's crimes, an explanation and identification of the Third Murderer, a scene in which Macduff explains to his wife why he is leaving for England, and so on. As Muir wisely argues, "The play would greatly suffer from any one of these additions" (1964, xxiii). The play comes at us in lurid flashes, a version of montage where the whole is greater than the parts and in which some questions remain for actors and directors to answer. Inasmuch as both Macbeth and Lady Macbeth attempt to subvert the laws of the universe in which they live, the whole is invariably larger than any actions they take. *Macbeth* is not existential drama, and Shakespeare keeps telling us that there is much more "in heaven and earth" than is dreamt of in their human wills, certainly much more than the content of "these terrible dreams that shake us nightly."

G. K. Hunter says of Hecate, "Not only do the Hecat lines *sound* different; they refer to a different relationship between Macbeth and the Witches" (1994, 819). Peter Hall, who has ever been a stickler for fidelity to the inherited text, defends Hecate: "She gives metaphorical presence to God or, rather, anti-God" (quoted in Brown 1982, 242), partly because, as Hall says, "one has to accept the authenticity of Folio text" (243). Hecate's appearance in 3.5, says Hall, is "a deliberately and theatrically exciting contrast" (243). With an eye and an ear for dramatic values, Bernice W. Kliman argues that if original versions of the play included the Hecate scenes, "Shakespeare's production avoided the unified greyness and tone of modern productions" (quoted in Brown 1982, 17). Some scholars dismiss the notion of "an authentic text," accepting "Shakespeare" as a term that incorporates a lot of collaboration (Orgel 1988; Bristol 1990). On the authenticity of the Hecate scenes, see J. M. Nosworthy (1965) and G. Wilson Knight (1953, 326–32). See also J. R. Brown's spirited but, I think, unconvincing case for Hecate (1963, 11–13).

The play reverberates with the unexploded charge of the Gunpowder Plot of November 1605 and specifically with allusions to the trial of the Jesuit, Henry Garnet (28 March 1606). I agree with Henry N. Paul who argues (1950, 37) that the last two acts of the play were written after the enactment of the Profanity Statutes (27 May 1606), which prohibited the use of specific names like Jesus and God on stage. The play was probably presented at court in the summer of 1606 for the entertainment of King James's brother-in-law, Christian IV of Denmark. A court presentation, which would have been part of banqueting and other formalities, would of necessity have been short. A short production would also have coincided with King James's well-known dislike of long plays. There is no doubt from the allusions we find in *Macbeth* that Shakespeare was doing the research for *Antony and Cleopatra*. Gary Wills argues (1995, 103–5) for a later date with a performance at Christmas 1606, seven months after Garnet's execution. J. L. Barroll says that the theaters were closed by plague after June 1606 (1991, 148–49). If so, a court performance would still have been possible.

Works Cited

Barroll, J. Leeds. 1991. *Politics, Plague, and Shakespeare's Theater*. Ithaca, N.Y.: Cornell University Press.

Bristol, Michael. 1990. *Shakespeare's America, America's Shakespeare*. London: Routledge.

Brown, John Russell, ed. 1963. *Macbeth*. Great Neck, N.Y.: Barron's.

———, ed. 1982. *Focus on 'Macbeth.'* London: Routledge and Kegan Paul.

Hunter, G. K., ed. 1994. *Four Tragedies*. London: Penguin.

Knight, G. Wilson. 1953. *The Shakespearean Tempest*. London: Metheun.

Muir, Kenneth, ed. 1964. *Macbeth*. London: Metheun.

Nosworthy, J. M. 1965. *Shakespeare's Occasional Plays: Their Origin and Transmission*. New York: Barnes and Noble.

Orgel, Stephen. 1988. "The Authentic Shakespeare." *Representations* 21: 1–25.

Paul, Henry N. 1950. *The Royal Play of Macbeth*. New York: Macmillan.
Wills, Gary. 1995. *Witches and Jesuits*. Oxford: Oxford University Press.
Wilson, J. Dover, ed. 1947. *Macbeth*. Cambridge: Cambridge University Press.

DIFFERENT EDITIONS

Most modern texts contain introductions of varying degrees of value and an edited modern version of the text. I quote useful insights from several introductions in the survey of criticism presented below. To keep up with the proliferation of texts of one of the most frequently taught plays is impossible. Some of the modern texts mentioned below may be out of print, and others may have been superseded by revisions. I make no claims for inclusiveness, nor are these comments intended as recommendations. I find it surprising how often obscure editions turn up in the hands of students.

The Blackfriars edition, edited by R. W. Dent (Wm. C. Brown, Dubuque, Iowa) contains brief essays on Shakespeare's life, times, and language. The notable feature of this folio-size edition is the room in the right-hand margins of the text left for notes for academic purposes or for blocking a production.

The Bantam edition, edited by O. J. Campbell, Alfred Rothschild, and Stuart Vaughan (Bantam Books, New York), contains a glossary, extensive and usefully speculative notes, a chapter on Shakespeare's life and times by Campbell, and a chapter on Shakespeare's theater by Vaughan. According to Vaughan, "The plays are as related to the theater of Shakespeare's day as a shooting script is to modern film techniques. The structural evolution of that theater, and the way it was used, profoundly influenced the nature of the plays themselves" (1961, 15). The text contains more complete stage directions than most editions. For the banquet scene, for example, "Macbeth conducts Lady Macbeth to the throne. She seats herself but Macbeth remains standing" (65) and later, "descending from her throne . . . she draws Macbeth aside" (68). This edition includes brief critical commentaries by William Hazlitt, J. H. Siddons, Thomas De Quincey, Edward Dowden, A. C. Bradley, Lascelles Abercrombie, J. Q. Adams, Caroline Spurgeon, and H. B. Charlton.

The Folger edition (Washington Square, New York) has been revised and updated under the editorship of Barbara Mowat and Paul Werstein. This edition contains chapters on Shakespeare's language, life, theater, and the publication of his plays. It continues to have very useful notes and an occasional illustration on the left-hand page facing the text. It contains a good chapter by Susan Snyder, which I will cite later, and brief notations of other mostly recent criticism, so that little sense of the critical history of this play is conveyed. The binding seems to be more durable than it was on previous Folger editions, which tended to become collections of unattached pages.

The Oxford School edition, edited by Roma Gill, contains text and notes in facing columns of the same page. The notes, appearing in smaller type on the left-hand one-third of each page, include notes on the sources, a summary of the play, an essay on Macbeth as character, other brief background materials, exam questions, and activities, some of which are silly, such as: "Give full TV coverage for the murder of Duncan—don't forget to interview the Porter and the Old Man, and to check the weather reports for that night. If possible, arrange that there should be signing for deaf people" (1993, 97). The text includes drawings by Coral Mula, including a mousing owl about to knock down a falcon.

The Cambridge School edition, edited by Rex Gibson, contains text on the right-hand page and notes, illustrations, and suggested activities on the left. Unfortunately, not all of the photographs from productions are completely identified (Olivier and Leigh on page 76, for example). The activities are based on decisions for production: "Work out how, in your own production, you would stage the approach of the camouflaged army" (1993, 142). The edition includes brief notations on meanings, themes, images, history, witchcraft, language, and staging. The text is that of A. R. Braunmuller, which follows the Folio more closely than most modernized texts.

The Kittredge version (Ginn and Company, Boston) has a solid introduction by the great Harvard scholar and very useful notes at the end of the edition. Of the Messenger who says, "I say, a moving grove," Kittredge says, "Not every man could face Macbeth down in his present mood with a stout-hearted 'I say'" (1939, 224).

The New Penguin edition, edited by G. K. Hunter (Penguin, London; Viking Penguin, New York), includes a solid scholarly introduction by Hunter, notes on sources, and, at the end, the useful and complete notes on the text characteristic of this series, along with an account of the text.

The Pelican edition (Penguin Books, Baltimore), edited by Alfred Harbage, has brief and not particularly informative introductions on Shakespeare's life, stage, and text, as well as a good general introduction to the play by Harbage. The great virtue of the Pelican edition is its compactness.

The Laurel edition (Dell, New York), edited by Francis Fergusson, contains an introduction to the play written by the editor, a chapter on the play for a modern audience by Flora Robson, the text as edited by C. J. Sisson, a chapter by Fergusson on Shakespeare's life and theater, and a glossary by H. H. Smith. The advantage of this edition is the large and readable type of the text itself. Another factor that makes the text easy to read is that it is unencumbered by notes, which are always likely to lead a reader's eye away from the script itself.

The Signet edition (Penguin, London and New York), edited by Sylvan Barnet, contains an introduction about Shakespeare's life and times, selections from the sources, ample excerpts from critics (Dr. Johnson, A. C. Bradley, E. E. Stoll, O. J. Campbell, Cleanth Brooks, Mary McCarthy, and Joan Larsen Klein), and a more complete list of further references than most paperback editions. What makes this edition unique and valuable is Barnet's chapter, "*Macbeth* on Stage and Screen," which I cite further below.

The Houghton Mifflin edition, edited by Joseph Quincy Adams, contains historical material, relating both to Scottish history and to King James's ascension as James I of England, along with a detailed summary of the events of the play. Adams cuts the Hecate scenes from his text, giving a full explanation in his chapter, "Omitted Scenes and Passages." He also cuts the scene between Lennox and a Lord (IV. 6) on the grounds that "the scene adds to the play not a single fresh fact nor the smallest new thought" and that "the style is hardly worthy of Shakespeare" (1931, 271). Adams also includes a skeptical account of Simon Forman's visit to the Globe, suggesting that it may be a forgery of J. P. Collier.

The Yale edition, edited by Eugene M. Waith, contains a good note on the date of the play and a useful defense of the Folio lineation. "In a large number of passages," Waith writes, "I have preferred to accept the Folio arrangement as possibly deliberate and meaningful" (1954, 120). Waith uses as his example Folio's "which you had thought to be our innocent self." "This reading," he writes, "with its heavy emphasis on Macbeth's deceptive portrayal of himself, seems to me a good one" (119).

The Oxford Shakespeare, edited by Nicholas Brooke, is a well-arranged scholarly edition, with extensive notes on line meanings and text, an appendix on the lineation of the Folio, and an appendix on musical adaptations that includes some of Henry Johnson's actual music. Brooke's introduction provides cogent arguments on the play's "baroque" (1990, 34) qualities, a very useful analysis of Stuart politics, and a good summary of the play's stage history.

The Mercury edition (Harper), designed to accompany phonograph records that featured Orson Welles and Fay Bainter in the major roles, has headnotes from Holinshed for each scene, some very explicit stage directions that tell us what is to be heard, an introduction by Welles, and, of course, Welles's pen-and-ink drawings. He talks (as of 1941) about how Shakespearean staging gave way to the proscenium format: "The fore-stage having dwindled into an apron, the playing area was now one gigantic *inner-stage*" (25, Welles's emphasis).

The New Swan Shakespeare (Longman), edited by Bernard Lott, was last revised in 1965, although the "Advice for Examination Candidates" was updated in 1986. This section accounts for students who may have worked on the issues of staging the play for performance. The textual notes, although indicated by potentially distracting numbers, are helpful, as is the glossary. The illustrations are sometimes useful, as in the case of the Stone of Scone on page 88, but occasionally are misleading, as the drawing of a "bank and shoal," which is a reification of the emendation of Folio's "Banke and Schoole."

The Shakespeare Made Easy edition (Stanley Thornes, Cheltenham), rendered into modern English by Alan Durband, offers Shakespeare's text on the left-hand page and the translation on the right. "To know my deed, 'twere best not know myself" becomes "Better to be lost in thought than face reality." "O, by whom?" becomes "Oh, no. Who did it?" "She should have died hereafter" becomes "She had to die sometime. It had to happen." The modernizations are suspect, reduced to a single meaning. They can show, however, when confronted by a skillful teacher, the options that the original script offers an actor. In all probability, though, the students will stay closer to the right-hand side of the page.

The Heinemann Educational Books edition, edited by Maynard Mack and Robert Boynton, claims that "reading Shakespeare is not a poor substitute for seeing Shakespeare well performed, but rather a different arena of experience with its own demands and rewards" (1981, v). This attractive edition is printed on paper that will accept notes without seeping through to the next page. Its notes are placed at the bottom of the page. It contains an outline of the play intended "to suggest ways of internally *visualizing* and *feeling* the play, which are essential if the reading is not to be merely an intellectual exercise" (111). It also includes a list of study questions: "In what sense are Macbeth's own last hours, seemingly totally different than his wife's (he is all action in Act V, and he scorns suicide), not so different as the surface view suggests?" (136). Regardless of its emphasis on reading, this edition creates a solid preproduction context.

The Shakespeare on Stage edition (Swan Books, Fair Oaks, California), edited by Diane Davidson, features extensive and interpretive stage directions: "(A cat meows, and she answers, "I come, Graymalkin!"). This would be a very good text for students working on staging the play, particularly if they question the stage directions, rather than merely follow them. The directions tend not to suggest placement on stage or, indeed, what stage is optimal for the suggested interpretations. Those issues would qualify many of the suggestions that Davidson offers. This edition, however, would serve as a valuable starting point for a production.

A very recent entry is the Applause edition (Applause Books, New York) which uses a text edited by R. A. Foakes and a scene-by-scene commentary by John Russell Brown. Brown is judicious, relying on stage directions where they exist, on Elizabethan stage conventions when they can be ascertained, on a sensitivity to the relationship between language and action, and on analysis of the options provided by the script, as in the instance of Lady Macbeth's faint, the appearance of Banquo's ghost, and the Third Murderer. Since Brown's notes will involve students in asking questions about how the text becomes performative, this will prove to be an extremely valuable edition in the classroom. The citations, however, are inadequate—"*Shakespeare Survey, 30,*" for example, is all we get for a critic's comment on the Trevor Nunn production—and no list of other materials to be studied is provided.

A parallel text edition, edited by Daniel Leary (Perfection Learning, Logan, Iowa), has a solid, brief account of Shakespeare's career and a text that on the left-hand side is Folio's (with modernizations—we are not told whose text this is) and a paraphrase on the right-hand page. Some of the translations seem unnecessary. "What need I fear of thee?" becomes "Why should I fear you?" "Fillet of a fenny snake, In the caldron boil and bake" becomes "Throw a slice of swamp-snake into the boiling kettle and let it cook." "I have a strange infirmity'' becomes ''I have a peculiar illness.'' The parallel text tends to suggest why Shakespeare made the choices he did. This edition includes questions and conclusions, vocabulary, factual questions, and matching questions, for example, ''Match the character with the proper description.''

A modernized text is A. L. Rowse's in the Contemporary Shakespeare Series (University Press of America, Lanham, Maryland). Rowse offers a mostly sane, occasionally idiosyncratic, rationale for a modernized text (substituting ''burdens'' for ''fardels'' in *Hamlet*, for example), a brief introduction, and a text that is not radically altered from the Folio version. ''Ronyon'' becomes ''rascal,'' which I would consider an illegitimate change given the meaning of ''rascal.'' ''If th' Assassination / Could trammell up the Consequence, and catch / With his surcease, Successe'' becomes ''If the assassination / Could gather up the consequence, and catch / With the event success,'' an alteration which flattens meaning and sound. As Robert Frost once said, ''Poetry is what evaporates from all translations.''

Another modernization is offered by Pocket Classics (Academic Industries, West Haven, Connecticut), a black-and-white comic book format with succinct translations: ''I am sorry to say that the boy has escaped.'' ''Well,'' says Macbeth, ''the main job is done. We'll take care of Fleance another time.''

The Folio Shakespeare (London, Ravette Books), edited by David Gibson, in the format of what used to be called Classic Comics, contains the complete text, arranged unconfusingly in bubbles above cartoon pictures by Von. The pictures inevitably reinforce stereotypes, but the eleventh-century garb, chain mail, helmets with horns and noseguards, for example, presses the play back into a noncontemporary setting, as opposed to the Folio *Twelfth Night*, for example. This edition makes the most conventional assumptions for placement of characters; for example, Lady Macbeth is at the banqueting table. One of the companies that purveys the Folio version (Writing Company, Culver City, California) makes the dubious claim that ''the comic book format 'explains' the action, making footnotes unnecessary'' (1996, 30).

I rely heavily in this guide on two editions: The New Variorum edition of 1873, edited by Horace Howard Furness, Jr., fifth edition of 1904, reprinted in 1963 by Dover, is a mine of useful nineteenth-century English and German criticism. The New Arden edition, edited by Kenneth Muir (1964), is highly recommended for its scrupulous textual editing and useful background material.

Another extremely valuable text is John Andrews's the Everyman Shakespeare (J. M. Dent, London). In his texts, Andrews attempts to go back to the punctuation and, to some extent, to the orthography of the original.

> Archeological excavations in London's Bankside have revealed that the
> foundations of playhouses such as the Rose and the Globe look rather different than what many historians had expected. And we're now learning from a close scrutiny of Shakespeare's texts that they too look different, and function differently, when we accept them for what they are and resist

> the impulse to normalize features that strike us initially as quirky, unkempt,
> or unsophisticated. (1990, xxvii)

Nineteenth- and twentieth-century editorial practices are analogous to eigh-
teenth-century efforts to clarify the meanings of the lines and to render the moral
meanings of the plays unambiguous.

Andrews offers some of the options for meaning and emphasis that inhere in
the Folio text. Folio's "Battaile" (1.1.4), for example, means "battle" *and*
"battalion," suggesting that when battles were lost, so were armies, as later in
"battell" (5.6.4). "Weyward" (1.3.30) means more than the usual "weird."
Weyward means "both (a) wayward (lawless, evil and misleading), and (b) fatal,
from the Anglo-Saxon *wyrd*, which meant 'fate' or 'destiny' " (12), so that their
contradictions and possibly complementary qualities are captured in a word. At
1.3.46, Andrews suggests that "hail" means

> both (a) salute, greet, and (b) health (from a related Anglo-Saxon word,
> *hale*, that means "whole," as in "hale and hearty"). Most editors place
> commas after this word [hail]; but there are ambiguities in the original
> phrasing that become obscured when commas are added. Among other
> things, the First Witch's greeting may mean "Let all salute Macbeth" (or
> "Everyone salutes Macbeth"), or "health to you as Thane of Glamis." (14)

The word "powr'd" (1.3.98), Andrews suggests, means "poured. But in this
spelling form could also be used for 'powered,' " a possible further meaning
in 1.5.28 ("that I may powre my Spirits in thine Ear") and 4.1.63 ("Powre in
Sow's Blood"). The phrase "unfix my heir" (1.3.133), Andrews suggests,
"means 'make my hair stand on end,' " but also, "make him heirless" (20).
Siward uses the same pun later (5.7.77). The executed Cawdor's "dearest thing
he ow'd" (1.4.10) means "owned," of course, but also "that what a human
being 'owns' in this world is actually 'owed' to Heaven" (22). The "milk of
Humane Kindness" points at the ethical dimension of being human, as does the
word kindness (28). (See Horowitz 1965, 117–18 on the ethical dimensions of
"kind.") "High thee hither" (1.5.27) means "hie," but, says Andrews, "with
wordplay similar to that in line 22 ['What thou wouldst highly']," that is "both
(a) earnestly, and (b) ambitiously" (29). "Thou sowre and firm-set Earth"
means "both (a) sour (morose, sorrowful, gloomy), and (b) sore" (48). The
word then glances at "tyrannical," as in Stephano's pun, "I should have been
a sore one then" in *The Tempest*. Andrews notes the irony of Macbeth's " 'Tis
better thee without, then he within" (3.4.13): "Soon 'then he within' will prove
ironically apt" (92). At 5.3.52, for "pristine," Andrews substitutes the original
"pristive," arguing that "it may be a Shakespearean coinage to combine *pristine*
and *pristly* (a variant of *priestly*). If so, it provides an ironic reminder that the
" 'Health' Macbeth seeks is the kind that only a 'Divine' (V.i.83) can minister"
(166). Andrews retains the Folio punctuation of "What need we fear? Who

knows it, when none can call our Powre to accompt?'' Who knows it, with this punctuation, means "Who dares acknowledge it?''

Works Cited

Adams, J. Q., ed. 1931. *Macbeth*. Boston: Houghton, Mifflin.

Andrews, John, ed. 1993. *Macbeth*. London: J. M. Dent.

Barnet, Sylvan, ed. 1986. *Macbeth*. New York: Penguin.

Brooke, Nicholas, ed. 1990. *Macbeth*. Oxford, Oxford University Press.

Brown, John Russell, ed. 1996. *Macbeth*. New York: Applause Books.

Campbell, O. J., Alfred Rothschild, and Stuart Vaughan, eds. 1961. *Macbeth*. New York: Bantam Books.

Davidson, Diane, ed. 1986. *'Macbeth' for Young People*. Fair Oaks, Calif.: Swan Books.

Dent, R. W., ed. 1969. *Macbeth*. Dubuque, Iowa: W. C. Brown.

Durband, Alan, ed. 1990. *Macbeth*. Cheltenham: Stanley Thornes.

Fergusson, Francis, ed. 1960. *Macbeth*. New York: Dell Laurel.

Furness, Horace H., Jr., ed. 1873. Variorum *Macbeth*. 1904 edition. Philadelphia: J. B. Lippincott. Reprint. New York: Dover, 1963.

Gibson, David, ed. 1984. *Macbeth*. London: Ravette Books.

Gibson, Rex, ed. 1993. *Macbeth*. Cambridge: Cambridge University Press.

Gill, Roma, ed. 1993. *Macbeth*. Oxford: Oxford University Press.

Harbage, Alfred, ed. 1960. *Macbeth*. Baltimore: Penguin.

Horowitz, David, ed. 1965. *Shakespeare: An Existential View*. New York: McGraw-Hill.

Hunter, G. K., ed. 1967. *Macbeth*. Harmondsworth, England: Penguin.

———, ed. 1994. *Four Tragedies*. London: Penguin.

Kittredge, G. L., ed. 1939. *Macbeth*. Boston: Ginn and Company.

Leary, Daniel, ed. 1983. *Macbeth*. Logan, Iowa: Perfection Learning.

Lott, Bernard, ed. 1986. *Macbeth*. London: Longman.

Mack, Maynard, and Robert Boynton, eds. 1981. *Macbeth*. Portsmouth, N.H.: Heinemann Educational Books.

Mowat, Barbara, and Paul Werstein, eds. 1992. *Macbeth*. New York: Washington Square.

Muir, Kenneth, ed. 1964. *Macbeth*. London: Metheun.

Pocket Classics. 1984. *Macbeth*. West Haven, Conn.: Academic Industries.

Rowse, A. L., ed. 1985. *Macbeth*. Lanham, Md.: University Press of America.

Waith, Eugene M., ed. 1954. *Macbeth*. New Haven, Conn.: Yale University Press.

Welles, Orson, and Roger Hill, eds. 1941. *Macbeth*. New York: Harper.

Writing Company. 1996. *Shakespeare Catalogue*. Culver City, California.

King James I. From *Shakespeare* (Philadelphia: Claxton, Remsen & Haffelfinger, 1879)

2

CONTEXTS AND SOURCES

Shakespeare's imagination was not watertight. While he researched *Antony and Cleopatra*, his reading began to seep into the play he was writing, *Macbeth*. This influence has long been noted (Spencer, 1964).

G. Wilson Knight has argued the contrast between *Macbeth* and *Antony and Cleopatra*. "In point of imaginative profundity, *Macbeth* is comparable alone to *Antony and Cleopatra*" (1957, 140), even if one is the other's "polar opposite" (1931, 327). Certainly they contrast on a huge scale. Macbeth would destroy the structure of the world—"the frame of things"—while he fights against the inevitable. Reality would dissolve before human will. Antony would "let Rome in Tiber melt," but Caesar comes unmeltingly after Antony, even as Antony and Cleopatra seek "new heaven, new earth." In very different ways the two plays challenge the limits of what is possible. Macbeth would destroy the world and cannot. Antony and Cleopatra would create a new world, and who knows where their triumphant metaphysics takes them? "Shakespeare's own imagination [in *Macbeth*] is preoccupied with the dissolution of the usual boundaries between mind and matter, imagination and reality," according to James Calderwood (1986, 131).

It is not surprising that the Geneva Gloss on Revelation XX 12 sounds as if it were appropriated for use in *Macbeth* ("Everie mans conscience is as a boke wherein his dedes are written, which shal appeare when God openeth the boke"), while the first line of the next chapter seems to be repeated at the beginning of *Antony and Cleopatra*: "And I sawe a new heaven, & a new earth: for the first heaven, and the first earth were passed away, & there was no more sea."

The nemesis that pursues Macbeth is a version of "Caesar." Shakespeare's mind must have been listening to the music of his new play even as he completed his old. *Macbeth* is a dark overture. In Plutarch, an astronomer of Egypt tells Antony that his "Demon . . . (the good angel and spirit that keepeth thee)

is afraid of his, and being courageous and high when he is alone, becometh
fearful and timorous when he cometh near unto the other'' (Spencer 1964, 215–
16). Shakespeare's Antony agrees: "He hath spoken true: the very dice obey"
Caesar. Macbeth uses Plutarch in complaining that "under [Banquo] / My *Genius* is rebuk'd, as it is said / *Mark Antonies* was by *Caesar.*" Dr. Johnson,
rightly sniffing out an allusion to classical history emerging from an eleventh-
century thane not characterized as well-read, notes that

> this passage . . . I believe was an insertion of some player, that, having so
> much learning as to discover to what Shakespeare alluded, was not willing
> that his audience should be less knowing than himself and has therefore
> weakened the author's sense by the intrusion of a remote and useless image
> into a speech bursting from a man wholly possessed with his own present
> condition and therefore not at leisure to explain his own allusion to himself.
> (quoted in Wimsatt 1960, 104)

Johnson later admitted that the passage "may still be genuine and added by the
author in his revision" (quoted in Wimsatt 1960, 104). It is probably truer, as
A. L. Rowse says of the allusion to Caesar, "that *Antony and Cleopatra* is not
far away in that teeming mind" (1985, 16). On this point, see H. R. Coursen
(1979).

The night of Duncan's murder resembles one that Antony's army suffered
during his arduous Parthian campaign. His army experienced "as ill and dreadful
a night as ever they had. For there were villains of their own company who cut
their fellows's throats for the money. . . . Thereupon all the camp was straight
in tumult and uproar" (Spencer 1964, 236). As in *Macbeth*, "the Hurley-
burley's done": "day began to break, and the army to fall again into good
order, and all the hurly-burly to cease" (237). During the campaign, Antony's
starving soldiers ate roots "that were never eaten before; among the which there
was one that killed them and made them out of their wits. For he that had once
eaten of it, his memory was gone from him, and he knew no manner of thing"
(233). Banquo, of course, talks of the "insane Root, / That takes the Reason
Prisoner."

Other parallels include the epic treatment that Macbeth and Antony are given
by the Captain and Philo before they appear. The forsaking of Antony by his
men (Spencer 1964, 276, for example) is an element more prominent in Plutarch's story of Antony than in Rafael Holinshed's of Macbeth. In Holinshed's
narrative, "Makduffe" refuses to come to Dunsinane to help "Makbeth" build
his hilltop fortress. In Plutarch's, the desertion by Domitius (Shakespeare's En-
obarbus) is rendered in the context of "certain kings also that forsook him, and
turned on Caesar's side; as Amyntas and Deiotarus" (253). Macbeth's scorning
to "play the Roman Foole with [his] sword" sneers at Antony's suicide. Antony
had earlier determined that "there was no way more honourable for him than
to die fighting valiantly" (273). Both Antony and Cleopatra refuse to be led in

triumph, paralleling Macbeth's unwillingness to "yeeld . . . and live to be the shew and gaze o' th' time."

Knight overstates the case to make his point: "Both plays are clearly dominated by a woman. In no other play do we find just this relationship existent between hero and heroine. Lady Macbeth and Cleopatra possess a unique power and vitality" (1931, 327). "Each woman is ultimate in her play: she is the whole play's universe, with its rich fascination and serpentine grace, as Macbeth and Antony are not. They are in it; their ladies are of it: 'it' being 'evil' and 'love' respectively" (336). Lady Macbeth "is herself serpentine, a temptress, like Eve, serpent-beguiled, serpent-propelled" (330). "*Macbeth* and *Antony and Cleopatra*," asserts Knight, "stand out from the other great tragedies by their excessive intensity, which is to be related to the idea of 'speed' " (334). " 'Nature' in both plays is transcended. The dominant spirit quality in both forbids a pure naturalism such as we find in *Lear*. In *Macbeth* what 'nature' there is mostly distorted, in *Antony and Cleopatra* it is outdistanced" (334). "In *Macbeth* nature is deformed, dislocated: in *Antony and Cleopatra* it is fulfilled and transfigured" (336). "In *Antony and Cleopatra* the universe is full, packed full of life-forms. But *Macbeth* is empty, void with a dread infinity, a ghastly vacuum which yet echoes 'strange screams of death.' In *Macbeth* all nature, all life-forms of birth, feast, honour, and kingly glory are opposed by this nothingness" (338). "Humanity is distorted in the one story: hence Macduff enters with Macbeth's head, the protagonist hideously decapitated. In the other, Cleopatra dies crowned and beauteous in a death which is but an added glory to life" (339). "[T]oo easily neglected [in] *Macbeth* [is] the fine love which binds the protagonists" (338).

> Antony and Cleopatra are presented as being so accustomed to the worship of sensual love as an absolute that they are unable to change this obviously fatal allegiance, that, in fact they would rather lose everything than change their ways. The tragic outcome of *Antony and Cleopatra* is as firmly shaped as that of Macbeth by the failure to alter misguided affections and destructive choices. (347)

Peter Hall notes another not merely coincidental contrast:

> opposed to Macbeth the warrior, is the intelligent ruler, Malcolm, somewhat as Antony is opposed by Octavius . . . the politically adroit, more modern man, Malcolm, does not engage in hand-to-hand fighting; that is left to Macduff . . . there is no suggestion that Malcolm is a warrior, wants to be, or is expected to be. (quoted in Brown 1982, 233)

He is, then, his father's son, dealing in lieutenantry, as Antony says scornfully of Octavius, who is himself no "sworder." But there is no suggestion that careful subordination of one's command is a bad thing. Edward III is not censured, even by his enemies, for watching the Black Prince triumph at Crecy.

It might be noted that Lady Macbeth and Cleopatra both say "husband" once.

Like all of Shakespeare's plays, *Macbeth* is informed by Elizabethan humor theory. We can assume that black bile, the fluid characteristic of the melancholic, predominated in Macbeth. Certainly, the melancholy tendency is accented as his introverted sensation feeds not just on horrible imaginings but on the imagery of his own crimes:

> why doe you keepe alone,
> Of sorryest Fancies your Companions making,
> Using those Thoughts, which should indeed have dy'd
> With them they thinke on?

According to Gary Wills, "black humors are nature's vulnerable point for the entry of any real devils" (1995, 61). Robert Burton, the great expert on the syndrome, says "This humor of melancholy is called the Devil's Bath . . . [since] melancholy persons are most subject to diabolical temptations and illusions, and most apt to entertain them, and the Devil best able to work upon them" (1628, 174–75).

In a work that influenced *Macbeth*, Samuel Harsnett asks,

> Why men of a melancholick constitution be more subject to fears, fancies
> and imaginations of devils, and witches, than other tempers be? . . . because
> from their black & sooty blood, gloomie fulginous spirits do fume into their
> brain, which bring black, gloomy, and frightful images, representations, and
> similitudes in them. (1603, 131–32)

It may be that King James I suggested the atmosphere for the play. The devil, says James, can "*thicken* and obscure so the air . . . that the beams of any other man's eye cannot pierce through the same to *see* them" (1597, 27). Burton, predictably, extends this murkiness to its psychological conclusion: "A thick air thickeneth the blood and humors. . . . Polydore calls it a *filthy* sky" (1628, 209), as, it might be added, do the Weird Sisters ("Hover through the fogge and filthie ayer"). In the first of his "Gunpowder" sermons, given in November 1606, Lancelot Andrewes talked of "black and dismal days, days of sorrow and sad accident . . . no-days—nights, rather, as having the shadow of death upon them. Or, *if* days, such as . . . which Satan had marred than which God had made" (1853, 207–8; sermon of November 1606). Presumably, such a day would have resulted from the miasma of the successful detonation of that vast store of powder. James himself provided the atmosphere for that explosion:

> And so the earth as it were opened, should have sent foorth of the bottome
> of the *Stygian* lake such sulphured smoke, furious flames, and fearefull
> thunder, as should have by their diabolicall *Domesday* destroyed and de-

faced, in the twinkling of an eye . . . our present living Princes and people. (*Workes* 1616, 224, quoted in Muir 1964, xviii)

Shakespeare conflates two episodes from Holinshed, episodes at times so similar that no conflation is necessary. The combination of Holinshed's narratives, however, creates a characterization that is lacking in their separate contexts.

In about 968, kinsmen of Donwald, "capteine of the castell," are put to death by King Duff for consorting with witches who were deemed responsible for Duff's wasting illness. Donwald

> begged their pardon; but having a plaine deniall, he conceived such an inward malice towards the king (though he showed it not outwardly at the first). [Thereafter] through setting on of his wife, and in revenge of such unthankefulness, hee found means to murder the king within the foresaid castell of Fores where he used to soiourne. For the king being in that countrie, was accustomed to lie most commonlie within the same castell, having a speciall trust in Donwald, as a man whom he never suspected . . . his wife . . . counselled him (sith the king oftentimes used to lodge in his house without anie gard about him, other than the garrison of the castell, which was wholie at [Donwald's] commandment) to make him awaie . . . Donwald . . . determined to follow hir advise in the execution of so heinous an act. Whereupon devising with himself for a while, which may hee might best accomplish his cursed intent, at length gat opportunitie [after] . . . the king . . . bestowed sundrie honorable gifts amongst them, of the which number Donwald was one, as he that had been ever accounted a most faithfull servant to the king. . . . Then Donwald, though he abhorred the act greatlie in heart, yet through instigation of his wife he called four of his servants unto him (whome he had made privie to his wicked intent before) . . . they entered the chamber (where the king laie) a little before cocks crow, where they secretlie cut his throte as he lay sleeping, without anie buskling at all. . . . [Donwald] foorthwith slew the chamberleins, as gultie of that heinous murder. . . . For the space of six moneths togither, after this heinous murther thus committed, there appeared no sunne by day, nor moone by night in anie part of the realm, but still was the sky covered with continuall clouds, and sometimes such outragious windes arose, with lightenings and tempests, that the people were in great fear of present destruction . . . horses in Louthian, being of singular beautie and swiftness, did eat their own flesh, and would in no wise taste anie other meate. . . . There was a sparhawke also strangled by an owl . . . all men understood that the abhominable murther of king Duffe was the cause thereof. (Holinshed 1587, 149–52)

This segment provides the outline for the murder itself. The outline is clear— the heinousness of the crime, the murderer's resistance to the deed, his wife's insistence on it, the king's trust in Donwald, the king's murder being done while he was a guest, the prodigies resulting from the crime, and even some local color, such as the cocks and perhaps the suggestion for the line, "The moon is down.'' Shakespeare, of course, removed the motive of revenge from his character, deepening both his struggle and the abhorrent nature of the crime. Shakespeare also isolates Macbeth and Lady Macbeth, who act without accomplices.

In a separate episode, from which Shakespeare borrows Macbeth's response to his crimes, King Kenneth slays his nephew and becomes like any

> such as are pricked in conscience for anie secret offense an unquiet mind. And (as the fame goeth) it chanced that a voice was heard as he was in bed in the night time to take his rest, uttering unto him these or the like woordes in effect: ''. . . For even at this present are there in hand secret practises to dispatch both thee and thy issue out of the waie, than other maie injoy this kingdome which thou dooest indevour to assure unto thine issue.'' The king . . . being striken into great dread and terror, passed that night without anie sleepe comming in his eies. (Holinshed 1587, 158)

From a sector that covers the years from 1054 to 1057, Duncan, Holinshed tells us, was ''negligent . . . in punishing offendors,'' and thus ''manie misruled persons tooke occasion thereof to trouble the peace and quiet state of the commonwealth, by seditious commotions'' (168). One of these was Makdowald, who called Duncan ''a faint-hearted milkesop, more meet to governe a sort of idle moonks in some cloister, than to have the rule of such valiant and hardie men of warre as the Scots were'' (168). Makdowald got

> together a mightie power of men: for out of the westerne Iles there came unto him a great multitude of people, offering themselves to assist him in that rebellious quarrel, and out of Ireland in hope of the spoile came no small number of Kernes and Gallowglasses, offering gladlie to serve under him. (168–69)

Macbeth defeats Makdowald and orders ''the head to be cut off, and set upon a poles end, and so sent as a present to the king.'' Meanwhile, ''Sueno king of Norway [but thereafter in Holinshed labeled a Dane] was arrived in Fife, with a puissant armie, to subdue the whole realm of Scotland'' (168–69). The Scots divided into ''three battels. The first was led by Makbeth, the second by Banquho, & the king himself governed in the maine battell or middle order'' (169). After the Scottish victory,

> Makbeth and Banquho journeid towards Fores, where the king then laie, they went sporting by the way togither without other company, save onelie themselves, passing through the woods and fields, when suddenlie in the middest of a laund, there met them three women in strange and wild apparell, resembling creatures of elder world, when they attentivelie beheld, woondering much at the sight of them, the first of them spake and said: All haile Makbeth, thane of Glammis (for he had lately entered into that dignitie and office by the death of his father Sinell). The second of them said: Haile

Makbeth thane of Cawder. But the third: All haile Maketh that heereafter shalt be king of Scotland. (170)

Banquho demands why these women "seeme so little favourable unto me" and is told,

> [W]e promise greater benefits unto thee than unto him, for he shall reigne in deed, but with an unluckie end: neither shall he leeave anie issue behind him to succeed in his place, where contrarilie thou in deed shalt not reign at all, but of thee those shall be borne which shall govern the Scotish king-dome by long order of continuall descent. Herewith the foresaid women vanished immediatlie out of their sight. This was reputed at the first but some vaine fantasticall illusion by Mackbeth and Banquho. . . . But after-wards the common opinion was, that these women were either the weird sisters, that is (as ye would say) the goddesses of destinie, or else some nymphs or feiries, indued with knowledge of prophesie by their necroman-ticall science, bicause everie thing came to passe as they had spoken. For shortlie after, the thane of Cawdor being condemned at Fores of treason against the king committed; his lands, livings, and offices were given of the kings liberalitie to Mackbeth.
>
> Mackbeth revolving the thing in his mind, began even then to devise how he might atteine to the kingdome; but yet he thought with himselfe that he must tarie a time, which should advance him thereto (by the divine provi-dence) as it had come to passe in his former preferment. But shortlie after it chanced that king Duncane having two sonnes . . . he made the elder of them called Malcolme prince of Cumberland, as it were thereby to appoint him his successor to the kingdome, immediately after his decease. Mackbeth sore troubled therewith, for that he saw by this his hope sore hindered (where, by the old lawes of the realme, the ordnace was, that if he that should succeed were not of able age to take the charge upon himself, he that was next of bloud unto him should be admitted) he began to take counsell how he might usurpe the kingdome by force, having a just quarrell so to doo (as he tooke the matter) for that Duncane did what in him lay to defraud him of all manner of title and claime, which he might in time to come, pretend unto the crowne.
>
> The woords of the three sisters also . . . greatlie incouraged him hereunto, but speciallie his wife lay sore upon him to attempt the thing, as she that was verie ambitous, burning in unquenchable desire to beare the name of a queene. At length therefore, communicating his purposed intent with his trustie friends, amongst whome Banquho was the chiefest, upon confidence of their promised aid, he slue the king at Enverns or (as some say) at Botgosuane . . . in the yeare after the birth of our saviour, 1046. (170–71)

Duncan's sons flee, Malcolm to the court of Edward in England and Donald to Ireland.

After a decade of just rule, "the pricke of conscience (as it chanceth ever in tyrants, and such as atteine to anie estate by unrighteous means) caused him ever to feare, lest he should be served at the same up, as he had ministered to his predecessor.'' Fearing the sisters's prophecy to Banquo, he ''willed therefore the same Banquho with his sonne named Fleance, to come to supper,'' but he arranges an ambush beforehand: ''[I]t chanced yet by the benefit of the darke night, that though the father were slain, the sonne yet by the helpe of almightie God reserving him to better fortune, escaped that danger [and] to avoid further perill he fled into Wales'' (172).

Holinshed then lists the Scottish monarchs descended from Fleance.

''At length [Macbeth] found such sweetnesse by putting his nobles to death, that his earnest thirst after blud in this behalfe might in no wise be satisfied'' (173). Having built his fortress at Dunsinane but fearful of Macduff, Macbeth seeks out ''certeine wizzards,'' who tell him

> that he should never be slain with man borne of anie woman, nor van-
> quished till the wood of Bernane come to the castell of Dunsinane. By this
> prophesise Mackbeth put all fear out of his heart, supposing he might doo
> what he would, without anie feare to be punished for the same, for by the
> one prophesie he beleeved it was unpossible for any man to vanquish him,
> and by the other unpossible to slea him. [Still] Makbeth had in everie noble
> mans house one slie fellow or other in fee with him, to reveale all that was
> said or doone within the same, by which slight he oppressed the most part
> of the nobles of his realm. (174)

Macbeth kills Macduff's wife, children, and servants. Macduff goes to En-gland ''to trie what purchase hee might make by means of [Malcolm's] support to revenge the slaughter so cruellie executed on his wife, his children, and other friends.'' He hears Malcolm's detractions, accounts ''himself a banished man for ever, without comfort or consolation,'' but he is resolved by Malcolm's statement that ''I have none of these vices before remembered, but have jested with thee in this manner, onlie to proove thy mind'' (175).

''Malcolm purchased such favor at king Edwards hands, that old Siward, earle of Northumberland, was appointed with ten thousand men to go with him into Scotland'' (175). Malcolm orders his soldiers ''to get a bough of some tree . . . that on the next morrow they might come closelie in such wise and without sight in this manner within viewe of his enimies'' (176). Macduff responds to Macbeth's boast that he was ''not appointed to be slaine by anie creature that is borne of a woman'':

> It is true Makbeth, and no shall thine insatiable crueltie have an end, for I
> am even he that they wizzards have told thee of, who was never borne of
> my mother, but ripped out her wombe: therewithall he stept unto him, and
> slue him in the place. Then cutting his head from his shoulders, he set it
> upon a pole, and brought it unto Malcolme. . . . [Macbeth] was slain in the
> yeere of the incarnation 1057, and in the 16 yeere of king Edwards reigne
> over the Englishmen. (176)

Malcolm appoints his chiefest followers earls—"the first earles that have beene heard of amongst the Scotishmen" (176). Siward makes sure that his son was wounded "in the forepart of the body. . . . He greatly rejoised thereat, to heare that he had died so manfullie" (192).

According to Herbert Grierson, Shakespeare drew his theme from Holinshed: "Story after story told him of men driven by an irresistible impulse into deeds of treachery and bloodshed but haunted when the deed was done by the spectres of conscience and superstition" (1914, xix). Obviously, Shakespeare puts his sources to work as a play. The differences between Holinshed's history and *Macbeth* are too numerous to mention, but a few are worth noting.

Shakespeare exchanges the murder of Duff for the killing of Duncan—apparently during an ambush. Shakespeare eliminates Macbeth's successful decade as king. That Sueno becomes Norway in the play means that Shakespeare refused to substitute Sueno, king of Denmark, for his father, Seuno, king of Norway, who had given his son his crown. As Michael Hawkins argues, "It does not require the visit of a Danish king to account for the substitution of Norwegians for Danes in the play: the existence of a Danish queen of England would have been sufficient" (1982, 186).

Shakespeare rejects the version of the "weak king dilemma" that Holinshed offers (cf. Manheim 1973), unless we accept the materialist view of Duncan as a "weak king." According to Muir, "By making the victim old and holy and by passing over his weaknesses, Shakespeare deliberately blackened the guilt of Macbeth" (1964, xli). Rossiter considers that "[t]he *wilfulness* of the murder is thus isolated" (1961, 210). In Holinshed, word of the slaughter of Lady Macduff and her children is not brought to Macduff in a scene which follows the murders and during which we wait for the terrible news to arrive. Holinshed gives no hint of Macbeth's guilt about the murders when he faces Macduff at the end.

Emphasizing Macbeth's violation of the rules of hospitality, Harry Morris notes that Shakespeare's "most pointed addition to Holinshed is to place the murder carefully within the doors of Macbeth's castle" (1994, 491). That borrowing comes, however, from the story of Donwald. The play opens into *current* seventeenth-century history.

Muir points out that Holinshed's "marginalia read almost like a running commentary on the play and they may have given hints to Shakespeare on the dramatic treatment of the subject" (1964, xl). Indeed, the glosses suggest thematic emphases: The Weird Sisters are "a thing to wonder at." "Prophesies moove men to unlawfull attempts." Lady Macbeth typifies "Women desirous of high estate." People guess who the murderer may be—"Some wiser than other. The matter suspected." "The king had a giltie conscience." "A voice heard by the king." "Prodigious weather." "He remembered also the words of the weird sisters." "Makbeths confidence in wizzards." "Makbeth recoileth." "Makbeths trust in prophecies."

The account in Holinshed is reinforced by George Buchanan's *Rerum Scoticarum Historia*. Muir says that Shakespeare's "hero is perhaps nearer to Buchanan's portrait of Macbeth than Holinshed's'' (1964, xxxix). Buchanan's narrative was available in Latin during Shakespeare's lifetime.

> Donald's wife . . . by her persuasion incited him to murder the king; telling him that as keeper of the royal castle he had the life and death of his sovereign in his hands, and that he might thereby not only perpetrate the act, but conceal it when it was done. . . . Macbeth was a man of penetrating genius, a high spirit, unbounded ambition, and, if he had possessed moderation, was worthy of any command, however great; but in punishing crimes he exercised a severity which, exceeding the bounds of the laws, appeared oft to degenerate into cruelty. . . . On a certain night, when he was far distant from the king, three women appeared to him of more than human stature, of whom one hailed him thane of Angus, another, thane of Moray, and the third saluted him king. His ambition and hope being strongly excited by this vision, he revolved in his mind every way by which he might obtain the kingdom, when a justifiable occasion, as he thought, presented itself. Duncan had two sons . . . Malcolm Canmore (great head) and Donald Bane (white). Of these, he made Malcolm, while yet a boy, governor of Cumberland. This appointment highly incensed Macbeth, who thought it an obstacle thrown in the way of his ambition, which—not that he had obtained the two first dignities promised by his nocturnal visitors—might retard, if not altogether prevent, his arriving at the third, as the command of Cumberland was always considered the next step to the crown. His mind, already sufficiently ardent of itself, was daily excited by the importunities of his wife, who was the confidant of all his designs. Wherefore, having consulted with his most intimate friends, among whom was Bancho, and having found a convenient opportunity, he waylaid the king at Inverness, and killed him, in the seventh year of his reign; then, collecting a band together, he proceeded to Scoon, where, trusting to the favour of the people, he proclaimed himself king. . . . But when he had strengthened himself by so many safeguards, and thus gained the favour of the people; the murder of the king—as is very credible—haunting his imagination, and distracting his mind, occasioned his converting the government which he had obtained by perfidy, into a cruel tyranny. He first wreaked his unbounded rage on Bancho, his accomplice in the treason, instigated, as is reported, by the prophecy of some witches, who predicted that Bancho's posterity would enjoy the kingdom. Wherefore, fearing that so powerful and active a chief, who had already dippt his hands in royal blood, might imitate the example which he himself had set, he familiarly invited him, along with his son, to an entertainment, and caused him to be assassinated on his return, in such a manner, as if he had been accidentally killed in a sudden affray. Fleanchus, his son, being unknown, escaped in the dark, but, informed by his friends that his own life was sought after, fled secretly to Wales. [Informed by Malcolm of all the latter's imperfections, Macduff] exclaimed, away! dishonor of thy royal blood and name, more fit to dwell in a desert, than to reign; and was about to retire in anger, when Malcolm taking him by the hand, explained to him the reason of his simulation, that he so often been deceived by the

emissaries of Macbeth, that he dared not rashly trust himself to every body. . . . The report of [Malcolm's] army's march, excited a great commotion in Scotland, and many daily flocked to the new king. Macbeth, being almost wholly deserted, when in this so sudden defection he saw no better alternative, shut himself up in the castle of Dunsinnan . . . [Malcolm's] soldiers joyfully seized [the acclamations of the people] as an omen of victory, and placing green boughs in their helmets, represented an army rather returning in triumph, than marching to battle. Astonished at this confidence of the enemy, Macbeth immediately fled and the soldiers, deserted by their leader, surrendered to Malcolm. Macduff having followed the tyrant, overtook him, and slew him. Here some of our writers relate a number of fables, more adapted for theatrical representation, or Milesian romance, than history, I therefore omit them.[1] (Buchanan 1829, 73–81)

It is difficult to sort witchcraft as source from the way in which the Weird Sisters are depicted in the play, since contextualization is interpretation. I will, however, deal with interpretations of Shakespeare's sorority later. Witchcraft is not a source of the play, but, rather, the source is society's fascination with and debate about witchcraft. It was a firing of Shakespeare's imagination that took him toward the unknowable and certainly kept him from "answering" the questions the Weird Sisters raise. They become a seemingly endless source of response, since critics are quick to enlist their partial answers at the service of a thesis.

Jane Jack has examined the parallels between *Macbeth* and the story of the Witch of Endor in 1 Samuel 28 (1955, 173–93). My own sense of the relationship between the narratives is less explicitly theological than hers. 1 Samuel (25: 23) does link two concerns of *Macbeth*: "For rebellion *is as* the sinne of witchcraft." The Geneva Gloss to this passage says that "God hateth nothing more than the disobedience of his commandment, though ye intent seme never so good to man." A desperate Saul, deserted by God, goes to the Witch to seek advice of the ghost of Samuel. Both Reginald Scot (1584, 8: 8–14) and James I (1597, 2–5) agreed that the ghost could not be Samuel. The Geneva Gloss talks of Saul's "gross ignorance, not considering the state of the Saints after this life, and howe Satan hath no power over them." It follows that it was not Samuel who appeared but "Satan, who to blind eyes toke upon him the forme of Samuel, as he can do of an Angel of light." James, of course, accepted that interpretation, while the more skeptical Scot argued, according to Henry N. Paul, that "it was a trick practiced by a cozening old woman" (1950, 53). Paul goes on to say that "Shakespeare . . . pictures just such a distraught and frightened king seeking by the worst means to know the worst and learning that he is to lose his kingdom" (53). *If* the ghost of Samuel had been the devil in a pleasing shape, he might have persuaded Saul of some positive but double-edged prediction, as do the Weird Sisters in *Macbeth*. Instead, Samuel's shade is unequivocal: "the Lord will rent the kingdome out of thine hand, and give it to thy neighbour David. Because thou abeiedst not the voyce of the Lord, nor

executest his fearce wrath upon the Amalekites, therefore hathe the Lord done
this unto thee this day'' (1 Samuel 28: 17–18). That sounds like Samuel to me,
regardless of his violation of later doctrine that says that saints must be permitted
to sleep. What Shakespeare does is to complicate the source, making the prophecies ambiguous and thus susceptible to a positive interpretation by a Macbeth
deceived by his own need for reassurance. The moral that James applies to Saul
could better be applied to Macbeth: ''Consult therefore with no necromancier
nor false prophet upon the success of your warres, remembering on King Saul's
miserable end'' (James I, *Basilikon Doron*, 57). Saul's end was preordained.
Samuel merely fills in the blanks of God's silence. Macbeth's end is also inevitable, but his knowledge of it comes with shuddering insights when a ''hidden
meaning'' is announced to his circumscribed ego. We as an audience share these
moments from the double position of knowing that the prophecy has already
been fulfilled—in the instance of the moving grove—and of experiencing,
through Macbeth's vivid response, what it is to learn of such a thing for the
first time. Macduff's revelation about his birth, of course, is news to both spectators and Macbeth.

Terry Hawkes points at the king himself as a source of the play:

> James was to be the second Brutus, destined to reunify the land founded
> by the first Brutus, and then riven by him in folly. And it was that edifice
> of imminent unity that the Gunpowder plot seemed designed to reduce to
> rubble. That the conspirators were foreign-backed Catholics, their confes-
> sions appeared to confirm. That they were also (and therefore) agents of the
> devil intent upon the destruction of God's divine plan for Great Britain and
> her people followed without question. Inspired by Lucifer, the conflagration
> they purposed had its analogue in the flames of Hell. (1977, 3)

Philip McGuire adds another historical analogue that set James's reign apart
from Elizabeth's. Augustus was employed ''to give it a style that, in contrast
to Elizabeth's, is Roman, imperial, and specifically Augustan'' (1994, 35). The
analogy is also drawn by Jonathan Goldberg (1983), but it helps explain Macbeth's otherwise curious allusion to Augustus (3.1.68), which I discuss below.
David Bergeron suggests that civic spectacles in the early years of James's reign
in England emphasized his Stuart heritage and would have encouraged a playwright's exploration of Scottish history (1993, 13–18).

Shakespeare probably read James's *Daemonologie* (1597). If so, James would
have reinforced the devilish motives of the Weird Sisters:

> For as the means are divers, which allure them to these unlawful arts of
> serving of the devil, so by divers ways use they their practices, answering
> to these means which first the devil used as instruments in them—though
> all tending to one end: to wit, the enlarging of Satan's tyranny and crossing
> of the propagation of the kingdom of Christ, so far as lies in the possibility,
> either of the one or other sort, or of the devil their master. (1597, 2: ch. 3)

James would also have contributed to the play's notorious misogyny:

> What can be the cause that there are twenty women given to [witchcraft] where there is one man? . . . The reason is easy, for as that sex is frailer than man is, so it is easier to be entrapped in these gross snares of the devil, as was over well proved to be true by the serpent's deceiving of Eve at the beginning, which makes him [more at home] with that sex since [then]. (2: ch. 5)

James's assertions stem from the even more misogynistic *Malleus Malefica-rum*:

> [I]t is no matter for wonder that there are more women than men found infected with the heresy of witchcraft. . . . She is more carnal than man . . . as she is a liar by nature, so in her speech she stings while she delights us . . . her heart is a net, and her hands are bands. He that pleaseth God shall escape from her; but he that is a sinner shall be caught by her . . . can he be called a free man whose wife governs him . . . nearly all the kingdoms of the world have been overthrown by women. (quoted in Stallybrass 1982, 204)

According to Peter Stallybrass, "All of these statements have analogues in *Macbeth*" (204), as well as some strong echoes in the next play, *Antony and Cleopatra*.

James also attributes elements to the devil and to witches that do appear in *Macbeth*: "he knows well enough what humor dominates in any of us. And as a spirit he can subtly wake up the same, making it peccant or to abound as he thinks meet for troubling of us, if God will so permit it" (1597, ch. 5). The qualification at the end of James's assertion suggests that he is not going to commit the Manichean heresy, which posits evil as a separate power. *Macbeth* also occurs in an explicitly non-Manichean world. Other qualities of witches include the raising of "storms and tempests upon sea or land, but not universally; but in such a particular place and prescribed bounds as God will permit them to trouble," "having affinity with the air as being a spirit, and having such power of the forming and moving thereof," and the making of "spirits either to follow and trouble persons, or haunt certain houses and affray oftentimes the inhabitants" (1597, ch. 5).

In his preface to *Daemonologie,* James precisely expresses the conceptual basis from which the play emerges: "For where the devilles intention in [evil deeds] is ever to perish, either the soule or the body, or both of them, that he is so permitted to deale with: God by the contrarie, draws every out of that evill glorie to himselfe" (1597, sig. A4). Thus, as Stallybrass argues, both Lady Macbeth and the Weird Sisters "are constructed so as to manifest their own antithesis . . . [Lady Macbeth experiences] the reassertion of 'the compunctious visitations of nature' if only in sleep. . . . Cursed witches prophesy the triumph of godly rule'' (1982, 198–99). The point of view of the world is inevitably structured into the characters who inhabit it.

Donald Nugent says that the two

> common denominators [of] witchcraft [are] sexuality (in symbol or in fact) and power. . . . Witchcraft is a means of artificially heightening the will in ages when men feel flattened by misfortune. It is hubris-enhancing, and it can tempt men to be ''as gods.'' (1971, 73)

Possible sources of Macbeth's ''Stones have beene knowne to move, & Trees to speake'' can be found in Scot (1584, bk. 8, chap. 6, p. 165): ''the okes of Dondona . . . was a wood, the trees thereof (they saie) could speak,'' and in book 11: ''trees spake, as before the death of *Caesar*'' (chap. 18, p. 208).

G. L. Kittredge, an authority on witchcraft, proposes that,

> in adopting the term ''Weird Sisters'' from Holinshed, Shakespeare was obviously adopting also Holinshed's definition—''the goddesses of destiny.'' The Weird Sisters, then, are the Norns of Scandanavian mythology [who] shaped beforehand the life of every man . . . their office was not to prophesy only, but to determine. . . . Their presence is due to the large infusion of Norse blood in the Scottish blood, and their function is in full accord with the doctrines of Norse heathendom. . . . They were not ordinary witches or seeresses. They were great powers of destiny, great ministers of fate. They had determined the past; they not only foresaw the future, but decreed it. . . . Thus the tragedy of *Macbeth* is inevitably fatalistic, but Shakespeare attempts no solution of the problem of free will and predestination. . . . He never gives us the impression that man is not responsible for his own acts. (1939, xviii–xix)

Where, one must ask, does *choice* reside? If Macbeth's fate is predestined, his human decisions are superficial, merely a cooperation with what has been ordained. Unlike Oedipus, he does not try to avoid the predictions. He leaps to them. He is then overtaken by what A. C. Bradley calls ''Sophoclean irony'' (1904, 270).

Scot's witches are ''commonly old, lame, bleare-eied, pale, fowle, and full of wrinkles'' (1584, 1). Shakespeare uses part of that description, of course, but he gives them power beyond those of mere crones, perhaps to accord with King James's more diabolical interpretation of witchcraft.

Like Kittredge, Charlotte Carmichael connects the Nornae of Scandinavian mythology and the Weird Sisters. Of the Nornae, Carmichael notes,

> the Third is the special prophetess, while the First takes cognisance of the past, and the Second of the present, in affairs connected with humanity. These are the tasks of the Urda, Verdandi, and Skulda of Scandinavian

Mythology . . . their role is most clearly brought out in the famous "Hails."
(quoted in Furness 1873, 9)

Bernard McElroy disagrees: "Far from being awesome demons of implacable Norns, they are filthy old hags who possess very little grandeur of any kind. . . . The witches are not instruments of a power that *causes* destruction and suffering; they are instruments of a power that *enjoys* destruction and suffering" (1973, 212–13). That may be so, but the enjoyment has to be a by-product of the observation of the loss of a soul. One can trivialize the Weird Sisters on the basis of their appearance and some of their activities, but their purpose is diabolical. On the Weird Sisters, see also Bullough (1974), Griffin (1966), and Satin (1966).

Gary Wills goes so far as to create a genre, of which *Macbeth* is the chief example: "The typical Gunpowder play deals with the apocalyptic destruction of a kingdom (attempted or accomplished), with conclusions brought about by secret 'mining' (undermining), plots and equivocation. And witches are active in the process" (1995, 9). As Psalm 9, line 15 says, "They fell in the pit they themselves dug." By these criteria *Hamlet* and the spirit that may be a devil almost fit. While Wills shows the differences between James and Duncan (31), he also shows that anything can be adduced to prove a case. The importance of the Gunpowder plot, however, cannot be overemphasized. Lancelot Andrewes's sermon of 1606 on the subject called it "a religious, missal, sacramental treason. . . . Hallowing it with orison, oath, and eucharist—this passeth all the rest" (1853, 4: 214). Wills remarks the religious prelude to what was to have been the blowing up of King James "profanation of the Lord's Supper to a regicidal purpose" (1995, 36). Shakespeare, of course, had used this configuration before, in *Richard II,* where York complains, "A dozen of them here have ta'ne the sacrament, / And interchangeably set down their hands, / To kill the King at Oxford" (5.1.97–99).

John Donne delivered a Sermon on 5 November 1622 that James so liked that he ordered Donne to make a copy of it from his notes. This sermon, which stressed the Gunpowder plot on grounds even more fundamental than Andrewes's self-interested condemnation of sacramental perversion, shows Donne's enjoyment of the 'conceit': "they made that whole house [Parliament] one murdering piece and charged that piece with peers, with people, with princes, with the king and meant to discharge it upward at the face of heaven, to shoot God at the face of God" (1963, 108).

Another minor source—for 1.3 and the First Sister's allusion to "Aleppo," destination of the Tiger—has been uncovered by Samuel C. Chew:

Newbury's expedition left England in 1583. Their ship was the Tiger; the immediate destination Aleppo. When the Witch . . . refers to the wife of the "master of the Tiger" who had "to Aleppo gone" we have evidence that

Shakespeare had read the narrative of this voyage in Hakluyt. (quoted in
Coles, 1938, 18)

The Harrowing of Hell has been frequently cited as a source of the Porter
Scene (2.3).

> In *The Harrowing of Hell,* an often-performed Miracle play, Christ strikes
> at the gate and compels Lucifer to release the souls of the patriarchs and
> prophets. As Christ leads the tormented souls into the light, so Macduff
> (after enduring great pain himself) will enter the castle for the second time,
> kill the tyrant and proclaim that "the time is free." (Siddall 1988, 185–86)[2]

NOTES

1. On Shakespeare's use of Scottish history, see David Norbrook, "Macbeth and the
Politics of Historiography," in *Politics of Discourse: The Literature and History of
Seventeenth-Century England,* ed. Kevin Sharpe and Steven Zwicker (Berkeley: Univer-
sity of California Press, 1987), 78–116.

2. On the Porter and the Harrowing of Hell, see John B. Harcourt, " 'I Pray You,
Remember the Porter," *SQ* 12 (1961): 393–402, who explicates the farmer, equivocator,
and tailor; Glynne Wickham, "Hell-Castle and Its Door-Keeper," *Shakespeare Survey*
19 (1966): 68–74; Michael J. B. Allen, "Macbeth's Genial Porter," *ELR* 4 (1974): 326–
36; John Doebler, *Shakespeare's Speaking Pictures* (Albuquerque: University of New
Mexico Press, 1974), 132–37; Richard S. Ide, "The Theater of the Mind: An Essay on
Macbeth," *ELH* 42 (1975): 338–61; Frederic B. Tromly, "Macbeth and His Porter," *SQ*
26 (1975): 151–56; and Nicholas Brooke, ed., *Macbeth* (Oxford: Oxford University Press,
1990), 79–81.

Works Cited

Andrewes, Lancelot. 1853. *Workes.* Edited by Henry Parker. Oxford: Oxford University
    Press.
Bergeron, David. 1993. "The King James Version of *Macbeth.*" In *Shakespeare Set
    Free,* edited by Peggy O'Brien. New York: Washington Square Press.
The Bible. 1560. Geneva: Rovland Hall.
Bradley, A. C. 1904. *Shakespearean Tragedy.* London: Macmillan.
Brown, John Russell, ed. 1982. *Focus on 'Macbeth.'* London: Routledge and Kegan Paul.
Buchanan, George. 1582. *Rerum Scoticarum Historia.* Translated from the Latin by
    James Aikman. Edinburgh: T. Ireland, 1829.
Bullough, Geoffrey. 1973. *Narrative and Dramatic Sources of Shakespeare.* Vol. 7. Lon-
    don: Routledge and Kegan Paul.
Burton, Robert. 1628. *Anatomy of Melancholy.* Translated by Floyd Dell and Paul Jordan.
    London: Tudor, 1927.
Calderwood, James L. 1986. *If It Were Done: 'Macbeth' and Tragic Action.* Amherst:
    University of Massachusetts Press.
Coles, Blanche. 1938. *Shakespeare Studies: 'Macbeth.'* New York: Richard R. Smith.
Coursen, H. R. 1979. "Agreeing with Dr. Johnson." *Ariel* 10, no. 2 (April): 33–42.

Donne, John. 1622. "Guy Fawkes Day." In *Seventeenth Century Prose and Poetry.* Edited by Alexander M. Witherspoon and Frank J. Warnke. Harcourt, Brace & World. 2d ed., 1963.

Furness, Horace H., Jr., ed. 1873. Variorum *Macbeth.* Philadelphia: J. B. Lippincott.

Goldberg, Jonathan. 1983. *James I and the Politics of Literature: Shakespeare, Johnson, Donne and Their Contemporaries.* Baltimore: Johns Hopkins University Press.

Grierson, Herbert, ed. 1914. *Macbeth.* Cambridge: Cambridge University Press.

Griffin, Alice, 1966. *The Sources of Ten Shakespearean Plays.* New York: Thomas Y. Crowell.

Harsnett, Samuel. 1603. *Declaration of Egregious Popish Impostures.* London.

Hawkes, Terrence. 1977. Introduction, *Twentieth Century Interpretations of 'Macbeth.'* Edited by Terrence Hawkes. Englewood Cliffs, N.J.: Prentice-Hall.

Hawkins, Michael. 1982. "History, Politics, and *Macbeth.*" In *Focus on 'Macbeth.'* Edited by John Russell Brown. London: Routledge and Kegan Paul.

Holinshed, Rafael. 1587. *The Chronicles of England, Scotland and Ireland.* London.

Jack, Jane. 1955. "*Macbeth,* King James, and the Bible." *English Literary History* 22 (Fall): 173–93.

James I. 1597. *Daemonologie.* Edinburgh.

———. 1603. *Basilikon Doron.* Edited by James Cragie. Edinburgh: Edinburgh University Press, 1944.

Kittredge, G. L., ed. 1939. *Macbeth.* Boston: Ginn and Company.

Knight, G. Wilson. 1931. *The Imperial Theme.* Oxford: Oxford University Press.

———. 1957. *The Wheel of Fire.* New York: Meridian.

Manheim, Michael. 1973. *The Weak King Dilemma in Shakespeare.* Syracuse, N.Y.: Syracuse University Press.

McElroy, Bernard. 1973. *Shakespeare's Mature Tragedies.* Princeton, N.J.: Princeton University Press.

McGuire, Philip. 1994. *Shakespeare: The Jacobean Plays.* New York: St. Martin's Press.

Morris, Harry. 1994. "Hell and Judgement in *Macbeth.*" In *Shakespeare: The Christian Dimension.* Edited by Roy W. Battenhouse. Bloomington: Indiana University Press.

Muir, Kenneth, ed. 1964. *Macbeth.* London: Metheun.

———. 1977. *The Sources of Shakespeare's Plays.* Vol. 2. London: Methuen.

Nugent, Donald. 1971. "The Renaissance and/of Witchcraft." *Church History* 40, no. 1 (Spring): 49–73.

Paul, Henry N. 1950. *The Royal Play of Macbeth.* New York: Macmillan.

Rossiter, A. P. 1961. *Angel with Horns.* London: Longman.

Rowse, A. L., ed. 1985. *Macbeth.* Lanham, Md.: University Press of America.

Satin, Joseph. 1966. *Shakespeare and His Sources.* Boston: Houghton Mifflin.

Scot, Reginald. 1584. *The Discoverie of Witchcraft.* Edited by B. Nicholson. London, 1886.

Siddall, Stephen. 1988. "Ceremony in *Macbeth.*" In *'Macbeth': Critical Essays.* Edited by Linda Cookson and Bryan Loughrey. London: Longman.

Spencer, T.J.B. 1964. *Shakespeare's Plutarch.* Harmondsworth, England: Penguin.

Stallybrass, Peter. 1982. "*Macbeth* and Witchcraft." In *Focus on 'Macbeth.'* Edited by John Russell Brown. London: Routledge and Kegan Paul.

Wills, Gary. 1995. *Witches and Jesuits.* Oxford: Oxford University Press.

Winsatt, W. K., ed. 1960. *Samuel Johnson on Shakespeare.* New York: Hill and Wang.

Mrs. Siddons as Lady Macbeth. From *The Leopold Shakespeare* (London: Cassell, Petter, Galpin, n.d.)

3

DRAMATIC STRUCTURE

This chapter explains how the play builds as play, from scene to scene, from decision to consequence. Each of its five acts is, in a sense, a separate composition within a remarkably unified work of art.

The first section frames some of the questions raised by the play and suggests the range of interpretation within which critical discourse moves, with a specific emphasis on the imagery of the play. While some interpretation is inevitable, the issues touched on here will be treated in greater detail in chapter 5. The text used is that of the First Folio of 1623.

"WHEN DUNCAN IS ASLEEP . . ."

Three witches gather amid "Thunder and Lightning" to discuss their next meeting. It will be "upon the heath," "There to meet with *Macbeth*." The witches, or Weird Sisters, seem to hover with ominous neutrality over issues that might be important to mere humans: "When the Battaile's lost, and wonne," and "faire is foule, and foule is faire." Although Alfred Harbage claims that these are the "musty crones of popular superstition, not ministers of fate [but] nevertheless zealous in the cause of infiltration" (1963, 373), John Russell Brown remarks, "Little is certain here." The "audience . . . will not know what creatures these are, what powers they possess. . . . They might be three superstitious crones, or the Fates, or demons, or witches" (1963, 42). "They leave," according to Harbage, "to *hover* in the air, vulture-like, and ready to descend upon the one who carries the scent of spiritual death" (1963, 371). E. H. Seymour remains unimpressed: "The witches seem to be introduced for no other reason than to tell us they are to meet again" (quoted in Furness 1873, 7).

The scene introduces the atmosphere of moral ambiguity that, in particular, affects Macbeth during the opening scenes. The basic issues of the scene are as follows. What *are* these three Weird (or "weyward": 1.3.35) Sisters, and what do they look like? Unless a director is making the play a comment on the shallowness of modern politics, that is, a kind of cartoon, the Weird Sisters probably should "evok[e] tragic wonder," as Madeleine Doran notes (1941, 426). A wounded officer enters. "If the royal party enters from the opposite side to that at which the witches left," remarks Brown, "an unknown 'bloody man' will appear unheralded in the place of the strange women, and so, already, here is an impression of fateful timing and of implicit, portentous meaning in the stage movements alone" (1963, 43). The officer, who had defended Malcolm, the king's son, from being taken prisoner, describes to King Duncan the progress of the great battle swaying just out of sight. Macbeth, even in the face of a Fortune which seems to be smiling on the enemy's cause, carves his way to Macdonwald. Macbeth unseams him "from the Nave to th' Chops." The officer reports that Macbeth and Banquo defeated another attack, as if they would "memorize another Golgotha." Ross completes the narrative by describing Macbeth's victory at Fife—although some scholars say that Macbeth could not be at Fife and Inverness simultaneously and, if they were at Fife, should know of the capture of Cawdor, which Ross reports. Duncan commands Cawdor's execution and instructs Ross to greet Macbeth with the doomed thane's title.

The emphasis of the scene is certainly on the savagery of battle, but stresses even more the loyalty of Duncan's soldiers: the officer who defended Malcolm and the generals Banquo and Macbeth, who fought so heroically for king and country. Here the question is, how do the descriptions by the officer and Ross of Macbeth's behavior in battle condition our response to him and his actions?

The Weird Sisters meet again and kill time while waiting for their confrontation with Macbeth. One has been killing swine, another enacting petty revenge against a woman who refused to give the First Witch some of her chestnuts. She has a prize—"a Pilots Thumbe, / Wrackt, as homeward he did come." Macbeth enters, echoing the Witches: "So foule and faire a day I have not seene." Banquo notices the Witches "So wither'd, and so wilde in their attyre" and describes them as bearded, with "choppie finger[s]" and "skinnie Lips." They greet Macbeth as Glamis, Cawdor, and "King hereafter"—the Witches thus present a past, present, and future sequence. According to Banquo, Macbeth starts and seems to fear "Things that doe sound so faire." Banquo demands that, "if you *can* looke into the Seedes of Time" (my emphasis, suggesting his skepticism), they speak to him. They tell him that he will be "lesser than *Macbeth* and greater," "Not so happy, yet much happyer," and that he will "get Kings," though he be none. The Weird Sisters vanish. Banquo and Macbeth discuss their experience and question its reality. Ross and Angus enter. Ross greets Macbeth from Duncan as "*Thane* of Cawdor." Banquo attributes the prophecy to "the Devill" and warns Macbeth about the "Instruments of Darknesse," who "tells us Truths, / Winne us with honest Trifles, to betray's / In deepest consequence." Be that as it may, Macbeth begins to be entranced by the future suggested by the prophecies, which includes the "horrid Image" of the murder of the king. When he says, "Why doe I yeeld to that suggestion," he means more than "suggestion" in the generalized modern sense, as G. K. Hunter explains: " 'Suggestion' is a technical term of theology, meaning 'a prompting or incitement to evil; a temptation of the Evil One'; it is a thing itself external" (1994, 792). "And nothing is," Macbeth says, "but what is not," even as he recognizes the infernal source of "that suggestion." He considers that "Chance may crowne me, / Without my stir." Summoned back to the present by his companions, he says, "My dull Braine was wrought with things forgotten." The company moves toward Duncan.

The scene suggests to some that either Macbeth falls very quickly into the suggestive net that the Weird Sisters have begun to thread, or that his prior thoughts of killing Duncan and taking the throne have reemerged after the battle. A later conversation with Lady Macbeth suggests the latter, as does his excuse about "things forgotten." The issue here is central to whether *Macbeth* is a tragedy or not: Is Macbeth a basically good man who makes a fatal error in judgement? Or is he "an accomplished hypocrite" (quoted in Furness 1873, 71), already corrupted and, in a sense, merely eliciting from the Weird Sisters and later from Lady Macbeth what is already within him—"less reluctant than shy," as Harbage says (1963, 377)? Even if he *has* thought of killing Duncan— and the evidence suggests that he has—he has yet to make the decision. He can still, at this point, wait for "Chance" to act. Having thought of evil is not necessarily a sin, in spite of Christ's injunctions in the Sermon on the Mount. As Adam says in *Paradise Lost*, after Eve's dream: "Evil into the mind of God or Man / May come and go, so unapprov'd, and leave / No spot or blame behind." What she dreamed, he says, "Waking thou never wilt consent to do" (Hanford, 1953, 314). It is one thing to be tempted, another to fall, to paraphrase one of Shakespeare's characters, soon himself to fall. When Macbeth exits the scene, "he carries with him almost all the dramatic expectation, which is now supernatural, fateful, political, moral and psychological" (Brown 1963, 44).

Reporting to his father, King Duncan, who is perhaps "enthroned," as Brown suggests (1963, 44), Malcolm says that he has spoken with someone who witnessed Cawdor's execution. The account of Cawdor's repentance and plea for pardon has been filtered through at least two tellings, so it should be treated as a message conditioned for Duncan's consumption. The King regrets that "There's no Art, / To finde the mindes construction in the Face." He placed an "absolute Trust" in Cawdor as he does on his new Cawdor, who is already infested with thoughts of regicide. Macbeth enters on the word "Trust." Duncan wishes that Macbeth had "less deserv'd" so that the King could have made adequate "thanks, and payment." Having said that, Duncan names his son Malcolm, Prince of Cumberland. That title would make its bearer heir to the throne. Macbeth, perhaps startled, ruminates on "a step" that lies in his way. For all the "centralised grouping" in the scene, says Brown, "it has separated Macbeth from everyone else" (44–45). He seems to have advanced his thinking to a wish to achieve his "black and deepe desires," even if the "Eye feares" what must be done to achieve them. Harbage points at "the simultaneous evidence that he is struggling with his conscience and that the struggle is already lost" (1963, 375). Macbeth rides off to herald the King's arrival at Inverness.

The scene mirrors one treason with another, capturing the collision between past and future that the play explores so vividly: an executed Cawdor, a new Cawdor choking inside with a desire to be king. Duncan's action in elevating Malcolm may be "unconstitutional" (Henry Irving, quoted in Furness 1873, 66). It may also be like Lear's, taken "that future strife may be prevented now." Duncan makes his announcement at a moment of victory and without preamble. Perhaps this is a preemptive political move that belies the saintly old man image that wafts around Duncan. A new King of Scots would be a product of tanistry, whereby the chief thanes would have elected one of their own. Duncan attempts to impose the principle of primogeniture. Does the scene and the previous battle betray the insecurities of a system that has no orderly procedure for the transfer of title and property from one generation to another and that must rely on savage warfare to sustain itself? Certainly Duncan's political move incites Macbeth, so that we have action and counteraction here: The King of a now peaceful land confidently attempts to shape the future of Scotland even as Macbeth struggles with his deep desire to take Scotland's future violently into his own hands.

Lady Macbeth enters reading a letter which reports Macbeth's encounter with the Weird Sisters. He claims to have "*learn'd by the perfect'st report, they have more in them than mortall knowledge.*" She repeats their past, present, and future pattern: "Glamys thou art, and Cawdor, and shalt be / What thou are promis'd." Yet she fears Macbeth's "Nature, / It is too full o' th' Milk of humane kindnesse, / To catch the neerest way." *Humane* kindness is redundant, since one of the dimensions of "kindness" for the early seventeenth century would be "*of* human kind." An ethical and moral obligation resides in the word. R. G. Moulton suggests that the word should be " 'humankind-ness' "— suggesting "shrinking from what is not natural" (quoted in Furness 1873, 71), eschewing anything that is not of one's kind. Macbeth will reiterate this concept later. Modern editorial practice, in changing "humane" to "human," suggests that to be human is not necessarily to be kind. Lady Macbeth wants Macbeth to "High thee hither, / That I may powre my Spirits in thine Eare, / And chastise with the valour of my Tongue, / All that impedes thee from the Golden Round, / Which Fate and Metaphysicall ayde doth seeme / To have thee crown'd withall." Dr. Johnson sees Lady Macbeth shifting the grounds of the prophecies into an imperative of destiny: "which preternatural agents *endeavour* to bestow upon thee" (quoted in Furness 1873, 75). According to Mark Taylor, "What Macbeth puts into the letter is not, for the most part, what Lady Macbeth reads out of it" (1990, 35), an insight that carries over into much of the early dealings between the two. A messenger brings word that "The King comes here to Night," that is, not only tonight, but to spend the night. Lady Macbeth turns from her concern with Macbeth to her own need to be unsexed. She calls on the "Spirits, / That tend on mortall thoughts," that is, apparently, that await a summons, like Faustus's Mephistopheles. Harbage suggests that Lady Macbeth "could scarcely pray for release from womanliness and capacity for pity unless she supposed that she possessed these traits" (1963, 377). Like Macbeth, she invokes "thick Night" and hopes that "Heaven" will not be able to "peepe through the Blanket of the darke, / To cry, hold, hold." Macbeth enters. She greets him again with the process enunciated by the Weird Sisters: "Great Glamys, worthy Cawdor, / Greater than both, by the all-haile hereafter," and she leaps to that "all-haile": "I feele now / The future in the instant." Macbeth reports that the King is coming and purposes to leave in the morning. Lady Macbeth predicts that "never, / Shall sunne that Morrow see." She counsels Macbeth to "looke like th'innocent flower, / But be the Serpent under't." He merely says, "We will speake further." She promises to take care of "all the rest."

He is hesitant to mention murder, even if he is thinking about it. She is vehement, assuming first that fate has already made its decision and second that she must do whatever is necessary to become the handmaiden of destiny. The question of Macbeth's decision is raised again. Is it already made, and is he merely "the selfishly covetous and murderous coward still affect[ing] to hesitate"? (G. Fletcher, quoted in Furness 1873, 85). Or is he still in the throes of a struggle between his "virtuous understanding" and his "corrupt will," as E.M.W. Tillyard defines the terms of his inner conflict (1946, 315), much slower than Lady Macbeth in evaluating the issue, but in the process of pondering it? Is Lady Macbeth really possessed, as a few critics suggest, or does her demand to be unsexed argue that she is "resolutely repressing all that is inconsistent with [her] purpose," as Dowden suggests (1872, 251) and as the first scene of Act Five might confirm?

As Duncan and his party move toward Inverness, he and Banquo exchange remarks on the Castle's pleasant atmosphere. Of the "martlet" speech, L. C. Knights asserts, "What we are contemplating here is a natural and wholesome *order*, of which the equivalent in the human sphere is to be found in those mutualities of loyalty, trust, and liking that Macbeth proposes to violate" (1959, 136). Cawdor is a model of what must happen to such a violator. Lady Macbeth greets Duncan effusively. The King talks of Macbeth's "great Love (sharpe as his Spurre)."

The scene doubles in deception. Inside this place, where "the Heavens breath / Smells wooingly," where birds nest as if Inverness were a "Temple," murderous plots hatch. Lady Macbeth's greetings partake of a certain sincerity. Duncan *is* her benefactor, though in ways he does not glimpse. The ironies of the scene are straightforward, largely because Macbeth, the focus of confusion and struggle, is absent.

After he wanders out from the banquet held in Duncan's honor, Macbeth weighs the consequences of his crime. He rehearses the various reasons why he should *not* kill Duncan. Macbeth is Duncan's kinsman and host. Duncan has been "cleer in his great Office." The crime will have cosmic ramifications:

"Pitty, like a naked New-borne-Babe, / Striding the blast, or Heavens Cherubin, hors'd / Upon the sightlesse Curriors of the Ayre, / Shall blow the horrid deed in every eye, / That teares shall drowne the wind." The compassionate response, he says, has more power than the winds that the Weird Sisters control, and perhaps enough power to dissuade him from the deed. Lady Macbeth enters. Macbeth tells her that "Golden Opinions" and "their newest glosse" are not to be "cast aside so soone." She sneers at him. He claims that he "dare do all that may become a man, / Who dares do more is none." She rejects this distinction, reminding him that they had talked of killing Duncan earlier, when "Nor time, nor place / Did then adhere." She holds him to what she claims was that previous vow, telling him that she would have "dasht the Braines" of her nursing infant had she so sworn and, one assumes, reneged. Horace Furness, the Variorum editor, states, "This overcomes Macbeth. And here is the moral turning point in the drama" (1873, 108). "Macbeth's fear of the moment and of judgement," says Brown, "his pity, honour and knowledge of the world, cannot withstand his need to be a 'man' in his wife's sight" (1963, 46). Lady Macbeth explains how she will circumvent the failure he fears. He "bend[s] up / Each corporall Agent to this terrible Feat." His final couplet shows that he has acquired the language and techniques of Lady Macbeth: "Away, and mock the time with fairest show, / False Face must hide what the false Heart doth know."

Although Macbeth tumbled quickly to the conclusion that the Weird Sisters' projection of his kingship onto the blank screen of the future means that he must murder Duncan, he has been struggling with the morality of the deed. The soliloquy is the culmination of that struggle. He does not, however, argue a passive role, in which God might crown him without any action of his own. In fact, it can be argued that he is at least as worried about the consequences to himself as about the heinousness of the deed. Dr. Johnson paraphrases Macbeth thus:

> [I]f, once done *successfully*, without detection, it could *fix a period* to all vengeance and inquiry, so that *this blow* might be all that I have to do, and this anxiety all that I have to suffer . . . I would venture upon the deed without care of any future state. (quoted in Furness 1873, 95)

Still, who is so virtuous as to claim that fear of consequences has not been a deterrent? His excuse to Lady Macbeth—a materialistic reason for not pursuing an even more profitable course—is a phony one, but perhaps it is conditioned by his perception of what *she* can understand. It seems that, regardless of her desire to be unsexed, Lady Macbeth deploys a full panoply of feminine traits— sexuality ("Such I account thy love") and nurturing motherhood—however negatively, to compel Macbeth to kill the king. Macbeth bends his *corporal* agency to the murder, as if to say, I will do it, but my heart will not be in it.

He wills a certain detachment more consciously than does Lady Macbeth. But with a sword she, like Beatrice, her comic counterpart, is complete.

"A HEART SO WHITE . . ."

Banquo and Fleance enter. It is after midnight and very dark. Banquo cannot sleep, apparently because of "cursed thoughts / That Nature gives way to in repose." According to Edwin Booth, "Banquo is here conscious of the latent power of temptation, and seems wishful to rid himself of all incentives to dangerous thoughts, and all the means of mischief" (quoted in Furness 1873, 115). If so, he contrasts with Macbeth, but is surprisingly unsuspicious. Macbeth enters. Banquo tells him that he "dreamt last Night of the three weyward Sisters." Macbeth claims that he "thinke[s] not of them," but immediately contradicts himself by requesting that when Banquo has "an houre to serve," they "spend it in some words upon that Business." Twice, Macbeth uses the royal plural— "we"—as if he were already a king couching his orders in excessive courtesy. Banquo's response suggests that he has picked up Macbeth's assumptions: "At your kind'st leysure." Macbeth hopes that Banquo will "cleave to [Macbeth's] consent." "Cleave" is one of the few verbs in English to have opposite meanings—to bind together and to rend asunder. Shakespeare uses the word in its contradictory senses in *Antony and Cleopatra* and, here, predicts the "trenched gashes" that Banquo will suffer. During the conversation with Banquo, Garrick kept glancing at the door to Duncan's chamber. As Banquo and Fleance exit, Macbeth sees a dagger, at first pointing him toward Duncan and then covered with "Gouts of Blood." It is as if the deed has been done even as he hallucinates. He remarks the terrible silence. It is broken by the striking of the bell. Kemble had the clock strike two, in accord with Lady Macbeth's memory in her mad scene (Furness 1873, 126). For Duncan, "it is a Knell, / That summons [him] to Heaven, or to Hell." Edwin Forrest read the final couplet "with sadness, a tone of melancholy mixed with determination" (quoted in Furness 1873, 126).

Lady Macbeth enters, charged with the "fire" of alcohol. She starts when an owl shrieks, "the fatall Bell-man, which gives the stern'st good-night," that is, the man who would ring the bell for condemned persons so that they could make their final prayers and confessions. Duncan, like another sleeping king, Hamlet of Denmark, is not given that opportunity. Lady Macbeth hears Macbeth cry out. She fears that "th'attempt, and not the deed, / Confounds" them. She tells us that had Duncan "not resembled / [Her] Father as he slept, [she] had don't." Is this a betrayal of the sensitivity that will doom her? Or is it merely part of her objective discourse?—only a slight compunction kept me from doing the deed myself. "The murder is done offstage so that its effects upon the protagonists are the dominating impressions, not the short moment of horrible action" (Brown 1963, 47). That is true, of course. The continuing effects on Macbeth and Lady Macbeth become more powerful for us if we must *imagine* the deed on the basis of synechdoche and metonymy—blood as a part of the whole and as a closely related idea for the thing itself. The murder takes on its symbolic weight by horrified report rather than by our witness of it. The original images will be reinforced, of course, when the murder is discovered.

Kemble backed out of the murder chamber and collided with Lady Macbeth. "They both started and gazed at each other in terror" (W. A. Alger, quoted in Furness 1873, 126). Although Macbeth's reentrance is designated some five lines earlier, her "My Husband?" seems to convey doubt as to whom she sees. It may be that the delay in seeing him and then in recognizing him is meant to convey the physical darkness of the scene. "I have done the deed," he says. It is, as A. C. Bradley says, as if he has performed "an appalling duty" (1904, 284). Bodenstedt suggests that the scene is performed by "whispering . . . between the two who dare not meet each other's eyes" (quoted in Furness 1873, 131). Macbeth looks at his bloody hands and calls them "a sorry sight." Someone—Donalbain perhaps—cried, "God blesse us," but Macbeth "could not say Amen." His inability to do holily what he would highly troubles him. "Consider it not so deeply," says Lady Macbeth. If "these deeds [are] thought / After these wayes," she says, "it will make us mad." Macbeth continues, however, talking of the voice that cried, "Sleep no more." "*Glamis*," he says, "hath murther'd Sleep, and therefore *Cawdor* / Shall sleepe no more: *Macbeth* shall sleepe no more." Instead of continuing with the sequence suggested by the Weird Sisters, he comes back in horror to himself, the mere man who has destroyed his own ability to sleep. Bradley says that it is "as if his three names give him three personalities to suffer in" (1904, 283), but it is an existential flesh-and-blood Macbeth who will not sleep. Lady Macbeth notices with a shock that he has carried the daggers from the murder room. He refuses to take them back. She says, "Give me the Daggers," and, again, flings one of her moment-serving aphorisms at him: " 'tis the Eye of Child-hood, / That feares a painted Devill." She forgets that she has seen with the eye of childhood only moments before. S. T. Coleridge says "now that the first reality commences, Lady Macbeth shrinks" (quoted in Furness 1873, 134), but she does take the daggers back. Of the knocking at the gate, Thomas De Quincey has written in his famous essay of 1823,

> The murderers, and the murder, must be insulated—cut off by an immeasurable gulf from the ordinary tide and succession of human affairs—locked up and sequestered in some deep recess; we must be made sensible that the world of ordinary life is suddenly arrested—laid asleep, tranced, racked into a dread armistice; time must be annihilated; relation to things abolished . . . the knocking at the gate is heard . . . the pulses of life are beginning to beat again; and the re-establishment of the goings-on of the world in which we live first makes us profoundly sensible of the awful parenthesis that had suspended them. (1823, 326)

The sound of knocking "appalls" Macbeth. He looks at his hands and believes that all the water in the sea will not wash them clean, that, rather, his hand would "The multitudinous Seas incarnadine." Lady Macbeth comes back, her hands covered in blood, but scorning "a Heart so white." The knocking, she says, is "at the South entry," the direction from which retaliation for this murder and more will come much later. For now, "A little Water clears us of this deed." "To know my deed," says Macbeth, "'Twere best not know my selfe." If I acknowledge the deed, I must disavow my own identity. The deed erases my selfhood. "Wake *Duncan* with thy knocking," he shouts. "I would thou could'st." The actor has a choice here—"Wake Duncan" with the emphasis on "Wake" can be a command to the dead king. With the emphasis on the first syllable of "Duncan," the command is to the knocker at the gate. The actor looks either at the room in which the ineradicable deed has been done or at the gate from which discovery and, finally, retribution will come.

The knocking continues, overlapping into the next scene, suggesting the flexibility and fluidity of Shakespeare's dramaturgy. As Macbeth absorbs the dimensions of his crime, the Porter plays a variation on a theme by turning the South Entry into "Hell Gate." In "th'name of *Belzebub*," he admits several malefactors, including "an Equivocator, that could sweare in both the scales against eyther Scale, who committed Treason enough for Gods sake, yet could not equivocate to Heaven." This is an unmistakable reference to Fr. Garnet. Macduff and Lennox enter. Macduff will enter again later, to kill Macbeth. The Porter, like the Gravedigger in *Hamlet*, shows off his wit with his betters. Macbeth enters, takes Macduff to the door of Duncan's chamber, and agrees with Lennox about the prodigies of the night just ending. " 'Twas a rough Night," Macbeth says. Macduff emerges from Duncan's chamber shouting or whispering, "horror, horror, horror." He compares the sight to "the great Doomes Image"—Judgement Day—a suggestion that the scene continues in Lady Macbeth's reference to "a hideous Trumpet [that] calls to parley / The sleepers of the House." Macduff refuses to tell her what has happened: "The repetition in a Womans eare, / Would murder as it fell." To make Lady Macbeth a stereotypic female is ironic, of course. More deeply ironic is that, as John Andrews says, she "will in time prove unable to withstand the 'Repetition' of what she and her husband have done" (1993, 62). Macbeth enters and speaks what he knows to be true in a deeper sense than what can be understood by the other shocked thanes: "Had I but dy'd an houre before this chance, / I had liv'd a blessed time." He goes on to say that he has slain the grooms that had been guarding Duncan—"the Murtherers, / Steep'd in the Colours of their Trade." Lady Macbeth collapses: "[S]he may feign it as a means of deflecting interest from her husband or it may be a first sign of the price she is to pay" (Brown 1963, 48). The thanes resolve to get dressed and "question this most bloody piece of worke." Because "there's Daggers in mens Smiles," Malcolm and Donalbain resolve to flee to separate destinations.

Coleridge's vehement opinion about the scene—"the disgusting passage of

the Porter . . . I dare pledge myself to demonstrate an interpolation of the actors''
(1960, 1:69)—has been thoroughly refuted. The *themes* of the scene, particularly
damnation and equivocation, pervade the rest of the play. Furthermore, the scene
is a dramatic necessity. As W. E. Hales states, ''A monotony of horror cannot
be sustained. . . . If we retain [the knocking], we must retain him. . . . The sound
of a fresh voice after we have listened so long to that guilty conference is very
cordial'' (quoted in Furness 1873, 145). Harbage says that the Porter's ''glum
jocularities, the cadging for a tip, the subsequent ribaldries, draw a boundary
between night and day, between hell and earth, isolating the Macbeths in their
monstrous universe, and returning us to a seamy but sane normality'' (1963,
384). Macbeth, of course, draws suspicion upon himself by killing the grooms.
''Wherefore did you so?'' Macduff demands. Does Lady Macbeth faint or feint?
Her collapse or her act at least drives the scene in a different direction.

An old man who has lived for seventy years cannot remember anything as
''dreadfull'' or ''strange'' as this ''sore night.'' He and Ross discuss the unnatural ''Darknesse,'' the downing of a ''Faulcon'' by a ''Mousing Owle,'' and
the attack by ''*Duncans* Horses,'' ''Contending 'gainst Obedience, as they
would / Make Warre with Mankinde.'' Such things are ''unnaturall, Even like
the deed that's done.'' ''The audience has been brought from intense excitement
to general reflection,'' says Brown (1963, 49). Ross argues against the guilt of
Malcolm and Donalbain: ''Thriftless Ambition, that will raven up / Thine owne
lives meanes.'' We learn from Macduff that Macbeth has ''gone to Scone / To
be invested'' as King. Macduff, however, will not go to the coronation. He will
return to his home in Fife.

The scene suggests that nature itself either reflects or responds to the murder
of Duncan. It is as if order has been turned upside down. Nocturnal searchers
of fields rise up to down falcons. Horses that carry men into battle issue forth
as if to make war on them. The sun refuses to shine. Macduff betrays no suspicion—unless by tone of voice—but chooses not to attend Macbeth's coronation, that is, not to be there to pledge his fealty personally. He seems to have
reservations about Macbeth.

"BUT WHO DID BID THEE JOYNE WITH US?"

Certainly Banquo has reservations. He ''feare[s]'' that Macbeth has ''play'd
most fowly for'' the crown. Yet Banquo agrees to attend the ''great Feast'' and
''solemne Supper'' that Lady Macbeth and Macbeth mention. Banquo says that
his ''duties / Are with a most indissoluble tye for ever knit'' to the new king.
Macbeth elicits from Banquo information about Banquo's afternoon trip by
horseback, including the fact that Fleance will accompany Banquo. Macbeth
dismisses his retinue, including Lady Macbeth, and complains about all that he
has given up to make ''the Seedes of *Banquo* Kings.'' He has ''[de]fil'd [his]
Minde, Put / Rancours in the Vessell of [his] Peace,'' and has given his ''eternal
Jewell / . . . to the common Enemie of Man, / To make them Kings.'' Macbeth's

servant (probably Seyton) brings in two men to whom Macbeth has spoken earlier. Macbeth has convinced them that Banquo was their enemy and hopes that they are not "so Gospell'd to pray for this good man," that is, to "praye for them which hurt you, and persecute you" (Matthew 5:44). Macbeth convinces them to ambush Banquo and Fleance. As he had with Duncan, Macbeth talks of sending his victim to eternity: "*Banquo*, thy soules flight, / If it finde Heaven, must finde it out to Night."

Lady Macbeth enters. "Nought's had, all's spent," she says. "Better to be that which we destroy, / Than by destruction dwell in doubtfull joy." She tells Macbeth that "what's done is done." He replies that his mind is like a rack, a device of "torture" on which he lies "In restless extasie." He would rather let "Both the Worlds suffer, / Ere we will eate our Meale in fear, and sleepe / In the affliction of these terrible Dreames, / That shake us Nightly." In other words, he would destroy both heaven and earth rather than endure his fear and affliction. He envies Duncan, who "sleepes well . . . in his Grave." He complains of the continuing necessity of "mak[ing] our Faces Vizards to our Hearts, / Disguising what they are"; however, once having assumed a "False Face," he must continue to hide "what the False Heart doth know." His nature was once "too full o'th' Milke of humane kindness." Now, his mind is "full of Scorpions." He alludes to the murder of Banquo as "a deed of dreadfull note," but he refuses to inform Lady Macbeth. "Be innocent of the knowledge, dearest Chuck," he says, again, as in his earlier "dear Wife," incorporating terms of endearment into his black thoughts. He invokes "seeling Night" to "Scarfe up the tender Eye and pitifull Day" and to "Cancell and teare to pieces that great Bond, / Which keepes me pale." If Lady Macbeth would gladly call a halt to destruction, he claims that "Things bad begun, make strong themselves by ill."

Lady Macbeth and Macbeth exchange orientations as the play develops. This is not a constant process, as the banquet scene shows, but it does occur. What was "This Nights great Businesse" for her becomes for him the "Businesse" of Banquo's "execution." The fearful, hallucinating, blood-obsessed thane of the early portions of the play, appalled by "every noyse," becomes almost impervious to such sounds as "a Night-shrieke." The Lady Macbeth, who could say that "the sleeping, and the dead, / Are but as Pictures," becomes a sleepwalker describing her own damnation. This scene suggests a moment of transition. Macbeth, himself wandering the scarcely visible pathways of his own dark imagery, has planned a murder with all the thoughtful preparation—"In every point twice done, and then done double"—that went into her plotting of the assassination. But he does not confide in her. He has become an independent agent of evil, trying somehow to correct the problems raised by a previous crime through yet another crime. The manipulation of the two murderers

will seem to hang fire, to lack forward drive, if the actor does not take the opportunity Shakespeare has given him to show Macbeth's half-conscious prowling within the cage of his own deed: he is restlessly insecure, doubting

the murderers' resolve; he returns instinctively, as close as he may, to ideas
of goodness and love. (Brown 1963, 50)

What does he mean by "that great Bond"? Here, I think, he wishes that evil
were somehow a separate entity, a kingdom apart from God, that he lived in a
Manichean world which he could then rule. That he does not frustrates him,
but, as with his couplets just before the murders of Duncan and Banquo, he
continues to acknowledge what world he is in. Lady Macbeth begins to lapse
toward the next world. Her effort at the banquet scene is her final gesture toward
retaining her "doubtfull joy" as Queen. Clarendon says that Helen Faucit
"shuddered at the mention of the 'terrible dreams,' with which she too was
shaken. The sleep-walking scene was doubtless in the Poet's mind already"
(quoted in Furness 1873, 193).

The First Murderer asks the Third who has sent him: *"Macbeth."* Banquo
and Fleance enter. Banquo is struck down, but Fleance escapes.

Kenneth Muir calls the escape of Fleance "[t]he turning point of the play"
(1964, 91). Fleance's survival allows history to continue as a force superior to
Macbeth's efforts to subvert it. Harbage argues that "Macbeth's *perfect spy o'
th' time* [to the Murderers in the previous scene] may be taken to mean that his
agent would be present to direct them" (1963, 388). The Third Murderer does
know that "all men" begin to walk "from hence to th'Pallace Gate." Most
modern productions make the Third Murderer the attendant who brought the
two Murderers to Macbeth. That attendant becomes Macbeth's armor-bearer,
Seyton. Arguments that the Third Murderer is Macbeth (see Furness 1873, 200–
203) break down against Macbeth's reaction to the news that Fleance has escaped ("Then comes my Fit againe"). Still, the Third Murderer introduces a
note of mystery. Three Murderers correspond with the three Weird Sisters. That
fact alone lends an eeriness to the brief assassination scene. It is probable that
whoever played the Third Sister doubled as Third Murderer. Shakespeare's
dramaturgy—his writing of plays in which smaller parts were doubled—suggested the Third Murderer to him.

The banquet scene—one of the big court scenes that Shakespeare sometimes
places in the middle of his plays (the "Gonzago" scene in *Hamlet*, for example)—
finds the guests being seated by Macbeth. Lady Macbeth "keepes her State"—a
throne with a canopy over it—but Macbeth promises to "mingle with Society."
Instead, after he promises that they will all "drinke a Measure / The Table round,"
he approaches the door and tells the First Murderer, "There's blood upon thy
face." Macbeth learns that Fleance has escaped, but then he is called back to his
duties as host by Lady Macbeth. As Macbeth prepares to join his guests, the Ghost
of Banquo enters *"and sits in Macbeths place."* He does not see it, however, until
he attempts to find a place at the table. He becomes very upset.

The Knight of Burning Pestle, a play assigned to 1607, alludes to the Ghost's
appearance:

When thou art at thy table with thy friends,
Merry in heart and fill'd with swelling wine,
I'll come in midst of all thy pride and mirth,
Invisible to all men but thyself,
And whisper such a sad tale in thine ear
Shall make thee let the cup fall from thy hand,
And stand as mute and pale as death itself. (Nethercot, Baskervill & Heltzel,
    1971, 550)

Lady Macbeth rushes forward to try to calm him, comparing his "Impostors to true feare" to a "womans story, at a Winters fire / Authoriz'd by her Grandam." Macbeth is paying, he thinks, for a transgression of progress. His killing of Banquo is a reversion to "th'olden time / Ere humane Statute purg'd the gentle Weale," where "gentle" is proleptic, a product of civilization. Again, he keeps before himself a sense of how things should be, regardless of his effort to wrench them from their proper frame. The Ghost exits. Macbeth begins a toast. "Give me some Wine, fill full." The Ghost reenters. Macbeth challenges it: "[B]e alive againe, And dare me to the Desart with thy Sword." He faces the second appearance, according to David Garrick, "with a recovering mind" (quoted in Furness 1873, 221). The one shape Macbeth cannot abide or stand up to, however, is "that," that is, the image of his own guilt, the archetype of God within him. Unlike "the rugged Russian Beare, / The arm'd Rhinoceros, or th'Hircan Tiger," that is something in himself he cannot subdue or combat. His odd line "If trembling I inhabit then" can be partially explained by his sense that Banquo inhabits him, and is not just an external and independent object. As A. Symons points out (quoted in Furness 1873, 216), he cannot say, as of the dagger, "There's no such thing," nor can he agree with Lady Macbeth when she equates whatever he is looking at now with "the Ayre-drawne-Dagger which you said / Led you to *Duncan*." Macbeth imputes unnatural qualities to Lady Macbeth, who can "behold such sights, / And keepe the naturall Rubie of [her] Cheekes." Banquo's ghost *is* Macbeth's "shadow" in a Jungian sense, a personality made up of all that Macbeth has repressed from his own persona—"his Royaltie of Nature." While he has gone about the assassination with Machiavellian craftsmanship, something in him remembers what is it to kill another human being. The banquet scene is, for Macbeth, an analogue to Lady Macbeth's mad scene. The "good meeting" breaks up in "most admir'd disorder." As the thanes line up to make a ceremonial departure, Lady Macbeth tells them to "Stand not upon the order of your going, / But go at once." She bids them a "kinde goodnight" after Macbeth has proved his *un*kindness, his alienation from his kind, in murdering Banquo, and in claiming "What man dare I dare" while having gone beyond what "may become a man." It is too late to make the claim of such humanity. If the murder of Banquo is "strange"—that is, beyond comprehensible boundaries—Banquo's appearance at the banquet is "more strange / Then such a murther is." But something deep down in the web

of "understood Relations" has "brought forth / The secret'st man of Blood"—
that is, the victim, thought "safe in a ditch," and his killer, believing himself
safe, to whom the victim appears, in a terrible simultaneity. Macbeth mentions
to Lady Macbeth that Macduff "denies his person / At our great bidding."
Macbeth uses a plurality which the scene just ending, along with Macduff's
defection, is denying him. His reliance now cannot be on kingly prerogative but
on "the three weyard Sisters" to whom he will go "to morrow," that is, on
the next day, and find out about the future. He will continue, he says, to "wade"
in "blood" and to act the "strange things" he has "in head." Again using a
plural pronoun, as if assuming a role in his own kingdom of night, as opposed
to Scotland, he says, "We are yet but yong indeed," as if he is but an inex-
perienced adventurer in this new world. Most modern editors change "indeed"
to "in deed"—that is, I have only begun on this career of "strange things,"
and the line will obviously support that meaning. Brown suggests that "every
resolve seems to belong to purposes that are not wholly Macbeth's" (1963, 53).

The configuration of the banquet scene insists that Lady Macbeth not be at
the table. Peter Reynolds is simply wrong when he says that "Lady Macbeth
remains seated and, together with the rest of the company, waits to begin eating"
(1988, 75). Reynolds goes on to say that "she presumably also leaves the table
to confront her husband" (77). No. Macbeth says she "keepes her State," at
the beginning of the scene, meaning that, to calm Macbeth, she leaves the throne,
coming out from under the canopy (see Furness 1873, 207). An observer of
Helen Faucit's Lady Macbeth said, " 'She descends from her throne to pacify
the company' " (quoted in Carlisle 1983, 222). She is not at the table, nor does
she ever get there. The scene is modeled on Holy Communion, where the rubrics
say

> And if any of those be an open and notorious evil liver, so that ye congre-
> gation by him is offended, or have done any wrong to hys neighbours by
> word or dede: ye Curate havyng knowledge thereof, shall cal hym, and
> advertyse hym, in any wise not to presume to the Lordes table, until he
> have openly declared him self to have truely repented, and amended his
> former naughty lyfe. (Book of Common Prayer, 1605)

The opening prayer is to "Almighty God, unto whom al hartes be open, al
desires knowne, and from whom no secretes are hyd" The emphasis on blood
and wine, here horribly disjoined, reiterates the underlying archetype. Whether
the Ghost appears on the modern stage is a matter of debate, but the stage
direction and Forman's witness of it in April 1611 argue that it *did* appear in
Shakespeare's production. (See the discussion in Furness 1873, 210–16). According to Stuart Vaughan, "The ghost, on the Elizabethan stage, was visible
in full daylight. There was no way of making him seem intangible. What gave
him his aura of horror was the audience's knowledge that they were seeing a
dead person walking about" (1961, 192). According to J. Q. Adams, "The

apparition is nothing but the hallucination of Macbeth's overwrought emotions,'' but that we must "accept the visible presentation of the Ghost as a stage-necessity, but ever keep in mind the fact that what we see is merely one of the 'horrible imaginings' which are constantly torturing Macbeth, and which he cannot distinguish from reality" (1931, 194). We are in Macbeth's position here, knowing as we do about the murder, but also watching the guests and Lady Macbeth respond to Macbeth's outbursts. She is in a middle position, knowing of his guilt for Duncan's murder and his tendency to hallucinate. What the ghost *is*, of course, is another question. In the Roman Polanski film, it was still bleeding. It seems to be somewhere between a corpse ("Thou hast no speculation in those eyes / Which thou dost glare with") and the very articulate, emotional, and sensing ghost of King Hamlet. T. Campbell suggests that "Mrs. Siddons, I believe, had an idea that Lady Macbeth beheld the spectre of Banquo, and thereat her self-control and presence of mind enabled her to surmount her consciousness of the ghastly presence" (quoted in Furness 1873, 211). The sense of the scene, however, is that she could not see the ghost of a man she does not know has been murdered. In John Barton's *Hamlet* for the Royal Shakespeare Company (RSC) in 1980, Gertrude *did* see the ghost of her murdered husband, but hid the fact from Hamlet. Suffice it that the ghost of Banquo in the modern theater calls for an interpretation that will at least allow for Macbeth's terror and for his possible partial recovery at the ghost's second appearance. The allusion in *The Knight of the Burning Pestle* has the ghost visible only to Macbeth, whispering a sad tale, causing Macbeth's cup to drop and him to stand mute and pale. Part of that formula—the ghost's communication and Macbeth's silence—does not apply to the scene as scripted. A sixteenth-century commentator, Ludwig Lavater, describes the plastic versatility of ghosts. They could appear "berayde with bloud. . . . Sometimes a shadowe hath only appeared: sometimes a hand, sometimes an instrument, as a staffe, a sworde, or some such thing which the spirite helde in his hande. Sometimes . . . onley a hoarse kinde of voyce was heard" (1929, 92). One of the visual ironies of the end of the scene is described by Hunter: "The coda of the scene shows the King and Queen, now alone, slumped in their finery amid the debris of the 'great feast' " (1994, 799).

There follows the probably spurious Hecate scene.

Lennox and a Lord discuss events in Scotland and draw ironic morals: "Men must not walke too late." Suspicion of Macbeth has become open, and forces are gathering against him. Malcolm is in England. Macduff has gone there "to pray the Holy King" Edward. An army is being raised and a crusade "(with him above / To ratifie the Worke)" is forming. The purpose is not merely to depose Macbeth, but to "Give to our Tables meate, sleepe to our Nights: / Free from our Feasts, and Banquets bloody knives; / Do faithfull Homage, and receive free Honors." In other words, the goal of the crusade is to restore order in all senses of the word, with an emphasis on those rituals whereby the positive powers of the supernatural can be contacted and transmitted. Lennox prays that a "holy Angell" will fly to England "that a swift blessing / May soone returne to this our suffering Country, / Under a hand accurs'd."

The scene is "choric," both a commentary and a narrative, showing that a countermovement is forming against Macbeth's tyranny. Clearly, this impulse is endowed with the spiritual auspices necessary to its own success and is informed by a purpose of returning Scotland to spiritual well-being. Lennox, being an attendant lord, has no reason to depict the crusade in these terms. It is more than just political, or just historical. Harbage suggests that the scene "prepares us for the ambiguous prophecies that Macbeth will get from the Witches" (1963, 390).

"A DEED WITHOUT A NAME"

The Weird Sisters, knowing that Macbeth is on his way, prepare an unholy brew out of which will come the second set of prophecies that at once reassure Macbeth and predict the nature of his downfall. Of the ingredients, Dr. Johnson brilliantly observes that Shakespeare

> multiplies all the circumstances of horror. The babe, whose finger is used, must be strangled in its birth; the grease must not only be human, but must have dropped from a gibbet, the gibbet of a murderer; and even the sow, whose blood is used, must have offended nature by devouring her own farrow. (quoted in Furness 1873, 250)

It might be added that the "Baboones blood" used to "Coole" the "Cawdron" and the "Sowes blood" lend a distinctly antisacramental aspect to the occasion. Thomas Nashe points at what Macbeth insists on ignoring as he visits the Weird Sisters: "everything must be interpreted backward as Witches say their Paternoster" (1594, 294). Macbeth enters and asks, "What is't you do?" They reply, "A deed without a name." He demands that they answer his questions, even if the consequences amount to universal destruction, "Though you untye the Windes, and let them fight / Against the Churches." Macbeth is warned to "Beware the Thane of Fife." Here, the Sisters begin with something already known (like the treason of Cawdor) as an entrance to further predictions. Macbeth is told that "none of woman borne / Shall harme" him, that he will "never vanquish'd be, untill / Great Byrnam Wood, to high Dunsmane Hill / Shall come against him." Like Lady Macbeth with his letter much earlier, he interprets the prophecies *his* way. He insists on knowing, "Shall *Banquo's* issue ever / Reign in this Kingdome?" The Weird Sisters tell him to "Seeke to know no more." He threatens them with "an eternal Curse." They can laugh at him—we are cursed already—or cower at this creature suddenly more powerful and more evil than they. What Macbeth gets is a line of kings that seems to "stretch out to 'th'cracke of Doome," with Banquo smiling at Macbeth and pointing at the kings "for his." "Let this pernitious houre," Macbeth says, "stand aye accursed in the Kalender." His own future erased, he speaks as if he had the power to contaminate the future, at least to put a curse on this day to time's last syllable. When he says, "[D]amn'd all those that trust them," however, he pronounces his own damnation. As Hiram Corson explains, "He is now in the firm grip of fate. The free agency he might have exercised at the outset, which he received the wise caution of Banquo, he has forfeited; his self-determination is lost" (quoted in Furness, 1873, 273). Macbeth has even failed to find the doubtful comfort of hardness of which Richard Hooker speaks: "[S]ometimes the very custom of evil, making the heart obdurate against whatever instructions to the contrary" (593, 1039). The instructions to the contrary continue to live in both Macbeth and Lady Macbeth.

Macbeth learns that Macduff is "fled to England." Time, instead of something Macbeth controls, now "anticipat'st [his] dread exploits." He determines to "Seize upon Fife; give to th' edge o'th'sword / His Wife, his Babes, and all unfortunate Soules / That trace him in his Line." He enters to talk with "these Gentlemen," presumably those he has hired to commit the atrocity at Fife.

Not knowing what is coming toward her and her family, Lady Macduff complains of her husband's flight to England. "He wants the natural touch." She is "in this earthly world: where to do harme / Is often laudable, to do good sometime / Accounted dangerous folly." True of the world at large, her complaint is particularly true of Scotland. The Murderers break in and kill her and her son. In the 1995 Stratford, Ontario, production, one of Macduff's daughters looked on from downstage. As the Murderers closed in on her, the lights went out. We were left with the visualization of continuing brutality implanted in our retinas.

The scene shifts to England, where Malcolm and Macduff mourn for a Scotland where "each new Morne, New Widdowes howle, new Orphans cry, new sorowes / Strike heaven on the face." Malcolm is suspicious of Macduff. "Why in that rawnesse left you Wife, and Childe?" Malcolm asks. "Rawness" means, according to Dr. Johnson, "without maturity of counsel" (quoted in Furness 1873, 279). Malcolm alludes to the fallen angel, Lucifer: "Angels are bright still, though the brightest fell." If this is an echo of 2 Corinthians 11:14 ("Satan himself is transformed into an Angel of light"), then Malcolm signals his fear that Macduff may be an agent sent to trap him. 2 Corinthians 11:13 warns that "such false apostles are deceitful workers, and transform themselves into the Apostles of Christ." Malcolm proceeds to deny that he has any of "The King-becoming Graces, / As Justice, Verity, Temp'rance, Stablenesse, / Bounty, Perserverance, Mercy, Lowliness, / Devotion, Patience, Courage, Fortitude." A portion of his list seems to derive from Galatians 5:22–23: "But the frute of the Spirit is love, joye, peace, long suff'ring, gentlenes, goodnes, faith, / Mekenes, temperancie: against such there is no Law," because, as the Geneva Gloss says, "thei are under the spirit, or grace." In other words, Malcolm demonstrates that the "Graces" are endowed *by* grace, a concept he will reiterate more positively at the end of the play. Here, Malcolm sounds like Macbeth: "[H]ad I powre, I should / Poure the sweet Milke of Concord, into Hell, / Uprore the universall peace, confound / All unity on earth." Convinced, Macduff says that his "hope ends heere." But Malcolm, having delivered the "Childe of integrity" from Macduff, "Unspeake[s his] owne detraction." Has all this been a Machiavellian scheme that shows that Malcolm is little better than a modern politician? A Doctor enters to tell Malcolm that King Edward will cure "a crew of wretched Soules." Edward "solicits heaven," obviously in a different version of "supernaturall solliciting" than that Macbeth attributed to the Weird Sisters much earlier. Edward, curer of "the Evill," is the spiritual opposite of Macbeth. Ross enters to tell Macduff that his "Wife and Babes" have been "Savagely slaughter'd." When Malcolm urges "Revenge," Macduff says "He ha's no Children." That probably means Macbeth—I cannot revenge myself on *his* children—but it can refer to Malcolm, who is leaving Macduff no space in which to grieve. The actor must determine the meaning of the line. Macduff does decide to face "this Fiend of Scotland . . . Front to Front." Malcolm says, "This time goes manly," with the emphasis on *this* probably. In other words, now you sound like a man and align yourself with the time, which is a context for revenge. Later, Macduff, having killed Macbeth, will say that "the time is free." Malcolm's line works within the "discourse of manliness" that the play conducts and also contributes to the theme of time as distorted and wrenched out of its lineal sequence as opposed to its being one of the rhythms in which invisible supernatural sanctions and continuities can work their positive benefits. Most editors (see Muir 1964, 140) accept Nicolas Rowe's 1709 emendation of "time" as "tune." Why? Macduff has not alluded to music but has called on the *time* to be erased between the present and his meeting with Macbeth: "[G]entle Heavens, / Cut short all intermission." This is, says Tillyard, "a scene of order and stability, which gets much of its effect because it follows, and is interrupted by the report of Macbeth's culminating crime and supreme act of disorder, the murder of Macduff's family" (1946, 317).

"THE NIGHT IS LONG, THAT NEVER FINDES THE DAY"

The line with which Malcolm ends the scene in England is a further reference to time and its distortion in Scotland. The line makes a transition to the next scene which shows us precisely that long night—Lady Macbeth's madness. It will never find the day but must forever repeat the night of Duncan's murder, with an occasional reference to the concentric consequences of that murder, the killings of Banquo and the wife of the Thane of Fife. Her last line as sentient being had been, "You lacke the season of all Natures, sleepe."

Gary Wills convincingly compares Lady Macbeth, in nightgown "with a Taper," with the Duchess of Gloucester in *II Henry VI*. The Duchess, after dealing in black magic, must do penance "in a White Sheet, and a Taper burning in her hand." Elinor had wanted Gloucester to be king. She says, "Darke shall be my Light, and Night my Day. / To thinke upon my Pompe shall be my Hell." Lady Macbeth's entrance, Wills argues, "said, to Shakespeare's audience, repentant sorceress" (1995, 87). If so, the image of repentance belies the fact that it comes unconsciously, and therefore too late. Lady Macbeth's "damned spot" links her with Gertrude, won "with witchcraft of [Claudius's] wits," who sees "such black and grained spots, / As will not leave their Tinct."

The sleep-walking scene, like the first scene of *Antony and Cleopatra*, is framed, in this instance by a Doctor and a Lady in Waiting who has asked that the Doctor observe Lady Macbeth. Lady Macbeth is conducting an unconscious play-within-a-play in which the suspicions of all of Scotland are confirmed. Claudius looked at the nightmare of his murder of a king as Hamlet presented "Gonzago." Here, Lady Macbeth describes the nightmare of guilt she is having. Obviously, her trip back into the murder chamber made a terrible impression on her—"yet who would have thought the olde man to have had so much blood in him." This is not a question in the Folio, but rather a statement. She asks, "[w]hat need we feare? who knowes it, when none can call our power to ac-compt." The editorial change to "what need we fear who knows it?" is un-necessary; "who knowes it" means "who dares *acknowledge* the truth when we are all-powerful?" Here we get an assertion of invulnerability within a mo-ment of absolute *loss* of power, as Lady Macbeth wanders along pulled by the strings of a conscience—"a heart so white"—that she had denied earlier. She reiterates a lack of fear in the context of its realization. "She is now weak, sick, broken," according to Harbage (1963, 394). "Hell is murky," she says, as something in her realizes that this is damnation. Michael Gearin-Tosh adds, "We see Lady Macbeth's delicacy and sensuousness only now that it is lost, and we see the loss from the cruellest perspective, through her own eyes" (1988, 17). One of the scene's piercing ironies is "her delusion of closeness to her husband" (Brown 1963, 57). For her, "Memorie, the Warder of the Braine" is far more than "a Fume." It is total, and, with the exception of her interspersed recall of overconfidence which sharpens her despair, is totally negative. She had prayed, "Come thick Night, / And pall thee in the dunnest smoake of Hell." Now, as in the many curses of the first set of *Henry* plays, the prayer comes round to plague the inventor.

To feel the future in the instant and to anticipate it by murder is to deny oneself any future, indeed to be forced to repeat the past with all of its future implications vividly present in that past. As Bradley says, "Lady Macbeth, who thought she could dash out her own child's brains, finds herself hounded to death by the smell of a stranger's blood" (1904, 32). What she would "highly," she now does "holily"—within God's order, damnation. Like Macbeth before, but more profoundly, Lady Macbeth experiences the condition described by St. Bernard:

> [The soul] feels itself both like to God and faithful to itself, inasmuch as its aptitude for divine things subsists, but at the same time false to God and to its own true nature; and hence it is rent in twain and feeling itself still like and seeing itself in part unlike, it conceives that horror of self which is the inner tragedy of the sinner's life. (quoted in Gilson 1936, 236)

"A little Water cleares us of this deed," she had said. Now "all the perfumes of Arabia" will not suffice to "sweeten this little hand." "[W]hat's done, is done," she had said. Now she says, "What's done, cannot be undone." "More needs she the Divine, then the Physitian," says the Doctor. But it is too late for that.

The play moves into a quick montage sequence which alternates between Malcolm's approaching army and Dunsinane, where Macbeth becomes the focal point for bad news. Menteth, Cathness, Angus, and Lennox enter—Lennox being one of the latest defections from Macbeth's side—and announce, "The English powre is neere." Angus says that "minutely Revoltes upbraid [Macbeth's] Faith-breach." The "Breach in Nature, / For Ruins wastfull entrance" that Macbeth had made is being filled with soldiers, "the Med'cine of the sickly Weale."

Macbeth enters, buoyed by the prophecies of the "Spirits that know / All mortall Consequences" and crying "fly false Thanes."

A messenger brings him word of the approach of the English army. Macbeth pauses to mourn what he "must not looke to have": "Honor, Love, Obedience, Troopes of Friends."

Malcolm orders each of his soldiers to "hew him down a Bough" to "make discovery / Erre in report of us."

Macbeth is told that the "Queene . . . is dead." He delivers the famous "To morrow" soliloquy. Immediately, he is told that "a moving Grove" is approaching. He begins to "pull in Resolution" and to become aware that the "Fiend" has equivocated with him and "lies like truth."

Malcolm commands that his soldiers "throw downe" their "leavy Skreenes."

Macbeth complains that he is "tied . . . to a stake" and that "Beare-like [he] must fight the course." Still, he demands "What's he / That was not borne of Woman?" Macbeth dispatches Young Seyward. Macduff enters, searching for Macbeth. Seyward remarks that "the Castles gently rendered."

Macbeth refuses to "play the Roman Foole, and dye / On [his] owne sword." Macduff confronts him. Macbeth tells Macduff that his "soule is too much charg'd / With blood of thine already." Macduff informs Macbeth that Macduff "was from his Mothers womb / Untimely ript." Harley Granville-Barker says that Shakespeare refuses to give Macbeth a "finely worded end [which] might seem to redeem him. . . . He allows him one gleam of incorrigible pride, he leaves him his animal courage, he sends him shouting to hell" (1995, 63). They fight.

Malcolm and his officers enter. Macduff comes in with the head of Macbeth and hails Malcolm as "King of Scotland." This is followed by an acclamation. Malcolm promises to "reckon with [the] several loves" of his followers and to do "what needfull else / That call's upon us, by the Grace of Grace, / [To] perform in measure, time and place."

With a *Flourish, Exeunt Omnes.*

Works Cited

Adams, J. Q., ed. 1931. *Macbeth*. Boston: Houghton, Mifflin.

Andrews, John, ed. 1993. *Macbeth*. London: J. M. Dent.

Book of Common Prayer. 1605. London.

Bradley, A. C. 1904. *Shakespearean Tragedy*. London: Macmillan.

Brown, John Russell, ed. 1963. *Macbeth*. Great Neck, N.Y.: Barron's.

Campbell, O. J., ed. 1961. *Macbeth*. New York: Bantam.

Carlisle, Carol. 1983. "Helen Faucit's Lady Macbeth." *Shakespeare Studies XVI*: 205–234.

Coleridge, S. T. 1960. *Shakespearean Criticism*. Edited by Thomas M. Raysor. New York: E. P. Dutton.

De Quincey, Thomas. 1823. "On the Knocking at the Gate in 'Macbeth.' " *London Magazine* (October). Reprinted in *His Infinite Variety*, ed. Paul N. Siegel. Philadelphia: J. B. Lippincott, 1964: 323–27.

Doran, Madeleine. 1941. "That Undiscovered Country: A Problem Concerning the Use of the Supernatural in *Hamlet* and *Macbeth*." *Philological Quarterly* 20 (Summer): 138–47.

Dowden, Edward. 1872. *Shakespere: A Critical Study of His Mind and Art*. Reprint. New York: Capricorn, 1962.

Furness, Horace H., Jr., ed. 1873. Variorum *Macbeth*. Philadelphia: J. B. Lippincott.

Gearin-Tosh, Michael. 1988. "The Treatment of Evil in *Macbeth*." In *Macbeth*. Edited by Linda Cookson and Brian Loughrey. London: Longman.

Granville-Barker, Harley. 1995. *Preface to "Macbeth."* Portsmouth, N.H.: Heinemann.

Hanford, James Holly, ed. 1953. *The Poems of John Milton*. 2d ed. New York: Ronald.

Harbage, Alfred. 1963. *William Shakespeare: A Reader's Guide*. New York: Noonday.

Hooker, Richard. 1593. *Of the Laws of Ecclesiastical Polity. Tudor Poetry and Prose*. Edited by J. William Hebel, Hoyt H. Hudson, et. al. New York: Appleton, Century, Crofts, 1953.

Hunter, G. K., ed. 1994. *Macbeth. Four Tragedies*. London: Penguin.

Knights, L. C. 1959. *Some Shakespearean Themes*. London: Chatto and Windus.

Lavater, Ludwig. 1572. *Of Ghostes and Spirites Walking by Nyght*. Translated into English by R. H., 1572. Edited by J. Dover Wilson and May Yardley. Oxford: Oxford University Press, 1929.

Muir, Kenneth, ed. 1964. *Macbeth*. London: Metheun.

Nashe, Thomas. 1594. *Terrors of the Night*. Edited by Gossart. 2d ed. London.

Nethercot, Arthur H., Bashervill, Charles R. and Heltzel, Virgil B. 1971. *Stuart Plays*. Rev. ed. New York: Holt, Rinehart, and Winston.

Reynolds, Peter. 1988. "The Banquet Scene." *Macbeth*. Linda Cookson and Bryan Loughrey, eds. London: Longman.

Taylor, Mark. 1990. "Letters and Readers in *Macbeth, King Lear*, and *Twelfth Night*," *Philological Quarterly* 69.

Tillyard, E.M.W. 1946. *Shakespeare's History Plays*. New York: Macmillan.

Vaughan, Stuart. 1961. Notes. In *Macbeth*. Edited by O. J. Campbell. New York: Bantam.

Wills, Gary. 1995. *Witches and Jesuits*. Oxford: Oxford University Press.

Ellen Terry as Lady Macbeth. From *The Royal Shakespeare* (London: Cassell, n.d.)

4

THEMES

The play encompasses the themes of Shakespeare's great tragedies: fate versus free will, appearance versus reality, man's significance versus his cosmic insignificance, sanity versus madness, and damnation versus salvation. This play, like *Hamlet* or *King Lear*, reflects the collision of two paradigms that constituted the English Renaissance. Underlying these themes, in this play, more than in any other, is the depth of the structure of religious belief as embedded in the culture at the turn of the seventeenth century. What follows is not a guide to background but to the context that informs *Macbeth* in every line and between the lines as well.

It is difficult today to acknowledge the allegory of good versus evil that informed the literature of long ago. We live in a world in which evil exists, but it is inflicted by clerkish men like Adolph Eichmann whom Hannah Arendt discovered at the center of the Nazi spider web, or under the euphemism of "ethnic cleansing" in Bosnia, or by one tribe upon another in Rwanda, or by one drug dealer upon another in Brooklyn, with innocent pedestrians caught in the cross fire. The Devil has dropped out of the equation. Phyllis McGinley's modern minister, the Reverend Doctor Harcourt, seldom mentions sin. *Macbeth* narrowed to modern dimensions is still an exciting and intriguing play, as I will suggest in discussing recent productions, but it lacks the cosmic dimension that is irrefutably there in the inherited script. A deconstructionist, H. W. Fawkner, says "the 'Christian' issue in a drama like *Macbeth*—the reasons for and against viewing the play primarily in terms of Christian humanism—cannot be swept under the carpet during the process of deconstructing the play as a whole" (1990, 11). The saturation of the script in this material and the knowledge of it that most spectators would bring helps explain why, as Stephen Booth suggests, it is "impossible to find the source of any idea in *Macbeth*; every new idea seems already there when it is presented to us" (1983, 94). The materialist argument, with which I deal below, is that Duncan's world is hardly complete

and total, but flawed. Peter Stallybrass's more convincing suggestion (1982)—
also to be examined below—is that, if Shakespeare were to suggest how threat-
ening to the nature of things the assassination of a king could be, he had to
create a world that could be so threatened. This section looks at the sources of
that worldview.

The play may be partially syncretic—that is, partaking of different religious
premises—but it is more obviously Christian than such other syncretic plays as
Titus Andronicus or *King Lear*. The point is made by Stephen Siddall:

> The ceremonies in *Macbeth* have two major sources. One is the ancient
> war-like culture of the Anglo-Saxon epics, in which masculine virtues are
> celebrated in the lord's mead-hall. The other is specifically Christian and is
> evident through such powerful images as the Last Supper and the chalice
> which in I.7 Macbeth speaks of poisoning and which may be seen as re-
> curring in horribly parodic form as the cauldron the Witches fill with poi-
> soned entrails. (1988, 85)

Recent materialist criticism attempts to waft away the "essentialist" quality
of the script. It must, because the play seems to incorporate a consistent "world
picture." Unlike *King Lear*, where as Robert West says, we cannot be sure of
what the cosmic facts *are* (1968, 22), the cosmic facts here and Macbeth's battle
against them are vital to our grasp of *his* tragedy. For all of its margins and
problematizing, this play emerges from within the inherited and conservative
theological frame. It is therefore worth considering what that frame was as it
related to man and the destiny of man's soul within the Elizabethan reinterpre-
tation of the medieval Catholic worldview. Fine points of theology are unnecessary here, since Shakespeare was not writing for divines. The play, however,
does focus on the "inward man," which was Luther's emphasis and that of the
reformed church developing from Cranmer's prayer book after Elizabeth became
queen.

An attempt to recontextualize the play thematically is *not* to attempt to explain
the knotty issues of late sixteenth- and early seventeenth-century religious debate, but merely to suggest some of the commonplace assumptions of that moment and particularly the language in which the discussions were couched. These
words and metaphors flow into *Macbeth* more abundantly than most, if not all,
of the plays in the canon. It does not matter whether any of this is "what the
Jacobean believed" or "what Shakespeare believed." What matters is that
Shakespeare had this context available for dramatic purposes and used it here
even as he had discarded it in *King Lear*, in the latter case to ask what the
cosmic facts *are*, as opposed to exploring what happens when the traditional
sense of the cosmos is challenged.

I am convinced that Shakespeare decided that the dramatic impact of *Macbeth*
would be enhanced if he suggested that each of the major characters was
damned, or that *they* perceived themselves as damned. That each one does is

unequivocal. This element alone takes the play beyond the genre of the history play and tends to place it squarely within the framework of the Elizabethan world picture. *Macbeth* is one of the least "problematized" scripts in the canon. One must also bear in mind, however, Robert Ornstein's caveat that "the moral and providential platitudes that the Elizabethans and Jacobeans liked to see in print were not the piloting ideas at the forefront of their awareness" (1960, 20). In that sense, *Macbeth* can be seen as reactionary, as certainly this section will be labeled by postmodernist reviewers.

The Geneva Bible (1560) was the most popular Bible used during Shakespeare's lifetime. From "about 1596 on, [Shakespeare] more or less consistently used" it (Berry 1969, 20). (On this point, see also Noble, 1935, 75–76, and Shaheen, 1987, chap. 1.) It is the Bible I use here. Its consistent Calvinistic reading toward "election" does not seem to creep into the plays. One could argue, in fact, that *Macbeth* is almost Miltonic in its Arminianism, but where God must keep sending his Son on a new mission, finally inventing humility as a counter to pride, the world of *Macbeth* is self-correcting. In *Paradise Lost*, "had no remedy been provided, an active and eternal dualism would have been established, with God continuously losing ground as more and more of his weaker creatures were brought to Satan's side" (Hanford 1953, 195).

The play does, however, bring the

> tension between predestination and freewill . . . to an unusual pitch. . . . Shakespeare allows his work to approximate . . . the old story of Lucifer and the Lord . . . although the concern with the values of absolute Good and Evil is embodied in characters of excelling individuality and realism, yet the play's implications are universal. (Matthews 1962, 38)

The play does not, however, permit what Hanford calls an "active dualism" to develop. That is crucial to our understanding of Macbeth as tragic *hero*.

An age that stressed faith also emphasized the corollary of God's unknowability. The Joban imperative was reiterated in light of the necessities of a reformed church. Man can know God only by faith, or by fighting Him, in which case, God becomes a negative way of knowing, as for the damned in Dante's *Inferno*. Macbeth's quest for knowledge is heroic, quixotic. Because he does not accept unknowability, he is doomed to find out what he does not wish to know.

In Book 1 of the *Laws of Ecclesiastical Polity*, Richard Hooker, the great Anglican apologist, talks about the dangers of trying to understand the ways of God:

> Dangerous it were for the feeble brain of man to wade far into the doings of the Most High . . . our safest eloquence concerning him is our silence, when we confess without confession that his glory is inexplicable, his greatness above our capacity and reach. He is above, and we upon earth; therefore it behooveth our words to be wary and few. (1593, 1024)

The first part of the Sermon for Rogation Week repeats the contrast between man and God:

> And too much arrogancie it were for dust and ashes, to thinke that he can worthily declare his maker. It passeth for the darke understanding and wise-dome of a mortall man, to speake sufficiently of that divine Majestie, which the Angels cannot understand. We shall therefore lay apart to speake of the profound and unsearchable nature of Almightie God, rather acknowledging our weakeness, than rashly to attempt that is above all mans capacitie to compasse. (Rickey and Stoup 1966, 219)

"The little thereof which we darkly apprehend we admire," asserts Hooker, "the rest with religious ignorance we humbly and meekly adore" (1593, 1026).

Shakespeare makes evil equally unknowable in its workings, turning the mystery of God as urged by Hooker and others to advantage by maintaining the same silence toward the diabolical. Banquo comes closest with his awareness that "The Instruments of Darknesse" can "betray's / In deepest consequence," but it is a darkness that cannot be penetrated and a depth that cannot be plumbed by the finite mind. Banquo's response to the predictions is cautious. When he recognizes that a great betrayal *has* occurred, he insists that he stands "in the great Hand of God," perhaps looking at Macbeth as he says so. As Hooker argues, God is an indivisible God and, by implication, so is His world:

> Our God is one, or rather very Oneness and mere [absolute] unity, having nothing but itself in itself, and not consisting (as all things do besides God) of many things.

> The law whereby he worketh is eternal, and therefore can have no show or color of mutability. (1593, 1024, 1026)

God alone is creator: "So that we see it is the onely power of Gods word that maketh the earth fruitful, which else naturally is baren" (Geneva Gloss on Genesis 1:11). God is self-sufficient. He does not require anything from man, as Milton says in Sonnet XIX: "God doth not need / Either man's works or his own gifts." "Not that anything is made to be beneficial unto him, but all things for him to show beneficence and grace in them," says Hooker (1593, 1025), emphasizing the sacramental nature of creation.

Nothing is done without God's permission, or so argues the Geneva Gloss to Genesis 3:1: "God suffered Satan to make the serpent his instrument and to speak in him." When John says (14:30) that "the prince of this worlde commeth," the marginal Gloss informs us that "Satan executeth his rage & tyranie by the permission of God." The Second Sermon for Rogation Week informs us, "Hee hath good Angels, he hath evill angels, hee hath good men, and hee hath evill men" (Rickey and Stoup 1966, 226).

God is ubiquitous, as argued in the first part of the Sermon for Rogation Week:

> Hee is therefore invisible every where, and in every creature, and fulfilleth both heaven and earth with his presence. In the fire, to give heat, in the water to give moisture, in the earth to give fruit, in the heart to give his strength, yea in our bread and drinke is hee, to give us nourishment, where without him the bread and drinke cannot give sustenance, nor the hearbe health. . . . If it were not thus, that the goodnesse of God were effectually in his creatures to rule them, how could it bee that the maine sea, so raging and labouring to overflow the earth, could bee kept within his bounds and bankes as it is? . . . How could it be that the elements, so divers and contrary as they be among themselves, should yet agree and abide together in a concord, without destruction one of another to serve our use, if it came not onely of Gods goodnesse so to temper them? How could the fire not burn and consume all things, if it were let loose to goe whither it would, and not stayed in his sphere by the goodnesse of God, measurably to heat these inferiour creatures to their riping? Consider the huge substance of the earth, so heavie and great as it is: How could it so stand stably in the space as it doth, if Gods goodness reserved it not so for us to travell on? (Rickey and Stoup 1966, 221)

The frame and substance of nature and the place of man within it is captured by Hooker in a long periodic sentence which has its echoes in *Macbeth*:

> Now if nature should intermit her course . . . if the frame of that heavenly arch erected over our heads should loosen and dissolve itself; if celestial spheres should forget their wonted motions, and by irregular volubility turn themselves any way as if might happen; if the prince of the lights of heaven which now as a giant doth run his unwearied course . . . if the moon should wander from her beaten way, the times and seasons of the year blend themselves by disordered and confused mixture, the winds breathe out their last gasp, the clouds yield no rain, the earth be defeated of heavenly influence, the fruits of the earth pine away as children at the withered breasts of their mother no longer able to yield them relief; what would become of man himself . . . ? See we not plainly that obedience of creatures unto the law of nature is the stay of the whole world? (1593, 1028)

Macbeth can demand that "the frame of things dis-ioynte, / Both the Worlds suffer," but there *is* only one world, even if Macbeth would be willing to suffer in a self-created evil world. In pressing the words of ones "So wither'd, and so wilde in their attyre" toward "wither'd Murther," Macbeth suffers that withering that Hooker attributes to a mother's breasts.

The Bible reiterates the withering that attends a departure from God: "Thogh it were in grene & not cut downe, yet shal it wither before anie other herbe. So are the paths of all that Forget God. . . . His confidence also, shal be cut of, &

his trust *shalbe, as* the house of a spyder" (Job 8:12–14). The Geneva Gloss
to this passage reads, "Which is to day, and to morowe swept away." On the
departure of Christ and the disciples from Jerusalem, Peter cries, "[B]eholde,
the figge tre which thou cursedst, is withered" (Mark 11:21). The tree, according
to the Geneva Gloss on 11:14 had manifested "an outward shewe & appearance
without frute." "How sone is the figge tre withered!" cry the disciples in the
Matthew version of the story (21:20). Macbeth rejects the principle of "planting" that Duncan has enunciated and cancels his "Lease of Nature," jumping
immediately past time and into the latter days the Psalmist predicts for all men:
"[I]n the morning he groweth like the grass: / In the morning it florisheth and
groweth, *but* in the evening it is cut downe and withereth" (90:5–6). "[M]y
way of life," he says, "[i]s falne into the Seare, the yellow Leafe."

Macbeth's tragedy is not that he decides to kill Duncan but that he cannot
become independent. Even if a weaker agency than God, he would be his own,
himself alone. But he cannot fight free of his implication in the way things are
any more than Lady Macbeth can free herself of its embeddedness in her. The
world and all within it must be of a piece if their particular version of destiny
is to be acted out. Fate *cannot* "come . . . into the lyst." Fate is not an option
except as it—like "Chance"—is allied with God, a category properly defined
as the will of God.

Like Archimedes with his lever, Macbeth needs a place to stand. He would
wish a Manichean cosmos, an independent stance from which to wage his war.
"[T]hat great Bond / Which keeps me pale" is the unity of the world, the
oneness of God—*bonded*—and Macbeth's inevitable place there. Even if it
makes him pale, it proves him part of that nature. Fear is "pale-hearted Fear."
His cheek is "blanch'd with Fear"—the bond is coded in him. "[A] Heart so
White" is bloodless, and "Linnen cheekes . . . Are Counsailers to feare." He
keeps getting reminded what he is, where he is. Shedding blood makes *him*
bloodless. That is an inevitable consequence of his bonding to this order. The
irony is that the way to get rid of fear is to shed blood:

> Go pricke thy face, and over-red thy fear
> Thou Lilly-liver'd boy.

He can claim destruction as his own: "[W]hiles I see lives, the gashes / Do
better upon them," and then say, a moment later to Macduff, "[G]et thee back,
my soule is too much charg'd / With blood of thine already." He cannot escape
the order he is in because it is in him. What Saint Bernard says applies both to
Macbeth and Lady Macbeth: "The ills the soul now suffers after sin do now
replace that native goodness and distort it, deforming an order they can in no
wise destroy" (quoted in Gilson 1936, 295).

Macbeth recognizes, as Walter Curry says, that the acts of conscience that
torture him are really expressions of that outraged natural law, which "inevitably
reduces him as individual to the essentially human. This is the inescapable bond

that keeps him pale'' (1937, 127). Existentialism is not a philosophical stance available to Macbeth.

If he could become independent, he would lose, of course. The Geneva Gloss to Psalm 18 talks of ''the unspeakable power of his Father, thogh all the whole worlde shulde strive there against.'' That is what Macbeth *would* strive against, but he would do so from an independent, not a self-divided status where a ''soul . . . too much charg'd / With blood of thine already'' would neither be recognized nor necessary. As it is, his effort at independence becomes increasingly binding as ''that great Bond'' tightens in. As Curry says, Macbeth's actions lead ''to further irrationality . . . one of the penalties enacted is dire impairment of the liberty of free choice'' (1937, 134). In striving to be free, he becomes more engaged.

God is inescapable *in* even those who deny or oppose Him. Even as he plans his murders, Macbeth must phrase the results within the only dispensation available:

> Heare it not, *Duncan*, for it is a Knell,
> That summons thee to Heaven, or to Hell.
>
> It is concluded: *Banquo*, thy Soules flight,
> If it finde Heaven, must finde it out to Night.

With the Murderers, says J. R. Brown, Macbeth ''returns instinctively, as close as he may, to ideals of goodness and love'' (1963, 50). ''Are you so Gospell'd?'' he asks the Murderers. No other examples exist with which to communicate, which makes Macbeth's effort to shape ''the other examples'' so extraordinary. He tries to give word and action to ''A deed without a name.'' Banquo's ghost manifests ''an unnatural state of affairs against which Macbeth, architect of disorder himself, protests'' (Duthie 1966, 30). He must respond from a nature superior to his own disordering efforts, as Lady Macbeth will do later in her mad scene. ''The times has bene,'' he complains, ''That when the Braines were out the man would dye, / And there an end.'' Yes, he creates a ''strange'' opposite to what is natural and even claims to respond naturally to it, according to his ''disposition,'' but that opposite is never apart from him; indeed, it is his own projection, or, at least a thing that can manifest itself only *to* him. It is a thing coming from that part of the self that he would split off and divorce from himself. Since he must participate in God's order, it comes to him as a thing of horror. In a modern sense, of course, having forgotten what it is to kill a man, the repression leaps vividly before him as, in a Jungian sense, a ''horrible shadow.''

No other names exist, or, if they do, they are perversions or distortions of the truth that God is responsible for: ''the course of the yeere, the order of the starres, the thoughts of men, the differences of planets, the vertue of rootes, and whatsoever is hid and secret in nature'' (first part of the Sermon for Rogation

Week in Rickey and Stoup 1966, 222). Robert Burton describes this process of mimicry: "[W]here God hath a Temple, the Devil will have a chapel: where God hath sacrifices, the Devil will have his oblations; where God hath cere- monies, the Devil will have his traditions" (1628, III. vi. I, 1). No other models exist to emulate. Nor can they be invented. The knowledge upon which anti- ceremonies is based is inescapable:

> [E]ven the divels know and beleeve that Christ was borne of a virgin, that he fasted forty dayes and forty nights without meat and drinke, that he wrought all kinde of myracles, declairing himselfe very God: they beleeve also, that Christ for our sakes suffered most painefull death, to redeeme from everlasting death, and that hee rose againe from death the third day: they beleeve that hee ascended into heaven, and that he sitteth on the right hand of the father, and at the last end of this world shall come againe, and judge both the quicke and the dead. These articles of our faith the Divells beleeve, and so they beleeve all things that be written in the new and old Testament to be true: and yet for all this faith, they bee but Divells, re- maining still in their damnable estate, lacking the verie true Christian faith . . . a sure trust and confidence in Gods merciful promises, to be saved from everlasting damnation by Christ." (third part of the Sermon on Salvation in Rickey and Stoup 1966, 19–20)

The devils, however, have that knowledge only as a creed without the faith that informs belief.

The "Gospel," for example, to which Macbeth must allude in persuading the Murderers to do evil is Matthew 5:44: "Love your enemies: blesse them that curse you: doe good to them that hate you, and pray for them which hurt you, and persecute you." Macbeth's office as king *should* be similar to that of the bishops who, when consecrated in Elizabethan times, were thus enjoined:

> [G]raunte we beseche the, to this thy servante, suche grace that he may evermore be ready, to sprede abrode thy Gospel, and glad tidinges of rec- oncilement to God, and to use the aucthoritie geven unto him, not to des- troye, but to save, not to hurt, but to helpe, so that he as a wise and faithfull servaunt, geving to thy family meat in due season, maye at the last day be received into joye. (Book of Common Prayer, 1605)

Another obvious contrast between the function of a murderous tyrant and that of the efficacy of God's grace is drawn when Macbeth parodies the curate's exhortation to partake of the Eucharist: "I bydde you all that be heare present, and beseche you for the lorde Jesus Christes sake, that ye wyll not refuse to come thereto, beyng so lovingly called and bidden of God him selfe." Macbeth asks, "How say'st thou that *Macduff* denies his person / At our great bidding?"

A previous generation would have had no difficulty with G. Wilson Knight's assertion that the play represents "a wrestling of destruction and creation"

(1931, 153). In dealing with a single aspect of the play, Peter Stallybrass makes the same point: "Only by making his Sisters forces of darkness could Shakespeare suggest demonic opposition to godly rule" (1982, 194).

At some moments in the play the allusions to the Bible and to the theology of the day are particularly illuminating. In citing allusions, I will err in the direction of Peter Milward's inclusiveness (1987) since these plays were *heard*, as, for most people of Shakespeare's time, was the Bible. I roam beyond the "Criteria for a Valid Reference" defined by Shaheen, but, as Shaheen says, "the decision whether a passage is a reference to Scripture or has valid overtones of scripture is a subjective one, based on the reader's personal judgment" (1987, 59). Scripture was in the air, as were the Weird Sisters, and continues to ride the currents of this echoing script, which echoes not merely itself.

When Macbeth balances the words of the Weird Sisters, he begins to fall into a trap baited with apparent good: "This supernaturall soliciting / Cannot be ill, cannot be good." Hooker tells us that

> there is no particular evil which hath not some appearance of goodness whereby to insinuate itself. For evil as evil cannot be desired; if that be desired which is evil, the cause is the goodness which is, or seemeth to be, joined with it. Goodness dooth not move by being, but by being apparent, near, and present, which causeth the Appetite to be therewith most strongly provoked. (1593, 1038)

Macbeth recognizes that he has "no Spurre / To pricke the sides of [his] intent," intention here being the powerful steed that would carry the human will of "Vaulting Ambition." To that Hooker responds with the same metaphor: "For a spur of diligence, therefore, we have a natural thirst after knowledge ingrafted in us ... the very conceit of painfulness is as a bridle to stay us" (1593, 1038–39).

The encounters of Macbeth and Lady Macbeth in Act One are haunted by Biblical echoes, many from Genesis and Revelation, the first and last books. That is hardly coincidental. Christianity, according to Curry, "recognizes two tragedies of cosmic importance: (1) the fall of Lucifer and a third part of the angelic hosts ... and (2) the fall of Adam ... who set his will against God's will and so brought sin and limited freedom upon mankind" (1937, 67). Terry Eagleton points out that "someone must surely have proposed man's primal Fall as a mythic analogue to the murder of Duncan by Lord and Lady Macbeth" (1967, 91).

Lady Macbeth enjoins Macbeth to "looke like th'innocent flower, / But be the Serpent under't." The Bible calls Satan "That olde serpent called the devill and Satan, which deceiveth all the worlde" (Gloss to Revelation 12:9). Paul attributes a particular deception to Satan: the "serpent beguiled Eve through his subtiltie" (2 Corinthians 11:3). "As Satan can change himselfe into an Angel of light, so did he abuse the wisdome of the serpent to deceive man," states the Gloss to Genesis 3:1, a deception augmented by the skills attributed in the Gloss to 3:4: "This is Satans chiefest subtiltie, to cause us not to fear Gods threatenings." Macbeth's "Hath he ask'd for me?" reminds us of God's seeking of Adam in Genesis (3:9): "Where are thou?" The Gloss tells us that "The sinnefull conscience fleeth God's presence." The Gloss to Genesis 3:6 says that Adam acted "Not so much to please his wife, as mooved by ambition at her persuasion." After the Fall, as the Gloss to Genesis 3:7 says, "They began to fele their miserie, but they soght not to God for remedie."

"Your Face, my *Thane*," says Lady Macbeth, "is as a Booke, where men / May reade strange matters." In Revelation 20:12, we read, "And I sawe the dead, bothe great & smal stand before God: and the bokes were opened, & another boke was opened, which is *the boke* of life, and the dead were judged of those things, which were written in the bokes, according to their workes." The Gloss reads, "Everie mans conscience is as a boke wherein his dedes are written."

When Macbeth mentions "Heavens Cherubin, hors'd / Upon the sightlesse Curriors of the Ayre," that "Shall blow the horrid deed in every eye, / That teares shall drowne the winde," he echos Psalm 18:10: "And he rode upon Cherub and did flie, and he came flying upon the wings of the winde." The passage deals with "how horrible Gods judgements shalbe to the wicked. Darkness signifieth the wrath of God, as the clear light signifieth Gods favour" (Gloss to Psalm 18: 7–9). The rest of Psalm 18 testifies at length to God's skill in retribution in behalf of those who praise Him, as we assume Duncan has done. "His Vertues," as Macbeth says, "Will pleade like Angels, Trumpet-tongu'd against / The deepe damnation of his taking off." (One wonders how Shakespeare knew how to tongue a trumpet. It is done by the tongue's making 't' sounds.)

The angels of judgement in Revelation 9 capture much of the imagery and atmosphere of *Macbeth*: "And the fift Angel blew the trumpet, & I saw a starre falle from heaven unto the earth, and to him was given the keye of the bottomles pit" (9:1). The Gloss says that these are priests "who forsake the worde of God, & so fall out of heaven, & become Angels of darkness" and, of course, "the Pope." Verse 2 continues: "And he opened the bottomles pit, and there arose the smoke of the pit, as the smoke of a great fornace, and the sunne, and the ayre were darkened by the smoke of the pit."

When Macbeth says, "I am settled, and bend up / Each corporall Agent to this Terrible Feat," he is saying, in effect, that he will do the deed physically, but his heart will not be in it. According to Hooker, "another law there is, which toucheth [natural agents] as they are sociable parts united into one body; a law which bindeth them each to serve unto other's good, and all to prefer the good of the whole before . . . their own particular" (1593, 1031). That means that "Each corporall Agent" must unite with a spiritual goal. The distinction between the corporal and the spiritual is one aspect of Macbeth's effort to divide an inviolable unity.

As would be expected, Saint Paul develops this point at length. In Romans 6, he says, "Let not sinne reigne therefore in your mortal bodie, that ye shulde obey it in the lustes thereof" (6:12). "Neither give ye your membres as weapons of unrighteousness unto sin: but give your selves unto god, as they that are alive from the dead, and give your membres as weapons of righteousnes unto God" (6:13). "For sin shal not have dominion over you: for ye are not under the Law, but under grace" (6:14). The Geneva Gloss reads, "The mind first ministereth evil motions, whereby mans wil is entised: thence burst forth the lustes, by them the bodie is provoked, and the bodie by his actions doeth solicite the mind: therefore he commandeth that we rule our bodies." "Know ye not," says Paul in verse 16, "that to whomesoever ye give your selves as servants to obey, his servants ye are to whome ye obey, whether it be of sinne unto death, or of obedience unto righteousnes?" He goes on in verse 23 to say that "the wages of sinne is death." In 7:23, he says, "I see another law in my membres, rebelling against the law of my minde, & leading me captive unto the law of sinne, which is in my membres." The corporal agents to which Macbeth assigns the deed are, of course, those which die and can be damned: "O wretched man that I am, who shal deliver me from the bodie of this death!" (7:24), or, as the Gloss puts it, "This fleshlie lump of sinne and death." Flesh alone, says Paul, can only serve "the law of sinne" (7:25).

The Parable of the Talents (Matthew 25:14–30), which deals with what is owed to God, is reiterated in *Macbeth*. Both Macbeth and Banquo acknowledge their debt to Duncan and their dependence on his system of rewards:

> The service, and the loyaltie I owe,
> In doing it, payes it self.
> Your Highnesse part, is to receive our Duties.
>
> There if I grow,
> The Harvest is your owne.

Macbeth's is a pro forma statement of the feudal contract. Banquo picks up Duncan's metaphor of planting and makes of the King a creator. Lady Macbeth's response to Duncan is also pro forma, but it carries an implication that she does not perceive:

> Your Servants ever,
> Have theirs, themselves, and what is theirs in compt,
> To make their Audit at your Highnesse pleasure,
> Still to return your owne.

The parable says that "after a long season, the master of those servants came, and rekened with them." The Gloss reads, "The master receiveth him into his house to give him parte of his goods and commodities." Matthew says,

"Blessed *are* those servants, whome the Lord when he cometh shall find waking" (Matthew 25:19).

The parable, of course, deals with judgement, for which Lady Macbeth's "compt" is another word. As John Andrews argues, "by implication, she acknowledges that her duty to the king is rooted in her relationship to God" (1993, 34). Furthermore, her violation of that duty leads to the coming of the deeper version of "compt": "who knowes it, when none can call our powre to accompt."

Merchant W. Moelwyn suggests "Last Judgement" in "compt" and "make their audit" (1966, 78) but does not suggest the Parable of the Talents as a source of the motif. It is the *specific* version of the Last Judgement that Duncan's "You shall bid God 'ield you," Lady Macbeth's "Your servants ever," and her belated recognition of an accounting suggest. "This similitude teacheth how we oght to continue in the knowledge of God, and do good with those graces that God hath given us," says the Gloss. The result of the discarding of those graces, of course, is the command, "Cast therefore that unprofitable servant into utter darkness: there shalbe weping, and gnasshing of teeth" (Matthew 25:30).

The reward / punishment concept is reiterated, of course, in the Bible, as in Romans 9:28: "For he will make his account, & gather it into a short sume with righteousnes: for the Lord wil make a short count in the earth." In Matthew 25, those who do not take in "the least of these my brethren" (25:40) are ordered to "Departe from me ye cursed, into everlasting fyre which is prepared for the devil and his angels" (25:41).

At the end of the play, Malcolm promises, "We shall not spend a large expence of time, / Before we reckon with your severall loves, / And make us even with you." He does not claim, as his father had done, "More is thy due then more than all can pay." Instead, Malcolm puts himself in the place of the master of the parable: "But after a long season, the master of those servants came, and rekened with them" (Matthew 25:19).

A Judgement Day occurs in II.1. Macduff calls what he has seen "The Great Doomes Image" and commands that Malcolm and Banquo, "As from your Graves rise up, and walke like Sprights, / To countenance this horror." Although Macduff has commanded that "the Bell" be rung, Lady Macbeth mentions an instrument within the Judgement Day configuration:

> What's the Business?
> That such a hideous Trumpet calls to parley
> The sleepers of the House?

The parallel with 1 Corinthians 15:51–52 is clear: "We shal not al slepe. . . . In a moment, in the twinkling of an eye at the last trumpet: for the trumpet shal blowe, and the dead shal be raised up." Matthew, speaking of the Second Coming, says, "And he shal send his Angels with a great sounde of a trumpet" (24:30).

Macbeth and Lady Macbeth both command, "Let there be darkness" but in different ways. He would obviate knowledge of the murder both for God and for that sector of God within him, even as he recognizes that sector as his own fear:

> Starres hide your fires,
> Let not Light see my black and deepe desires:
> The Eye winke at the hand; yet let that bee,
> Which the Eye feares, when it is done to see.

Lady Macbeth's invocation fears prevention:

> Come thick Night,
> And pall the in the dunnest smoake of Hell,
> That my keene Knife see not the wound it makes,
> Nor heaven peepe through the Blanket of the darke,
> To cry hold, hold.

For her, even the knife might object, if it could see what it was doing, to the deed. The deed is not prevented, of course, but she notices "the dunnest smoake of Hell"; later, in her madness: "Hell is murky."

The play's participation in darkness is deeply theological.

> And yet darke Night strangles the travailing Lampe:
> Is't Nights predominance, or the Dayes shame,
> That Darkeness does the face of Earth intombe,
> When Living Light should kisse it?

Andrews reads "travailing Lampe" with the emphasis on lamp, that is, "the Sun . . . a lonely overburdened traveller, who has been assaulted and strangled by 'dark Night' " (1993, 70). Another reading would make the sun the lamp by which we travel, as it is usually edited, or by which we *travail*, as in the Folio. The latter reading has the resonance of "The Comfortable Words" of the Communion service: "Come unto me all that travaile and be heavy laden, and I shall refresh you." As Andrews notes, the lines "recall the Gospels' account of the Crucifixion" (70). At the death of Christ, according to Luke 23:44, "there was a darkness over all the land, until the ninth houre."

The damned, according to the second part of the Sermon of Falling from God,

> shall bee deprived of the heavenly light, and life that they had in Christ,
> whiles they abode in him: they shall be (as they were once) as men without
> God in this world, or rather in worse taking. And to be short, they shall
> bee given into the power of the devill, which beareth the rule in all that be
> cast away from God, as hee did in Saul and Judas, and generally in all

such, as worke after their owne willes, the children of mistrust and unbe-
liefe. (Rickey and Stoup 1966, 57)

The third part of the Sermon of Faith says that "He that loveth his brother,
dwelleth in the light, but he that hateth his brother, is in darkness, and walketh
in darkness, and knowethe not whither hee goeth: for darkenesse hath blinded
his eyes. . . . Hereby we manifestly know the children of God from the children
of the devill" (1966, 28).

In the Sermon on the Mount, Christ says, "But if thine eye be wicked, then
all thy bodie shalbe darke. Wherefore if the light that is in thee, be darknes,
how great is that darkenes!" (Matthew 6:23).

In Job, God "discovereth the depe places from *their* darkness, & bringeth
forthe the shadowe of death to light" (12:22). Job's complaint (10:18–22)
stresses darkness:

> Wherefore then hast thou broght me out of the wombe? Oh that I had
> perished, and that none eye had sene me! / *And* that I were as I had not
> bene, *but* broght from the wombe to the grave. / Are not my dayes few?
> let him cease *and* leave of from me, that I may take a little comfort, /
> Before I go and shal not returne, *even* to the land of darknes, and shadowe
> of death / Into a land, I *say*, darke as darkenes it selfe, and into the shadow
> of death, where is not order, but the light *is there* as darkness.

We have a hint here of Faustus's wish for annihilation and of the illumination
of Milton's Pandemonium ("darkness visible"), but Macbeth does not complain. He lists what he will not have ("Honour, Love, Obedience, Troopes of
Friends") and what he will lose (his "eternal jewell").

Macbeth's lines "The Eye winke at the Hand; yet let that bee, / Which the
Eye feares, when it is done to see" has a specific source, Matthew 13:15: "with
their eyes they have winked, lest they shulde se with their eyes, and heare with
their eares, and shulde understand with their hearts, and shulde returne, that I
might heale them." Verse 16 goes on to say, "But blessed *are* your eyes, for
they se." The Gloss tells us what the blessed eyes do see: "To wit, the glorie
of the Sonne of God."

"But wherefore could I not pronounce Amen?" Macbeth asks after killing
Duncan. The "Homilie of Common Prayer and Sacraments," advocating a liturgy conducted so that "all understand the tongue wherein the prayer is sayd"
(as opposed to Latin), says, "For the unlearned hearing that which he understandeth not, knoweth not the end of the prayer, and answereth not *Amen*: which
word is as much to say, as trueth, that the blessing or thanksgiving may bee
confirmed" (Rickey and Stoup 1966, 139). The homily reinforces the point by
quoting Saint Paul: "*How shall he answer, Amen, to the prayer of that he
understandeth not?*" (139). Macbeth "understands" the words "God Bless
Us!" in a formal sense, of course, but his deeper understanding—that which

allows him to participate—has been blocked, so that "Amen" must stick in his throat. Final cause in the Aristotelian sense is not acceptance of blessing but horror. He begins to experience what he has willed upon himself, the status that Saint Bernard describes: "The ills the soul now suffers after sin do now replace that native goodness and distort it, deforming an order they can in no wise destroy" (quoted in Gilson 1936, 295). The process Macbeth suffers early is the same that Lady Macbeth undergoes later. Hers, a function of a deeper repression (or rending in twain), is a more profound "inner tragedy." It is important to note here that each victim wills his or her victimization—in Lady Macbeth's case, in Dantean terms, as Revelation 14:11 says, "And the smoke of their torment shal ascende evermore: & they shall have no rest day nor night."

The shaking of the earth mentioned by Lennox ("Some say, the Earth was fevorous, / And did shake"), accompanied by the "darknesse" reported by Ross—prodigies surrounding Duncan's murder—have many analogues in the Bible, including, of course, those reported at Christ's death. The point, again, is that this murder has cosmic ramifications.

In 1 Samuel:16, "[T]he earth trembled: for it was *stricken* with fear by God." The Gloss explains, "In that the insensible creatures tremble for feare of Gods judgement, it declareth how terrible his vengeance shalbe against his enemies." In Job 9:6, "He removeth the earth out of her place, that the pillers thereof do shake." In Matthew 27:51, "[T]he earth did quake, and the stones were cloven." In Psalm 18, "Then the earth trembled, and quaked: the fundaciouns also of the mountaines moved and shoke, because he was angry." Matthew predicts, "And immediately after the tribulations of those dayes [before the Second Coming], shall th sunne be darkened, & the moone shal not give her light, and the starres shall fall from heaven, & the powers of heaven shall be shaken" (24: 29). The Gloss tells us, "He meaneth the horrible trembling of the world, & and as it were an alteration of the ordre of nature."

A Lord in *Macbeth* prays that "we may againe / Give to our Tables Meate, sleep to our Nights / Free from our Feasts, and Banquets bloody knives; / Do faithful Homage, and receive free Honors, / All which we pine for now." "When night returns [to Scotland]," asserts Paul Jorgensen, "it will be a natural night in which the stars shine and in which there is not only a freedom from prodigious tumult but a freedom from nightmare and a return of innocent sleep" (1971, 137). Even night has its place in the positive rotation of God's order. It is not just a zone of assassination by "black Agents." Thomas Nashe in 1604 suggested that "the divell is a speciall predominant Planet of the night, and . . . our creator for our punishment hath allotted it to him as his peculiar segniorie and kingdome" (1958, 346). Nashe emphasizes not just darkness as the venue of evil but also God's permission of evil. A more recent critic argues the temporary nature of the *satanic* darkness of this play: "The kingdom in *Macbeth* shadows forth the kingdom of heaven on earth, obscured for a time by the blanket of the dark but never sundered from heaven" (Roy Walker 1949, xv).

With some reservations, that is the view of this study. The Prayer Book's *Benedicite ominia opera Domini domino* exhorts, "O ye nightes and daies, blesse ye the Lord: praise him, and magnifie him for ever. / O ye light and darknes, blesse ye the Lorde: prayse him, and magnifie him for ever."

Christ explains in Matthew 13:14 why He speaks in parables: "By hearing, ye shal heare, and shal not understand, and seing ye shal se, and shal not perceive." The second set of prophecies, which Macbeth interprets but does not understand, are a disjunctive analogy to Christ's parables. The "hidden meaning" of Christ's allegories is salvation; of the prophecies of the Weird Sisters, death and damnation.

> And all our yesterdayes have lighted Fooles
> The way to dusty death. Out, out breefe Candle,
> Life's but a walking Shadow

Macbeth's soliloquy after hearing of his wife's death is filled with hints of Biblical negatives, particularly from the psalmist who consistently places dust and shadow in contrast to the help and light of the Old Testament God: Psalm 144:4: "Man is like to vanitie: his daies *are* like a shadowe, that vanisheth." Psalm 22:15: "[T]hou hast brought me into the dust of death." (This may be a doubtful allusion because the psalm predicts the crucifixion with remarkable specificity, as Christ knew when he quoted it from the cross, "My God, my God, why hast thou forsaken me?") Psalm 39:6: "Douteless man walketh in a shadowe."

In Job 8:9, Bildad, the Shuhite says, "For we are but of yesterday, and are ignorant: for our days upon earth *are* but a shadow." The Gloss says, "Meaning, that it is not ynough to have the experience of our selves, but to be confirmed by the examples of them that went before us." In 18:6, Bildad reiterates his pessimism: "The light shalbe darke in his dwelling, and his candel shalbe put out with him."

In the Apocryphal Wisdome of Salomon, chapter 2, "The imaginations and desires of the wicked," we read in verse 4, "Our life shal passe away as the trace of a cloude" (cf. the "horrible Shadow" that "overcome[s him] like a Summers Clowd") and in verse 5, "For our time is as a shadowe that passeth away, and after our end there is no returning."

Some critics have discerned in *Macbeth* allusions to specific episodes and characters. William Burgess sees in the play parallels to 1 Kings: "Jezebel and Lady Macbeth each succeed in their respective guilty purpose. Ahab secures Naboth's vineyard after a treacherous murder of its owner, and Macbeth obtains the crown of Scotland" (1903, 89).

Susan Snyder finds a debt to the story of Hazael and Elisha in 2 Kings (1994, 289–300). The sick king of Aram, Benhadad, sends Hazael to Elisha, who tells Hazael that Benhadad will surely die but tells Hazael to *tell* Benhadad that he will recover. The Geneva Gloss to 2 Kings 8:10 says, "Meaning that he shulde recover, of this disease: but he knewe that this messenger Hazael shulde slaie him to obteine the kingdome." Hazael does so, smothering Benhadad with a damp cloth. Was Hazael's decision a function of destiny or of free will? Hazael becomes king and defeats Joram, a son of Ahab, in Ramoth, Gilead. Hazael, as Elisha had prophecied, remains a successful enemy of Israel (because "the Lord began to loathe Israel": 10:32), is given a vast sum of gold to spare Jerusalem, finally dies, and is succeeded by his son, also named Benhadad. Israel regains its lost cities thereafter. Hazael may have been fated to kill his king, but his career is more like the successful king of Holinshed's Chronicles than Shakespeare's Macbeth. The story does raise enticingly, as Snyder argues, the question of fate and human decision that the play explores but does not answer.

Roy W. Battenhouse notes that

> "When my drink is ready, . . . strike upon the bell" and . . . "The bell is sounded," parodies a Christian mass, in which traditionally a bell is sounded to mark Christ's offering to God of his body and blood as a saving sacrifice. Macbeth's vision of the handle of a dagger as emblem of his mission is an evident perversion of devotion to the cross.

Macbeth's ending the scene with " 'It is done' [echoes] *consummatum est*, Christ's words from the cross" (1994, 49–50). Macbeth's later "It is concluded" does the same.

Shakespeare imports an earlier sound into Lady Macbeth's madness, when she says, "[T]here's knocking at the gate." But here the knocking takes on larger implications. "A Commination Against Sinners" in the 1559 Prayer Book says that "because they hated knowledge, and receyved not the feare of the Lorde, but abhorred my counsail, and dispised my correcyon, then shall it be too late to knocke, when the dore shalbe shutte, and to late to crye for mercye, when it is the time of Justice." Lady Macbeth is on the wrong side of Hellgate. Matthew 15:41 says, "Depart from me ye cursed, into everlasting fyre which is prepared for the devil and his angels." The Gloss to Matthew 17:3–4 refers to Judas: "Over late repentance bringeth despaireticn." He "dispaireth in Gods mercies, and seketh his owne destruction." One can ask, of course, as *Hamlet* does, whether a creature "incapable of her own distress" *can* commit suicide.

Constantly, of course, Macbeth is compared with Lucifer, a linkage perhaps first noticed by Coleridge. "It is a fancy," Coleridge muses, "but I can never read [Duncan's appointment of Malcolm as the Prince of Cumberland] and the following speeches of Macbeth, without involuntarily thinking of the Miltonic Messiah and Satan" (quoted in Bradley 1904, 433). That is a comparison only, but it is also the only comparison equal to the challenge Macbeth has launched. (See also John W. Hales 1891.) Macduff taunts Macbeth as a subordinate fiend: "Tell the Angell whom thou still hast serv'd." The Porter seems to call to his visitors from *inside* an infernal region: "Who's there i'th'name of *Belzebub?*"

"Beelzebub [is] the prince of devils," according to Matthew 12:24. "Angels are bright still," says Malcolm, "though the brightest fell." Matthew 11:14 says, "And no marveile: for Satan himself is transformed into an Angel of light." The Gloss discusses the "fetches of false apostles." Malcolm's reaction to Macduff, of course, suggests that Macduff may be an agent of Macbeth's.

One major point of the consistent reinforcement of this script with Biblical references is to suggest the world against which Macbeth is struggling and to which he refuses to surrender. The play makes sense only if he can *also* wish, as John Andrews says, "for a disintegration of Creation itself" (1993, 173)— "I wish the Estate o' th' World were now undone." He reiterates the wholeness of creation and that his only escape is a *universal* destruction that includes him.

The examples could be multiplied, but these should suffice to suggest how deeply *Macbeth* reaches into the inherited religious tradition to amplify its meanings. The materialist objections to this point of view will be considered below.

In an analysis which places Macbeth's decision to kill Duncan within the play's theological context, Charles Moseley says that "not to see Macbeth as a free agent is to destroy any coherence and dignity the character might have" (1988, 22). Moseley refutes the concept of predestination. "God," he asserts, paraphrasing Boethius,

> exists by definition in an Eternal Present, where there is no time, has knowledge of events in time but not *fore*knowledge of them, for all times are equidistant from him as all points on the circumference of a circle are equidistant from the central point of no dimension round which it is described. (23)

The question is "*how* Macbeth was trapped into becoming the willing agent of his own damnation" (24; Moseley's emphasis). The play, Moseley asserts, exemplifies the conservative view that "every being has its allotted place and job to do, and sin consists, basically, in refusing to do it" (24). Pride, says Moseley, paraphrasing Thomas Aquinas, is "the root cause of sin . . . the commitment of the self to a good which is changeable and imperfect" (24). The result is the "terrible despair and aloneness [which] theologians define as hell . . . for hell is a state and not a place" (25). Macbeth "assumes that the knowledge of the future the Witches seem to have leaves him no escape from his destiny" (25). It is "a grave mistake, as St. Augustine demonstrated . . . to see evil as independent, self-existing, a rival army . . . to the hosts of heaven. . . . Evil, rather, is a privation of good, an emptying, rather than a filling with something else" (25). For Macbeth, evil is a filling with "Scorpions." "Seyton (pronounced Satan) . . . is an image of the real relationship between the Prince of Darkness and the moral being," notes Moseley (27), as I have argued (1967, 385–86). Suffice it to say that Macbeth's fall "proceeds from his own moral choice rather than merely from things done to him . . . we have to feel a sense of terrible waste of human greatness and potential" (Moseley 1988, 27). The play shows us "a being making an initial and entirely free wrong choice, and gradually being rendered less and less free by the consequences of that choice, to the point where he is unable to leave the prison of his own self" (27).

An excellent essay, which brings together much of this background material under a single heading, written by Huston Diehl, deserves a full hearing here, since it reiterates so many of the points I have made.

Macbeth, according to Diehl, is "centrally concerned with the problematics of vision" (1983, 191). The "characters fail to realize ... that sight is both objective and ethical" (191). Diehl's thesis is amplified by contemporary theory. As Pierre de la Primaudaye informs us "[E]ies were given to man ... chieflie to guide and leade him to the knowledge of God by the contemplation of his goodly workes" (1605, 68). According to John Calvin, God "leads us to himself even by these earthly elements, and in the flesh itself causes us to contemplate the things that are of his Spirit" (1536, 118). Francis Quarles writes, "Before the knowledge of letters, God was knowne by *Hieroglyphicks*: and indeed, what are the Heavens, the Earth, nay every creature, by *Hieroglyphicks* and *Emblemes* of his Glory?" (1634). *Macbeth* can be said to go back in time to an emblematic or iconographic system—very much Catholic in its premises—as opposed to the print media, and expectation of literacy, of Calvinism. According to Henry Estienne, "[M]en have within their soules ... some Symboles and marks of his Divinity, which God imprints in us, by the Species of all those objects which he sets before our eyes" (1646, 2). Our innate knowledge is reinforced by the reflection of Divine majesty which our senses perceive. John Donne speaks of "the gallery of the soul, hang'd with so many, and so lively pictures of the goodness and mercies of thy God to thee, as that everyone of them shall be a *catechism* to thee" (1955, 2:237). The litany is conducted between any question of God's goodness and mercy and the affirmative answer the landscapes, still lives, and portraits of the soul provide as painted from Platonic forms. If "rest and sleepe," "which but [Death's] pictures be" bring "much pleasure," as Donne suggests, "from [Death], much more must flow" (Holy Sonnet X).

Diehl's argument finds ample evidence in the liturgy. The passage from Matthew (5:16) is the first of the sentences laid out for the curate after the Communion sermon: "Let your light so shyne before men, that they maye see your good workes, and glorifye youre father whyche is in heaven." A prayer to be said in the morning says, "[S]o that, thou giving us light, wee may see what things are truely good indeed ... for wee having nothing but mistrust in our selves, doe yeeld and commit our selves full and whole unto thee alone, which workest all things in all creatures, to thy honour and glorie. So be it" (*Book of Common Prayer,* 1605). A prayer for trust in God asks,

> Graunt us, that as we be blind and feeble in deed, so we may take and repute our selves, that we presume not of ourselves, to see to ourselves, but so far to see that alway wee may have thee before our eyes, to followe thee, being our guide, to bee readie at they call most obediently, and to commit

> our selves wholy unto thee; that thou, which only knowest the way, maist leade us the same way unto our heavenly desires. (*Book of Common Prayer* 1605)

A prayer to be said at night upon going to bed says,

> Wherefore I beseech thee hartily that thou wilt vouchsafe to take care and charge of me, and not to suffer me to perish in the workes of darknesse, but to kindle the light of they countenaunce in my heart, that thy godly knowledge may daily increse in mee, through a right and pure faith, and that I may alwayes bee found to walke and live after thy will and pleasure. (*Book of Common Prayer* 1605)

A prayer to be said at the hour of death asks, "Graunt me, merciful Saviour, that when death hath shut up the eyes of my bodie, yet that the eyes of my soule may still beholde and looke upon thee" (*Book of Common Prayer* 1605). To suggest that this emphasis is nonsectarian, I quote a portion of the Catholic Supreme Unction: "By this holy unction, may the Lord pardon and forgive all the sins that you have committed through the sense of sight."

"Images strike the memory," Diehl suggests, "leaving deep and lasting impressions on it, and memory, in turn, uses those stored images to mediate and interpret man's experience of the external, visual world" (1983, 192). Sight "involves ethical judgment. Visible images are for him always potentially signs of invisible truths" (192). "Although images may awaken the memory, excite men to virtue, and lead men to God, they may also deceive" (192). Thus sight was also a means of rejecting *false* knowledge, as Job says to his counsellors: 13:1 and 4: "Lo, mine eye hathe sene all *this* . . . in dede ye forge lyes."

Duncan, reinforced by Banquo, has a "sacramental vision." But even within the Godlike circumference of which he is the center, evil can exist. Eden had its serpent. The attack on the play's essentialism might launch itself through Duncan, who is *wrong* about Inverness. He is not wrong about the world in which he lives, however. He just fails to note the exceptions, which seem always to be named Cawdor. He "sees only surfaces and appearances" (Diehl 1983, 193) which *should* reflect grace. But Lady Macbeth knows how to control the "brows of grace." It follows, as Diehl argues, that Shakespeare emphasizes the "fallenness" of Scotland. "To the men of the Christian Renaissance, especially in the Protestant countries of Northern Europe, the physical world was a fallen world: darkened, illusory, treacherous. The eye of fallen man could misunderstand what it perceived, and the devil could, and often did, tempt through the eye" (192–93).

> The forms of temptation are many and varied; wicked conceptions of the heart . . . become temptations through the devil's devices, when they are thrust before our eyes that by their appearance we are drawn away or turn aside from God . . . riches, power, honors . . . often dull men's keenness of sight by the glitter and seeming goodness they display, and allure with their

blandishments, so that, captivated with such tricks and drunk with such sweetness men forget their God. (193)

Stephano and Trinculo are good examples of men falling for "honest trifles."

"Images," says Diehl, "may lead man to truth and persuade him to virtue; they may, on the other hand, tempt and delude him, causing his damnation. Such seeing and interpreting in the fallen world is central to the conflict in *Macbeth* and . . . equally important in the audience's relationship to the play" (1983, 193). "These characters pervert the interpretive process, ignoring potential meanings in the things they see, imposing their own willful desires onto the visual world, and forgetting traditional symbolic associations of the visual images" (193). "Lady Macbeth fails to perceive spiritual meaning in physical images or to believe in the ethical power of pictures" (194–95), even as she admits that power in an aside to her conscience. "Corpses, sleeping bodies, pictures," are to her, "harmless, physical images, easily removed from the seeing eye, and once removed, gone" (195). But "she has internalized the image of the bloody hands and, is finally, haunted by its essential, moral significance" (196). The image becomes negatively sacramental. "While she sees what no one else can see, [she] ceases altogether to see the external, physical world. . . . The sleeping and the dead *are* pictures" (196). "The audience, too, is involved in seeing, interpreting, and remembering these sights" (197). In completing the incomplete for Macbeth at the banquet, and for Lady Macbeth, we become her consciousness, with alter egos on stage.

"Unlike his wife," says Diehl, "who, until her madness, sees nothing but the physical phenomena of the external world, Macbeth generates mental images all the time. Although he creates such images, he fails to understand them; images haunt him rather than enlighten him" (1983, 197). He understands them but represses them and therefore they haunt him. "The Eye winke at the Hand"—Macbeth would detach knowledge from morality. But that cannot be done. "Though Macbeth denies pity, his savage actions activate pity in the world" (199). "The audience is forced to confront the limits of visual interpretation, both Macbeth's and its own" (199). The audience is forced to go beyond those limits, to fill in the visual or the moral dimension of deeds without names.

"The 'shadows' Macbeth sees (IV.i.111) deceive him because he interprets them narrowly and simplistically, according to his own personal needs and desires" (1983, 200). It can also be argued, of course, as H. W. Fawkner says, that the Ghost is "produced neurotically by the deepening of metaphysical servitude" (1990, 64). His needs and desires pull him into the vortex of evil and make him increasingly helpless. Diehl contends that "life is a walking shadow to Macbeth because he fails to perceive spiritual and ethical truths shadowed in the visible world" (1983, 200). The walking shadow is, among other things, Banquo's ghost, a "horrible shadow," and a "shadow" in the Jungian sense of a personality formed by repressing aspects of the persona, as Macbeth's grudging admiration of Banquo suggests Macbeth has done.

The "Playgoer . . . is asked to find in the visible world what Macbeth fails to find—reminders of invisible truths" (Diehl 1983, 200).

> Since the sacrament of communion is, according to Protestant interpretations, a visible sign "to put us in remembrance" of Christ [Calvin 1536, 148] the allusions to it may remind the audience of what Macbeth has failed to see in the visible world: signs of the spiritual. . . . The presence of Banquo's ghost, in the context of this communal feast, forces Macbeth to experience the reality of the ethical and spiritual world he tried to deny. (1983, 201)

In "a fallen world of illusions, seeing is problematic and therefore always interpretive" (201).

I would suggest that vision was problematized in this age by doubt about what the elements of the communion *were*. They were sacramental, that is, visible significations of invisible power and grace, but no longer magically transformed *into* the body and blood of Christ. We "receive his body and blood through faith" (Jewel 1954, 172). Martin Luther's emphasis on the "inward man" was translated by Hooker into a "co-existence," and that resulted in what Stephen Greenblatt calls "eucharistic anxiety" (quoted in Begley 1993, 34). "Truth" lay obscured by argument, and it was easy enough to argue oneself out of *the* truth.

Works Cited

Andrews, John, ed. 1993. *Macbeth*. London: J. M. Dent.

Battenhouse, Roy W. 1994. "Shakespeare's Augustinian Artistry." In *Shakespeare's Christian Dimension: An Anthology of Commentary*. Edited by Roy W. Battenhouse. Bloomington: Indiana University Press.

Begley, Adam. 1993. "The Tempest around Stephen Greenblatt." *New York Times, Magazine*, 28 March.

Berry, Lloyd, ed. 1969. *The Geneva Bible*. Madison: University of Wisconsin Press.

Book of Common Prayer. 1605. London.

Booth, Stephen. 1983. *'King Lear,' 'Macbeth,' Indefinition in Tragedy*. New Haven, Conn.: Yale University Press.

Bradley, A. C. 1904. *Shakespearean Tragedy*. London: Macmillan.

Brown, John Russell. 1963. *Macbeth*. Great Neck, N.Y.: Barron's.

Burgess, William. 1903. *The Bible in Shakespeare*. New York: Thomas Y. Crowell.

Burton, Robert. 1628. *Anatomy of Melancholy*. Edited by Floyd Dell and Paul Jordan. London: Tudor, 1927.

Calvin, John. 1536. *Institution of the Christian Religion*. Basel, Switzerland. Translated by F. L. Battles. Atlanta: John Knox Press, 1947.

Coursen, H. R. 1967. "In Deepest Consequence: *Macbeth*." *Shakespeare Quarterly* 18, no. 4:375–88.

Curry, Walter C. 1937. *Shakespeare's Philosophical Patterns*. Baton Rouge: Louisiana University Press.

Diehl, Huston. 1983. "Horrid Image, Sorry Sight, Fatal Vision: The Visual Rhetoric of *Macbeth.*" *Shakespeare Studies* 16:191–204.

Donne, John. 1955. *Sermons.* Edited by George R. Potter and Evelyn M. Simpson. Berkeley: University of California Press.

Duthie, G. I. 1966. "Antithesis in *Macbeth.*" *Shakespeare Survey* 19:25–33.

Eagleton, Terry. 1967. *Shakespeare and Society.* New York: Schocken Books.

Estienne, Henry. 1646. *The Art of Making Devises.* Translated by Thomas Blount. London.

Fawkner, H. W. 1990. *Deconstructing 'Macbeth': The Hyperontological View.* Cranbury, N.J.: Associated University Presses.

Gilson, Etienne. 1936. *The Spirit of Mediaeval Philosophy.* New York: Scribner.

Hales, John W. 1891. "Milton's *Macbeth.*" *Nineteenth Century* 30 (December).

Hanford, J. Holly, ed. 1953. *The Poems of John Milton.* 2d ed. New York: Roland Press.

Hooker, Richard. 1593. *Tudor Poetry and Prose.* Edited by J. William Hebel, Hoyt H. Hudson, et. al. New York: Appleton, Century, Crofts, 1953.

Jewel, Bishop John. 1954. "An Apology." In *The Renaissance in England.* Edited by Herschel Baker and Hyder E. Rollins. Boston: Heath.

Jorgensen, Paul A. 1971. *Our Naked Frailties.* Berkeley: University of California Press.

Knight, G. Wilson. 1931. *The Imperial Theme.* Oxford: Oxford University Press.

La Primaudaye, Pierre de. 1605. *The Second Part of the French Academy.* Translated by T. Bowes. London.

Matthews, Honor M. V. 1962. *Character and Symbol in Shakespeare's Plays.* Cambridge: Cambridge University Press.

Milward, Peter. 1987. *Biblical Influences in Shakespeare's Tragedies.* Bloomington: Indiana University Press.

Moelwyn, Merchant W. 1966. "His Fiend-Like Queen." *Shakespeare Survey* 19.

Moseley, Charles. 1988. "Macbeth's Free Fall." In *Macbeth.* Edited by Linda Cookson and Bryan Loughrey. London: Longman.

Nashe, Thomas. 1604. "The Terrors of the Night Or, A Discourse of Apparitions." In *The Works of Thomas Nashe.* Edited by R. B. McKerrow, with additions by F. P. Wilson. Oxford: Oxford University Press, 1958.

Noble, Richmond. 1935. *Shakespeare's Biblical Knowledge.* London: J. M. Dent.

Ornstein, Robert. 1960. *Shakespeare's Moral Vision.* Madison: University of Wisconsin Press.

Quarles, Francis. 1634. *Emblems.* London.

Rickey, Mary Ellen, and Thomas B. Stoup, eds. 1966. *Certaine Sermons and Homilies,* 1623 edition. Gainesville, Fla.: Scholar's Facsimiles.

Shaheen, Naseeb. 1987. *Biblical References in Shakespeare's Tragedies.* Newark: Delaware University Press.

Siddall, Stephen. 1988. "Ceremony in *Macbeth.*" In *Macbeth.* Edited by Linda Cookson and Bryan Loughrey. London: Longman.

Snyder, Susan. 1994. "Theology as Tragedy in *Macbeth.*" *Christianity and Literature* 43, nos. 3–4 (May):27–41.

Stallybrass, Peter. 1982. "*Macbeth* and Witchcraft." In *Focus on 'Macbeth,'* Edited by John Russell Brown. London: Routledge and Kegan Paul.

Walker, Roy. 1949. *The Time Is Free: A Study of 'Macbeth.'* London: Andrew Dakers.

West, Robert. 1968. *Shakespeare and the Outer Mystery.* Lexington: Kentucky University Press.

5

CRITICAL APPROACHES

THE WORLD OF MACBETH

Macbeth has drawn such diverse, brilliant, and sometimes idiosyncratic response
that it is difficult to establish categories in which to fit that criticism. Furthermore, the play is not susceptible to easy categorization. So, it is at the risk of
oversimplification and even distortion that I establish "the world of *Macbeth*"
as a category. It is no longer fashionable to speak of a play as if it *had* a world
of its own, that is, as if it were an imaginative construct that drew on a set of
generic assumptions. Those assumptions are based on something called drama
and on its subcategories and on the crossings and mergings within those loose
definitions—tragedy and the revenge play, for example. Today, of course, a
play-text is a document within the flux of other documents, or a work that is
not univocal, but full of margins to explore, or a fiction in which the tensions
it explores are not resolved within the play itself. Be it so. Certainly the anxieties
of a sixteenth century full of dynastic and religious conflict in England are both
consciously reflected *and* unconsciously embedded in the dramatic texts. They
become an aspect of the world of the play. The play also has such distinct
characteristics apart from its suffusion with religious issues that those elements
are worth looking at in themselves.

The model essay for my generation of graduate students was Maynard Mack's
"The World of *Hamlet*" (1952). Mack saw the work itself as a context in which
actions occurred. He demonstrated that the play was full of questions, as any play
of Shakespeare's is, and suggested that the interrogation in *Hamlet* is about identity, about what lies behind the smiles of a king or the apparent voice of a dead father, for example. The questions in *Macbeth* also deal with appearance versus
reality, but ask not "Who's there?" but *what* is there. "What are these / So
wither'd, and so wilde in their attyre . . . ?" "Are ye fastasticall, or that indeed /
Which outwardly ye shew?" "What's the Boy *Malcolme?*" "Geese Villaine?"

How does the world of a play shape reality for its inhabitants? Why, as Mack asked, can Gertrude *not* see the Ghost of King Hamlet when it appears to her son? Questions about the world of the play may provide answers about who inhabits or *can* inhabit this world, about the range of their decisions and the ramifications of their decisions. The world of *Richard II* probably does not argue Richard's assertion that those who have betrayed him are "thrice worse than Judas," but it does suggest that deposition will lead to terrible civil wars and a version of "Golgotha, and dead men's skulls." The world of *Othello may* support Othello's belief that he is damned. The world of *Macbeth* goes farther and permits us to agree with Lady Macbeth that she is in the "murky . . . Hell" she dreams she is in. A discussion centered on the world of the play permits generic debate and also allows attacks on the premise itself, that argue, as Macbeth says of the dagger, "There's no such thing."

Genre

An approach to literature by way of genre would ask, What kind of work is this? If drama, is it comedy or tragedy? In comedy, the issues raised can usually be resolved without bloodshed. The Shakespearean comedy invariably ends with reconciliation, celebration, and marriage. Its issues may be personal, but personal issues invariably are absorbed in the *social*. Shakespeare usually leaves someone out of the comic ending that most of the characters enjoy—Shylock, Jaques, Malvolio. The tragedy, of course, ends with isolation, despair, and death for the tragic figure, or, in the case of *Macbeth*, tragic figures. Both male and female are implicated in different ways in the fatality that tragedy entails. In spite of feminist arguments about the subjugation of Ophelia and the passivity of Desdemona, women can be agents in tragedy, as in the instances of Juliet, Goneril and Cordelia, Volumnia, and Lady Macbeth. Genre helps us understand what can happen in a given world—the socially constructive world of comedy, which involves the surrender of foibles and misconceptions before a "new society" is formed, and the destructive world of tragedy, which demands the sacrifice of the tragic hero before any new society can be considered, assuming that the ending posits a further history. *King Lear*, for example, seems to question any future, or at least any positive future beyond its "cheerless, dark, and deadly" conclusion. Shakespeare's plays are probably sui generis—of their own genre— but the generic question can be a useful starting point for a discussion of the play as literature and as play-text. Furthermore, dealing with the issue of genre helps us understand our relationship to the characters.

I agree with Gary Waller's statement that

> today most Shakespeareans would recognize as unsatisfactory any criticism
> (or teaching) that dehistoricizes the Shakespearean script into a static mon-
> ument. . . . We recognize perhaps that even in his own age, each time Shake-
> speare himself saw one of his own plays performed, he would have seen it

in a new guise, modified by factors over which he had no control. (1992, 103)

It may be helpful, however, to explore certain generalizations or possibilities before they must be modified. Genre, or *type* of literature, is one question to raise. Shakespeare's plays are probably more *unlike* each other than similar, but asking the generic question can help establish what can happen in the "world of the play." Genre is a platonic form awaiting contextualization. One of those contextualizations is, as Waller suggests, a play-in-history, subject to the pressures of changing times and of specific audiences, playing spaces, and zeitgeists. The question of genre can help define what those pressures are and what they cannot be.

Genre helps define the world. Errors are made in comedy, but they are resolvable and are resolved when mistaken identities are cleared up or when initial folly is corrected by reformation. In tragedy, the error cannot be erased. Duncan cannot awake with the knocking at the gate. The protagonist, having made his error in judgment, cannot return. Both Macbeth and Lady Macbeth know that. What is done is done. What is done cannot be undone.

> Tragedy, we are told, is expected to raise but not ultimately to accept the emotions of pity and fear. These I take to be the sense of moral good and evil, respectively, which we attach to the tragic hero. He may be as good as Caesar, and so appeal to our pity, or as bad as Macbeth, and so appeal to terror, but the particular thing called tragedy that happens to him does not depend on his moral status. The tragic catharsis passes beyond moral judgement, and while it is quite possible to construct a moral tragedy, what tragedy gains in morality it loses in cathartic power . . . tragedy is really implicit or uncompleted comedy. (Frye 1961, 83–84)

Macbeth owes much to the late-medieval genre of the morality play, of which *Everyman* is the classic example. In this allegorical play, Everyman recognizes what is necessary for salvation. Macbeth and Lady Macbeth are themselves, not allegorical characters with labels like "Ambition" or "Moral Blindness" attached to them. Willard Farnham discerns the allegory underlying the play: "*Macbeth* is a morality play written in terms of Jacobean tragedy. Its hero is worked upon by forces of evil, yields to temptation in spite of all that his conscience can do to stop him, . . . and is brought to retribution by his death" (1950, 79). Hardin Craig says of Macbeth, "He is seduced by the witches, clearly powers of evil, who exemplify the morality doctrine that Satan is a deceiver" (1950, 66). Satan is no doubt a deceiver, but Macbeth undergoes an intense spiritual debate wholly uncharacteristic of a character in an allegory, who, says Craig, "lacks motivation or any inward struggle" (66). Paul Jorgensen cites the play's heritage as one reason for the diverse critical response it has elicited: "*Macbeth* lends itself, partially because of its descent from the morality play, to allegorical ecstasy in the critic'' (1971, 12). Stephen Booth maintains that "it is hard to understand how the traditional reading of the drama as a morality play can create the rich impact actually produced by the play" (1983, 39). Few read the play that way nowadays, unless Booth means reading the play against its religious background.

John Russell Brown suggests that the play is "a tragedy of the *De Casibus* or 'Wheel of Fortune' type" (1963, 24), as in the many examples cited by Chaucer's Monk and the vastly popular Elizabethan series *A Mirrour for Magistrates*. The moral of *King Cambises* (c. 1560) was that "the many wicked deedes and tyrannous murders, committed by and through him" were met "last of all" by "his odious death by gods justice appointed." This is also, of course, the pattern of Shakespeare's *Richard III*, which brings in actual speaking ghosts to torment their murderer.

A similar argument is put forward by David L. Pollard. In responding to Dr. Johnson's finding that the play has "no nice discriminations of character" (1960, 105), Pollard likens the play to *A Mirrour for Magistrates* and says that the lack of delineation of characters other than Macbeth and Lady Macbeth creates a counterprotagonist to Macbeth, "a nation . . . the commonweal of Scotland" (1988, 75). The early "Homeric ethic" (72) gives way to "a didactic art form" (76), like *A Mirrour*. *Macbeth* becomes a tragedy that Phillip Sidney would have applauded: It "maketh kings to fear to be tyrants" (1904, vol. 1, 170). No doubt the latter phases of the play would enforce that moral, but it would seem that the play would argue a thesis that "maketh subjects fearful to kill their monarch."

R. S. Crane, working from what he considers strict Artistotelian principles, asserts,

> I shall assume that we have to do not with a lyric "statement of evil" or an allegory of the workings of sin in the soul and the state or a metaphysical myth of destruction followed by recreation, or a morality play with individualized characters rather than types, but simply with an imitative tragic drama based on historical materials. (1953, 170)

Crane's formula might apply more aptly to *Richard III: Macbeth* is "a form of serious action designed to arouse moral indignation for the deliberately unjust and seemingly prosperous acts of the protagonist and moral satisfaction at his subsequent ruin" (170). I do not believe that we ever sense that Macbeth is "prosperous." Even with the physical crown on his head, he lives in torment. The characters quiver with the larger implications of the theological background which the play invites us to consider. As E. K. Chambers points out,

> This is cosmic tragedy. From the contemplation of good and evil in the individual soul, the philosophic mind passes to the contemplation of good and evil in the totality of things, or more precisely in the tangled web of

individual souls acting under material conditions . . . the speculation of the
dramatist is primarily directed to the working of powers conceived of as
transcending the purely human. (1958, 227)

The play does exploit the Jacobean taste for exploring the macabre, the bor-
derland of evil just beyond sanity and just this side of total madness, the "brutality of evil" (Robert Ornstein, quoted in Leech 1965, 217) so rampant in such
plays as *The Duchess of Malfi, The Revenger's Tragedy*, and *The Changeling*.
Allegory cannot deal with such subjects. They require development beyond type
and into the specifics of the unspeakable. Film versions of *Macbeth* (Polanski
1970) and *Richard III* (Loncraine 1995) suggest that the genre of some of the
plays has some correlations with the Hollywood horror film. To warp the scripts
into that category, however, is to surrender much that the scripts can still communicate to modern audiences—without necessarily giving up on the horror that
they undoubtedly contain.

One of the great genre critics, Dame Helen Gardner, in confuting New Critical
approaches, argues that *Macbeth* is not

a symbolic drama of retribution. The reappearance of "the babe symbol"
in the apparition and in Macduff's revelation of his birth has distracted the
critic's attention from what deeply moves the imagination and the conscience in this vision of a whole world weeping at the inhumanity of helplessness betrayed and innocence and beauty destroyed. (1959, 61)

Different imaginations are moved in different ways, and even the same imagination is moved in different ways by different productions. Enfolded within the
final two acts of *Macbeth* is Macduff's unproblematic revenge.

W. H. Auden suggests, "If Macbeth had listened [to the Witches' prophecies]
as a Greek would have listened to the Oracle, then he would have been able to
sit and wait until by necessity it came to pass" (1945, 1). The Greek world *is*
one of inevitability, as Oedipus discovers during the course of *Oedipus Tyran-
nus*. The Greek who waited would not have been "tragic." Nor would the
Macbeth who decides not to wait for "Chance to Crowne" him "Without [his]
stirre." We do not learn whether fate or free will rules in the Scotland of
Shakespeare's play. We do know that when Macbeth uses his free will to act
against what he knows to be right, he elicits "judgement heere" as well as the
"deepe damnation" beyond the here. Edward Dowden puts the conflict in Victorian terms of vigor versus inaction: "Those who lack energy of goodness and
drop into a languid neutrality between the antagonist spiritual forces of the world
must serve the devil as slaves, if they will not decide to serve God as freemen"
(1962, 250). The New Testament paradox is resolved by the Prayer Book's
Collect for Grace: "O God, whose service is perfect freedome." Macbeth's
moral lassitude, then, elicits the response of damnation. That makes him somewhat like Faustus, who alludes to the Thief on the Cross in John as an excuse

for not repenting. Macbeth, however, *refuses* to repent, preferring to wade on into the sea of blood he is creating.

For Cedric Watts, "*Macbeth* [is] royalist propaganda." The "play lacks the searching and problematic features which preserve the appeal for modern audiences" of other plays (1988, 102). Shakespeare's "constraint is clearly illustrated by *Macbeth*," according to Watts (103). "The play's grotesque endorsement of such superstition [as witchcraft] is clearly one of its most regressive and disappointing features" (104). Shakespeare "generate[s] a stereotype of hideous witchcraft which would endure for centuries in literature . . . falsifi[ng] the historical record in order to advocate a given political position" (105). The "play suppresses some sophisticated and skeptical questioning which was well within Shakespeare's imaginative range" (109). This is to assume that Shakespeare's Weird Sisters *are* stereotypical, an issue to be discussed below.

Peter Hall stresses the historical aspect of the play, saying that *Macbeth* is a redepiction of the Wars of the Roses, of "England torn apart by a series of tribal wars" (quoted in Brown 1982, 235). The history play is about *power* and who wins it and who loses it. The history play usually does not center on a single character—*Henry V* and *Richard III* are exceptions—but on the shifting balance of power, as first one and then another character dominates the action. *Julius Caesar*, for example, while it configures tragic decisions for both Caesar and Brutus, moves from memories of Pompey, to Caesar, to Cassius, to Brutus, to Antony, and finally to "another Caesar" who will defeat Antony at a later time. The shifting nature of the history play is suggested by Caesar, who "comes in triumph over Pompey's blood," but who falls at the base of Pompey's statue, "while all the while ran blood." *Macbeth* is a tragedy shaped from elements of history. "We are now encouraged to think," says Hall of *Macbeth*, "that all the characters are carefully framed to . . . present a complicated series of contrasted political and personal relationships that, in turn, sets up a complicated system of dependency and power in which all have to try to function" (251). R. A. Foakes links *Macbeth* to Shakespeare's career, calling it "the culmination of a long development of tragic writing on the theme of the rise and fall of an ambitious prince" (1969, ix).

H. W. Fawkner argues that the play is sui generis:

> Shakespeare created something totally new—something radically different, daringly suggestive, and absolutely original. The reason why Shakespeare's audience could appreciate and digest this absolute novelty is not that the dramatist and the audience shared certain belief-structures in an absolutely uniform way, but that the special spirit of discovery in the Renaissance permitted the two sides [Shakespeare and his spectators] to come together in the imaginative freedom of dramatic innovation. (1990, 40–41)

It is important, if we are to *respond* to Macbeth, that our relationship to him be clear to us. What are the specific factors that set this "tragic hero" apart from others? I do not agree that Macbeth is like us or we like him. I would agree, with qualifications, with Derrick C. Marsh, who says that Macbeth is "neither the puppet of evil forces that some critics would make of him nor the inhuman monster that Malcolm's final dismissal of him as 'this dead butcher' would suggest" (1983, 12). Alfred Harbage argues that our attachment to Macbeth results from his being "human in his reflections as he is inhumane in his acts" (1969, 1108). He commands, says Marsh, our "interest, sympathy, even admiration" (1983, 13). That is probably true, but do we recognize in Macbeth "all too human, ordinary fallibility" (13)? If so, it is not in the warrior Macbeth of the opening or closing, but in the hesitant and fear-soaked Macbeth of Acts One and Two. The "hero is almost, but not quite, transformed into a monster," asserts Crane (1953, 172). His enemies conveniently and understandably transmorgrify him; his soliloquies keep something else in view, as G. K. Hunter suggests: "[T]he idea of a 'good' Macbeth, buried somewhere beneath the activities of a will dedicated to evil, has not been allowed to perish altogether at any point in the play." We sense "the wasted potentialities beneath the wicked actuality" (1994, 804–5). Macbeth, says E.M.W. Tillyard, is caught in "the terrible discrepancy between his virtuous understanding and his corrupt will" (1946, 315) and never loses that understanding, as he *cannot* given the world he exists in. Nor, of course, can Lady Macbeth. A. C. Bradley suggests that *Macbeth*'s "tragic characters are made of the stuff we find within ourselves" (1904, 20). Macbeth and Richard III "are the only heroes who do what they themselves recognise to be villainous" (22), but with such a difference!

I do not find much of Macbeth within myself, but I do believe that the play presents him so vividly—as good fictions will do—that we understand him through his own senses, his language of fear and of panic and of bodily response to inner imagery. That is not to identify with him, except as a man caught in a terribly anima/animus conflict as Jung describes it. We have perhaps done things we knew were against our own natures, and we have perhaps convinced others to do the same. But I watch Macbeth from a detached point of view. I do not say, "There but for the Grace of God, or good luck, or genes, go I." I do say that when I see Hamlet, Othello, and Lear. Our response to tragedy, it follows, depends upon our own unique psychology of perception. Bradley may capture part of my response when he discusses Macbeth's conscience, "a conscience so terrifying in its warnings and so maddening in its reproaches that the spectacle of inward torment compels a horrified sympathy and awe which balance, at the least, the desire for the hero's ruin" (1904, 22). A part, because I would like to see Macbeth defeat Macduff, thus prove he is in his own world at last, and turn to us. The heroic fact is that he continues to fight. In the play as written he can never win because he has that in himself against which he fights but cannot defeat. And *that* is what is "like us." I do not find many critics who say that Lady Macbeth is "like us." Those who have had nightmares charted along the old archetypes may associate with the Lady of Act Five. I will deal with feminist response to the play below.

In a brilliant essay, Dame Helen Gardner places *Macbeth* in the category of "tragedy of damnation," thereby removing its title character from all but a cautionary relationship with the spectator and placing him in the company of John Milton's Satan, Christopher Marlowe's Dr. Faustus, and Thomas Middleton's Beatrice-Joanna (1948, 46–66). Gardner stresses "the deforming of a creature in its origin bright and good, by its own willful persistence in acts against its own nature" (47).

Of Macbeth's later soliloquies, William Scott offers that "we presumably draw our criteria for meaning in some fashion from the life that is here said to be meaningless" (1986, 174). The "Tomorrow" speech and Macbeth's list of what he must not look to have represent "a vision that compels us to join in understanding, though we would not or dare not in action" (174). Macbeth keeps us with him while he isolates himself from the world of the play, even if the soliloquies are not directed *to* us. Is there any that is? "Hee's heere in double trust" is a possibility, particularly for non-proscenium productions in a small auditorium. In most cases—again with the possible exception of Lady Macbeth's "I lay'd their Daggers ready," in exasperation to us—the soliloquies are stream of consciousness rather than shared revelations. We witness both Macbeth and Lady Macbeth talking to themselves, since neither can share his or her experience with the other in that they inhabit different psychological states at different moments of the play.

Karl Jaspers says of tragedy, "Something elemental is here made manifest: when the tragic hero freely chooses his doom and perishes a free man he reveals to the spectators what each of them could be" (1952, 78). In surrendering the myth of identity by which all people live, Macbeth must try to live by one that is consistent with who he would be but alien to who he is. He must still argue "Nature," who is, in a sense, another controlling woman. It is "natural," he argues, to be afraid of that which he has sent to peace to gain his peace, to have his cheeks "blanch'd with fear." His own nature is negative evidence of his distorted humanity. It is perhaps when Macbeth feels most unlike "himself"— as a human being who would narcotize his humanity, or as an almost inert human being suddenly startled into his skin again—that we most associate with him. It may be that we seek those instants of contact as the play progresses. It may also be that Macbeth excites our own inevitable inauthenticity into recognition.

Tragedy may involve the elevation of certain functions to the exclusion of others. Certainly Shakespeare as performed appeals to our imaginations and our senses. According to Bradley, "When we are immersed in a tragedy, we feel towards dispositions, actions, and persons such emotions as attraction and repulsion, pity, wonder, fear, horror, perhaps hatred; but we do not *judge*" (1904, 32; emphasis in original). Is not hatred a judgment? If so, it emerges from the emotions rather than from the rational faculty, which emerges in our evaluation of our experience and is part of the experience of drama, even if not our immediate response while the play is being performed.

Norman Rabkin stresses how little Macbeth gains by his actions. The "regicide's lack of pleasure in his accomplishments," says Rabkin, "is presented not moralistically, as a judgment on evil deeds, but as a defining fact of the deeds themselves" (1981, 102). That is true even *before*, perhaps even particularly before, the defining deed. And this is transmitted to us through Macbeth's terrified imagery. Unlike other tragic heros, Macbeth sees his fall in advance, almost experientially. J. V. Cunningham paraphrases Macbeth's "Had I but dy'd an houre before this chance / I had liv'd a blessed time": "My life had ended in the state of grace . . . if I had died before resolving to murder my King . . . for the fall from the state of grace was coincident with the moral decision" (1951, 20).

It is worth noting that *Macbeth*, except for the Porter scene, is not metadramatic (as *Othello* is not). It does not want to call attention to artifice but to action imitated. Sidney Homan calls *Macbeth* "almost atheatrical, unplayful" (1986, 101). The frame around V.1, the Doctor and Gentlewoman, is necessary as a mediator between the audience and the Madwoman. It is also a way of reframing the aberrations of this reign within a normative context. That context returns with Malcolm. The frame around I.1 of *Antony and Cleopatra*—Demetrius and Philo—calls attention to a performative inner scene, particularly on Cleopatra's part. *Macbeth* does not come out to us. It pulls us into it. See, however, John Andrews's list of the play's ten references to acting (1993, 152).

Marjorie Garber (1987) shows how Shakespeare continues to "haunt" us, having become profoundly embedded in our modes of expressing and understanding ourselves. Our culture continues to be conditioned by Shakespeare in many ways; some perceived, some unperceived. *Macbeth* flows beyond the borders of conventional fiction. Nothing stays where it should stay—neither trees, nor sleepers, nor the dead. The play itself prowls restlessly into history seeking ways of being informed by and of informing times as yet unborn.

Works Cited

Andrews, John, ed. 1993. *Macbeth*. London: J. M. Dent.

Auden, W. H. 1945. "The Christian Tragic Hero." *New York Times Magazine*, 16 December, 1–4.

Booth, Stephen. 1983. *'King Lear,' 'Macbeth,' Indefinition in Tragedy*. New Haven, Conn.: Yale University Press.

Bradley, A. C. 1904. *Shakespearean Tragedy*. London: Macmillan.

Brown, John Russell, ed. 1963. *Macbeth*. Great Neck, N.Y.: Barron's.

———, ed. 1982. *Focus on 'Macbeth.'* London: Routledge and Kegan Paul.

Chambers, E. K. 1958. *Shakespeare: A Survey*. London: Sidgwick and Jackson.

Craig, Hardin. 1950. "Morality Plays and Elizabethan Drama." *Shakespeare Quarterly* 1 (April): 23–30.

Crane, R. S. 1953. *The Languages of Criticism and the Structure of Poetry*. Toronto: University of Toronto Press.

Cunningham, J. V. 1951. *Woe or Wonder: The Emotional Effect of Shakespearean Tragedy*. Denver: University of Denver Press.

Dowden, Edward. 1872. *Shakespeare: A Critical Study of His Mind and Art.* Reprint. New York: Capricorn, 1962.

Farnham, Willard. 1973. *Shakespeare's Tragic Frontier: The World of His Final Tragedies.* Oxford: Basil Blackwell and Mott.

Fawkner, H. W. 1990. *Deconstructing 'Macbeth': A Hyperontological View.* Cranbury, N.J.: Associated University Presses.

Foakes, R. A., ed. 1969. *Macbeth.* Indianapolis: Educational Press.

Frye, Northrop. 1961. "The Argument of Comedy." In *Shakespeare: Modern Essays in Criticism.* Edited by Leonard F. Dean. New York: Oxford Galaxy.

Garber, Marjorie. 1987. *Shakespeare's Ghost Writers: Literature as Uncanny Causality.* London: Metheun.

Gardner, Helen. 1948. "Milton's Satan and the Theme of Damnation in Elizabethan Tragedy." *Essays and Studies I*: 46–66.

———. 1959. *The Business of Criticism.* Oxford: Oxford University Press.

Harbage, Alfred, ed. 1969. *Macbeth.* Baltimore: Pelican.

Homan, Sidney. 1986. *Shakespeare's Theater of Presence: Language, Spectacle, and the Audience.* Lewisburg, PA: Bucknell University Press.

Hunter, G. K., ed. 1994. *Macbeth.* London: Penguin.

Jaspers, Karl. 1952. *Tragedy Is Not Enough.* Translated by Harold A. T. Reiche, Harry T. Moore, and Karl W. Deutsh. Boston: Beacon Press.

Johnson, Samuel. 1960. *Samuel Johnson on Shakespeare.* Edited by W. K. Wimsatt. New York: Hill and Wang.

Jorgensen, Paul A. 1971. *Our Naked Frailties.* Berkeley: University of California Press.

Leech, Clifford, ed. 1965. *Shakespeare: The Tragedies.* Chicago: University of Chicago Press.

Mack, Maynard. 1952. "The World of *Hamlet.*" *Yale Review* 41.

Marsh, Derrick C. 1983. "*Macbeth*: Easy Questions, Difficult Answers." *Sydney Studies in English* 8: 19–31.

Pollard, David L. 1988. " 'O Scotland, Scotland': The Anti-Heroic Play of *Macbeth.*" *Upstart Crow* 8: 26–43.

Rabkin, Norman. 1981. *Shakespeare and the Problem of Meaning.* Chicago: University of Chicago Press.

Scott, William O. 1986. "Macbeth's—and Our—Self-Equivocations." *Shakespeare Quarterly* 37, no. 2 (Summer): 160–74.

Sydney, Phillip. 1904. "An Apology for Poetry." In *Elizabethan Critical Essays*, vol. 1. Edited by G. Gregory Smith. Oxford: Oxford University Press.

Tillyard, E.M.W. 1946. *Shakespeare's History Plays.* New York: Macmillan.

Waller, Gary. 1992. Review. *Shakespeare Quarterly* 42, no. 1 (Spring): 103.

Watts, Cedric. 1988. "*Macbeth* as Royalist Propaganda." In *Macbeth.* Edited by Linda Cookson and Bryan Loughrey. London: Longman.

Essentialist Criticism

The essentialist, often a "new critic," would see the world of plays as "of a piece," a conscious artifact crafted by the playwright. The essentialist critic would tend to approach the play as if it were "a trans-historical phenomenon" (Bristol 1990, 151), free of the biography of the writer and free of the contexts of his time. In the case of the new critic, a William Empson (1930), an L. C. Knights (1946), or a Cleanth Brooks (1947), this version of criticism would examine the play as if it were an extended poem, full of irony, paradox, and repeated images (blood, darkness, clothes that do not fit), and as if it emerged from a *theme*. This kind of criticism tends to ignore the plays *as* plays, but it can be valuable to a director seeking a unifying concept for production.

According to Derek Traversi,

> Duncan is the head of a "single state of man" ... whose members are bound into unity by the accepted ties of loyalty. By virtue of this position he is the source of all the benefits which flow from his person to those who surround him; receiving the free homage of his subjects, he dispenses to them all the riches and graces which are the mark of true kingship, so that the quality of his poetry is above all life-giving, fertile ... to which are joined, at his moments of deepest feeling, the religious associations of worship in a magnificent, comprehensive impression of overflowing *grace*. (1956, 154)

Duncan, then, embodies the positive virtues of a world which is, basically, positive and purposive. But against that elemental force, contends G. Wilson Knight, is an *almost* equal negative power. He sees the play as a "wrestling of destruction with creation ... a wrenching of new birth, itself disorderly and unnatural in this disordered world ... then creation's more firm-set sequent concord replaces chaos" (1931, 153).

If the world of the play is not something like this, its effects must be assigned to some version of existential experience or to the ingenuity of critics. One aspect of the play, among many, is defined by Paul Jorgensen: "The play ... achieves a remarkable expression of cosmic implications without leaving the stage of the world" (1971, 13). Ross's line, "Threatens his bloody Stage," points at the world as a focal point of cosmic response to both positive and negative actions, and, of course, to the stage as the emblem of the world.

This play, more than any other, seems compressed, uses the language of physical fear, employs oxymoron on the linguistic and intellectual level, and echoes its words to our ears as if we ourselves were exploring corridors of shadow and stone.

Kristian Smidt compares Macbeth and Marlowe's Dr. Faustus. Macbeth's bargain leaves him with a barren and frantic few months. Faustus has his time, in which he hops around performing tricks for the lesser nobility. Smidt remarks on the complexity of Macbeth's characterization compared to that of Faustus (1966, 235–48).

From just inside the parenthesis around the near end of the English Renaissance emerges another inevitable comparison from Michael Long:

> [W]e are drawn in sympathy to Satan's side as he fights his doomed, ridiculous, magnificent battles with God. Both heroes arouse the same contra-

dictory feelings about a destructive criminality which none the less compels some sort of admiration, and both arouse, very strongly, the same kind of pity. Macbeth looks at himself and his derelict life and decides that honour, love, and friendship are things "I must not look to have," while Satan looks at Eden or the unfallen Eve and, in his great soliloquies of his misery, thinks of everything he has lost and everything he has become. (1989, 42)

"The peculiar nature of time [in *Macbeth*]," maintains Robert G. Collmer, "is its compression. The past, the present, the future center on each action, as if the universe were pushed into a pyramid and the pyramid were upended so that each action bears the weight of all the universe. Such a situation is magnified by Macbeth's tremendous imagination" (1960, 491).

M. M. Mahood argues that time in *Macbeth*

is tempo, rhythm, measure, the fitness of the natural order—order, that is, seen as a recurrent succession of events, season after season, generation after generation, the revolution of the starry wheels under the law that preserves the stars from wrong. Fundamentally, it is a religious concept of time, in which the change of hour and season, the bow in the heavens, symbolises both the impermanence of things within time and their extra-temporal permanence. In the play it is associated with the powers of good—Duncan, Malcolm, Macduff—whereas the concept of time as the momentous event alone might be said to dominate the thoughts and actions of Lady Macbeth and Macbeth, the concept of time as duration alone might be said to belong to Macbeth. The confrontation of these notions of time, the religious and the irreligious, is the play's major dramatic conflict. (1957, 131–32)

Macbeth, having attempted to tamper with time as sequence can complain when time becomes *un*natural—"The times have been." Aristotelian time is poised against a timelessness in which the damned will know time as endless duration, "ever-during" pain, to borrow a word from John Milton.

William Hazlitt calls the play

a huddling together of fierce extremes, a war of opposite natures which of them shall destroy the other. There is nothing but what has a violent end of violent beginnings. The lights and shades are laid on with a determined hand; the transitions from triumph and despair, from the height of terror to the repose of death, are sudden and startling. (1930, 260)

Winifred Nowottny asserts that "the most striking thing about *Macbeth* [is] the prevalence [in the poetry] of images which provide a language for that least articulate of emotions, panic" (1964, 66). John Russell Brown notices "especially at moments of horror . . . the choice of simple and common words with the power of evoking strong sense-reactions . . . giv[ing] to unfamiliar horror a tangible quality. . . . Everywhere fear has a 'taste' and blood a 'smell,' light 'thickens' and the air is 'filthy' '' (1963, 32). ''Sudden transitions of subject and mood, showing that Macbeth's mind is drawn by unspoken thoughts and feelings, become more violent as the play proceeds'' (1963, 36).

The effect of the imagery and language of this play is, according to Jorgensen ''violently vivid, tactile, and generally sensory'' (1971, 2). The play manifests a ''dark and painful power resulting from unparalleled sensory artistry'' (4). G. K. Hunter adds that the play is ''lurid and violent,'' conveying ''the sense of an inferno barely controlled beneath the surface crust'' (1967, 28).

Knights, in discussing Lady Macbeth's ''dasht the Braines out,'' posits an organic reality under the surface of the script that becomes available to the alert reader: ''It is not only an image of violence, but of unnatural violence, and thus links with the insistence on 'unnatural deeds' so pervasive throughout the play'' (1959, 16). ''It is only when the mind of the reader is thoroughly 'roused and awakened,' that meanings from below the level of 'plot' take form as a living structure'' (19). Brown suggests that the evocative language of the play is responsible for this result: ''[I]t has become increasingly clear that the organizing principles . . . have to be sought at a level of consciousness in the characters below that which is expressed fully in the denotive meanings of the words they speak'' (1982, 249).

''Another frequent conception of evil in Shakespeare's plays,'' suggests G. I. Duthie, ''is that it produces inversion'' (1966, 26). It ''can produce a state of affairs in which a given entity is both one thing and the opposite thing simultaneously . . . a given object or person being both one thing and the opposite . . .'' and ''something is changed into its opposite . . . distinct [but] closely associated'' (25, 27).

Robert Wilson, like Knight before him, suggests how the play conflates opposites: ''[M]oments of horrific destruction are linked with an awareness of family and so reinforce our sense of a fundamental destruction of society at its very origins'' (1988, 36). Macbeth ''longs for the very thing he is everywhere destroying'' (38). ''Duncan's interest lies in valuing the person and the personal relationship'' (40). The ''foundation of government in Duncan's court is faith in the good will, the nobility and 'gentle' qualities of the other'' (44). The ''arts of trickery and guile . . . are necessary for survival in the wicked world'' (42), as Malcolm demonstrates. The play depicts ''a sensitive, humane society and a tragic hero who shares those values in the early episodes of the play and never entirely abandons the memory of them'' (42). Pity's ''moral force produces an obliterating flood, reminding us of the mythical purging of the world which Noah survived'' (46).

The issue of language itself is debated subtextually in the play, particularly by Macbeth. He would *like* to believe, as Martin Heidegger asserts, that ''[s]ince I am self-defining and autonomous . . . religion, occupation, and national origins are appendages or decorations that may be cast off. . . . My ethical and social relations are contrived, conventional devices superimposed over me through the demands of expedience'' (quoted in Guignon 1983, 118–19). He knows differently, of course. As Gary Wills points out, "The view of language as natural, not artificial, was still held in the sixteenth century. God had *named* creatures as he made them" (1995, 95), so the word was an event simultaneous with the fact. The word for John is prior, of course, to its incarnation, meaning that language, or the concept of language, is *super*natural, the invisible essence that creates a sacrament. It follows that Macbeth's defiance of this *essential* truth means that Macbeth tumbles into a linguistic trap. Heidegger also claims that "it is not we who play with words, but the nature of language that plays with us" (1968, 118).

In writing about the play's poetry, Madeleine Doran argues "if the plot is simple, the style is not" (1983, 154). The play's "few major themes are constantly repeated, yet varied with subtle changes of phrase or key or tone" (154). "Shakespeare writes to the ear" (154). "The proportion of couplet endings to the number of scenes," she writes, "is higher in *Macbeth* than in any of the tragedies except *Richard II*" (156), giving "an undertone of sound to the thought" (160). At the banquet, Macbeth surrenders, ironically, to Lady Macbeth: "[H]e has now adopted her sense, a bravado sense, of manliness" (169). If so, he is overmatched by "any shape but that." According to Doran, "What moves us so profoundly in this tragedy is Macbeth's making and living his own damnation" (155).

Robin Grove argues that ethical ambiguity lies at the heart of the "nature" of the world of the play. In that it is a fallen world, equivocal, involving choice, in which the combining form "and" can seem to erase the distinction between opposites, it may seem ethically ambiguous. If so, the easier it is for a confused person to become further confused. The Weird Sisters, according to Grove, "merely declare what the future *will* be" (1982, 116). "It's as though in the primitive region of the play such voices are in the air, part of the blowing northern cold of a wilder climate, inhospitable, murky, where fog and darkness come down, light thickens, days close in threateningly—a bleak, half-savage place: Scotland, not England," Grove writes, paraphrasing Wilbur Sanders (1978, 57–65). The early parts of the play come "close to the possibilities of something like a musical score" (Grove 1982, 116), and indeed, Sarah Caldwell's production of 1982 developed the musical possibilities in the Weird Sisters. Grove argues that "what the murder seems to come from, so the drama seems to show, is some equivocation or irresponsibility; not just in Macbeth himself, but (worse still) glimpsed at the heart of things" (1982, 119–20).

I disagree. Macbeth is confused, or he pretends to be, conveniently, but he *knows* the truth and he expresses it unambiguously. He also knows the nature of the deed itself. Perhaps he is enticed by its horror—on some level—but it is horrible, and we are to agree with him, *not* say, well, it is a murky world, old boy, go ahead. His and our moral compasses are aligned. He goes against it. We recoil with him, in horror. We are horrified *at* Lady Macbeth, horrified *with* Macbeth.

The "roughest Day" and the "rough Night" are products of Macbeth's action. If they are the *world's* action they are *re*action. Grove argues that "whatever humane statute may exist is founded in ourselves, Nature refusing that responsibility" (1982, 120). No. The play shows Nature in both places, as the "rough Night" and Lady Macbeth's "nature," "perturbed," though it be proven ultimately natural within God's comprehensive scheme of things. The chanting of the Weird Sisters "does its best to unseat the supposition that moral qualities might be real" (Grove 1982, 120). But they are.

"Cawdor too had been overtaken by the self-undoing reversals the first scene set in motion" (Grove 1982, 121). That may be, but Cawdor perceives his error and should therefore serve as an example *against* Macbeth's own "black and deepe desires."

Grove is excellent on the way in which the play works on us:

> Not being able to state clearly, and so gain some mastery over, our experience—being obliged instead to undergo it, as we half-hear echoes or intuit a rhythm in part, these open, shifting, moment-by-moment presentations of possibility are the means whereby "plot," "character," and the rest come to us in a play. (1982, 122)

"No other drama I can think of makes such play with the headlong plunge of tenses" (125). We experience Macbeth as "compulsively his imagination leaps the gap . . . between the opposites" (124), the "powerful, baffling continuities" (126). A. C. Bradley suggests that "there is in him something which leaps into light at the sound of [the Weird Sisters]; but they are at the same time the witness of forces which never cease to work in the world around him" (1904, 277).

The effect of the play is powerful, assuming that we are not sitting there sneering at royalist propaganda, and assuming the production is paying attention to and communicating the words of the play. Bradley, for example, talks of

> the "Sophoclean irony" by which a speaker is made to use words bearing the audience, in addition to his own meaning, a further and ominous sense, hidden from himself and, usually, from the other persons on the stage . . . the answer [for example] that Banquo, as he rides away, never to return alive, gives to Macbeth's reminder, "Fail not our feast." "My lord, I will not," he replies, and he keeps his promise. (1904, 270)

We do not know that he is fulfilling a fated pattern until we—and Macbeth—recognize him at the banquet. Caroline F. E. Spurgeon, in her classic study of Shakespeare's imagery, argues that "an appreciable part of the emotions we feel throughout of pity, fear and horror, is due to the subtle but repeated action of this imagery [dark versus light, for example] upon our minds, of which, in our preoccupation with the main theme, we remain often largely unconscious" (1935, 335). The play, she offers, creates "sound echoing over vast regions, even into the limitless spaces beyond the confines of the world'' (327). Macbeth's Scotland, writes Edith Sitwell, is a "vast world torn from the universe of night'' (1961, 27).

Although *King Lear* would be a candidate for the play in the canon in which evil is most powerful, Peter Hall argues that *Macbeth*

> is the most thorough-going study of evil that I know in dramatic literature. Evil in every sense: cosmic sickness, personal sickness, personal neurosis, the consequence of sin, the repentance of sin, blood leading on to more blood, and that, in a way, leading inevitably to regeneration. . . . I find it the most metaphysical of Shakespeare's plays. (1982, 244)

Sanders (1966) finds the play pessimistic because of the vitality of evil in the play. S. L. Bethel attributes this enormous energy partly to diabolic images "suggesting the notion of hell or damnation'' (1952, 37). Certainly the play's emphasis on damnation argues the specific nature of evil in *Macbeth*, as opposed to the seemingly more modern, existential variety exhibited in Goneril and Edmund.

One reason why evil can seem so potent in *Macbeth* is isolated by Sanders: "[I]t is Macbeth's self-accusation that speaks ['renown and grace is dead,' etc.], recognizing how he has uncreated something which it is not within his powers to recall to life either in Duncan or in himself. . . . For the world of the play, too, these things are dead'' (1968, 257–58). The economy of means in *Macbeth*, where all elements are held powerfully *and* delicately in a precisely defined relationship to each other, insists that striking at a *central* element harms all the others. Suddenly, horses are "free'' to war on mankind and on themselves, mousing owls are empowered to pull down falcons. Michael Gearin-Tosh deals with the *extremes* of nature depicted in the play: "tears . . . so forceful that, like torrential rain, they drown a gale'' (1988, 10). "The word 'wither' primarily refers to a plant which shrivels through lack of light and moisture. Murder's world has no sun'' (12). " 'Unfortunate' [in Macbeth's "all unfortunate Soules / That trace him in his Line''] is a sadist's caress'' (15). Our response is also extreme: "[N]o one knows what takes place during sleep and we are all subject to those strange processes of psychic reworking, guilt and regeneration which make sleep 'great nature's second course.' [We experience] both an eerie intensity at being witness to what is secret, and a shared vulnerability'' (17). We are witnessing helplessness, and we are ourselves helpless in our witness.

Works Cited

Bethel, S. L. 1952. "*Macbeth* and the Powers of Darkness.'' *Emory University Quarterly* 8 (Fall): 17–28.

Bradley, A. C. 1904. *Shakespearean Tragedy*. London: Macmillan.

Bristol, Michael. 1990. *Shakespeare's America, American's Shakespeare*. London: Routledge.

Brooks, Cleanth. 1947. "The Naked Babe and the Cloak of Manliness." In *The Well Wrought Urn*. New York: Harcourt, Brace.

Brown, John Russell, ed. 1963. *Macbeth*. Great Neck, N.Y.: Barron's.

————, ed. 1982. *Focus on 'Macbeth.'* London: Routledge and Kegan Paul.

Collmer, Robert G. 1960. "An Existentialist Approach to *Macbeth.*" *The Personalist* 41 (Autumn): 24–29.

Doran, Madeleine. 1983. "The *Macbeth* Music." *Shakespeare Studies* 16: 153–74.

Duthie, G. I. 1966. "Antithesis in *Macbeth.*" *Shakespeare Survey* 19: 25–33.

Empson, William. 1930. *Seven Types of Ambiguity*. London: Jonathan Cape.

Gearin-Tosh, Michael. 1988. "The Treatment of Evil in *Macbeth.*" In *Macbeth*. Edited by Linda Cookson and Bryan Loughrey. London: Longman.

Grove, Robin. 1982. "Multiplying Villainies of Nature." In *Focus on 'Macbeth'*. Edited by John Russell Brown. London: Routledge and Kegan Paul.

Guignon, Charles. 1983. *Heidegger and the Problem of Knowledge*. Indianapolis: Hackett.

Hazlitt, William. 1930. *Complete Works*. Vol. 4. Edited by P. P. Howe. London: Chatto & Windus.

Heidegger, Martin. 1968. *What Is Called Thinking*. New York: Harper and Row.

Hunter, G. K., ed. 1967. *Macbeth*. Harmondsworth, England: Penguin.

Jorgensen, Paul A. 1971. *Our Naked Frailties*. Berkeley: University of California Press.

Knight, G. Wilson. 1931. *The Imperial Theme*. Oxford: Oxford University Press.

Knights, L. C. 1947. *Explorations*. London: Chatto and Windus.

————. 1959. *Some Shakespearean Themes*. London: Chatto and Windus.

Long, Michael, ed. 1989. *Macbeth*. Boston: Twayne.

Mahood, M. M. 1957. *Shakespeare's Wordplay*. London: Metheun.

Nowottny, Winifred. 1964. "Shakespeare's Tragedies." In *Shakespeare's World*. Edited by Joel Hurstfield and James Sutherland. New York: St. Martin's Press.

Sanders, Wilbur. 1966. "The Strong Pessimism of *Macbeth.*" *Critical Quarterly* 15 (Fall): 57–65.

————. 1968. *The Dramatist and the Received Idea*. Cambridge: Cambridge University Press.

————. 1978. *Shakespeare's Magnanimity*. Cambridge: Cambridge University Press.

Sitwell, Edith. 1961. *A Notebook on William Shakespeare*. Boston: Beacon Press.

Smidt, Kristian. 1966. "*Dr. Faustus* and *Macbeth.*" *English Studies* 23 (Summer): 235–48.

Spurgeon, Caroline. 1935. *Shakespeare's Imagery and What It Tells Us*. Cambridge: Cambridge University Press.

Traversi, Derek. 1956. *An Approach to Shakespeare*. Garden City, N.Y.: Doubleday Anchor.

Wills, Gary. 1995. *Witches and Jesuits*. Oxford: Oxford University Press.

Wilson, Robert. 1988. "The Sense of Society in *Macbeth.*" In *Macbeth*. Edited by Linda Cookson and Bryan Loughrey. London: Longmans.

The Weird Sisters

A unique and powerful aspect of the world of the play is the treatment of the Weird Sisters, who, like so much else in Shakespeare, leave a lot of the interpretation to the production. They interpenetrate both cosmic and human sectors of the play and are crucial to any interpretation of what the play "means." What they are in the play is perhaps inseparable from how they got there—that is, what they were in their historical moment. Here the new historicists are right. They are not "source." They are context.

While evil is not an independent entity, as Macbeth would wish it or would wish to create it, evil was, according to Walter Clyde Curry a reality:

> evil was both [a] subjective and, so far as the human mind is concerned, a non-subjective reality . . . evil manifested itself subjectively in the spirits of men and objectively in a metaphysical world whose existence depended in no degree upon the activities of the human mind. . . . Such a system of evil was raised to the dignity of a science and a theology. (1937, 58)[1]

Reginald Scot is careful to place witches, however nonsubjectively real, within the larger dispensation:

> And yet so farre as Gods word teacheth me, I will not sticke to saie, that they are living creatures, ordeined to serve the estate, yet that they are the Lords ministers, and executioners of his wrath, to trie and tempt in this world, and to punish the reprobate in hell fier in the world to come. (1886, 433)

The Weird Sisters indeed represent different aspects of time—past, present, and future—a fact that makes their prophecies powerful because they simulate process. Once the Macbeths begin to play the "future" game, they are both lost, even if Macbeth considers waiting for "Chance [to] Crowne [him] / Without [his] stirre." His reliance on pagan fatality signals his yielding to the certainty that will bring uncertainty to all his days and nights to come.

A few critics attempt to suggest what the Weird Sisters *are*, as if they were independent of their subordination to a dramatic purpose, while others examine their possible origins. I have already dealt with witchcraft as *source*, but further discussion of the Weird Sisters will be useful, even if, as John Turner suggests, they "baffle the very categories that they invite" (1992, 14). The question is, what are they in this *play?*

According to Charles Moseley, Shakespeare avoids actual devils as laughable stage devices to get at "the terror and sublimity of a metaphysical world of evil" (1988, 60). The play betrays an "underlying skepticism about the powers supposedly deployed by witchcraft" (25), but shows what can happen to human beings who give "the mind's consent to the illusion" (29). The Weird Sisters' power becomes "parasitic upon Macbeth's own nature and ambition" (27). As with the Ghost in *Hamlet*, so is it with the Weird Sisters. The dramatic issue is what Hamlet or Macbeth *makes* of them. The contrast to Macbeth, says Moseley, is Banquo, who "highlight[s] the freedom of choice both men enjoy" (29).

James Bulman asserts that the "Weird Sisters are the source of linguistic uncertainty in the play" (1985, 172). Whether they create or reflect ambiguity, they are the *physical* manifestation of their metaphysics; as Sidney Homan suggests, the witches "embody the principle of equivocation" (1986, 113). According to H. W. Fawkner, "From the viewpoint of the play as a whole, [the Weird Sisters] distribute the economies of equivocation; from the viewpoint of the hero, they manipulate the question of Truth" (1990, 52). They are "agents of indeterminacy" (52). They are, claims Fawkner, "quintessentially Shakespearean and therefore not reducible to extra-Shakespearean entities" (53). "These females cannot immediately be ravaged for information by too-confident males used to extracting meaning from every object they choose to query" (53). They "dismantl[e] the opposition past-future" (54). Do they? They seem to have a precise sense of time and timing. It seems to me that they encourage that dismantling in those who listen to them.

A materialist critique must see the Weird Sisters as part of the dramatist's intention to validate the dominant ideology. If a king's death can destroy a world, Shakespeare must make such a world. Peter Stallybrass asserts that "*Macbeth* takes material eminently suitable for dialectical development (the weak ruler being overthrown by a ruler who establishes 'equal justice') and shapes it into a structural antithesis" (1982, 193). To "suggest that the monarchy was under demonic attack [he must] glorify the institution of monarchy, since that implied that it was one of the bastions protecting the world from the triumph of Satan" (192). "In England . . . there was already a clear connection between prophecy, witchcraft, and monarchy before James ascended the throne" (191). Indeed, Bishop Jewel, in a sermon circa 1560 had issued this warning to the young Queen Elizabeth: "It may please your Grace to understand that this kind of people, I mean witches and sorcerers, within these few last years, are marvelously increased within your Grace's realm, for the shoal of them is great, their doings horrible, their malice intolerable" (1847, 2: 446). The containment of subversion can be a means of continuation in power for any political system, as witness the "witch-hunts" of the 1950s and much of the Cold War, including the inexcusable wars in Vietnam: the first to maintain a colonial empire; the second, to contain the alleged spread of monolithic communism.

What follows from Stallybrass's argument is that, as Shakespeare invented the Weird Sisters so that he could posit the throne as a guarantor of protection from them, Shakespeare also places the Elizabethan world picture into the depth structures of the drama to show the positive virtues that the throne also guarantees. That may be so, but is it not more basic to Shakespeare's intention that the dynamic of the world picture functions to demonstrate what happens when individuals defy it? The power beyond any king was God, as Shakespeare had demonstrated directly in *Richard III* and within multiplying ironies in *Richard II*. Is Shakespeare positing God in *Macbeth* as one of the things the king guarantees? If *Richard II* is our example—the example of a willful king interrupting the flow of God's grace to his kingdom—then the answer is yes. Malcolm promises "the Grace of Grace" at the end. Stallybrass and the materialists place the entire play within a political frame, a surrounding and informing context dictated by the throned Jacobean. The context is there. How much it dictates or dominates content is a question to be asked. It seems to me that Shakespeare needs the world he creates in order to frame tragedy within it.

Ian Robinson claims that the Weird Sisters "have managed to put themselves forward as the chorus; at first they do represent what is normal in the play, and so are terrible. For if the witches are what is normal in the world, the world is hell, nor are we out of it" (1968, 102). I disagree. They represent a temptation to farther fall in a fallen world, just as Duncan represents a means toward grace (see Coursen 1967). They represent a distortion of normality, a perverse mirror of positive orders, as Robert Burton suggests: "[w]here God hath sacrifices, the Devil will have his oblations" (1628, III. iv. I.1). Their cauldron is a shadow of Communion: "Coole it with a Baboones blood''; "Powre in Sowes Blood, that hath eaten / Her nine Farrow."

Arthur R. McGee suggests that the Weird Sisters "act as agents of remorse and despair like the classical Furies, their aim being to insure Macbeth's damnation" (1966, 66). They are, he argues, "objective agents in a theological system" (66). He cites Timothy Bright as agreeing to "the religious view of conscience" (66).

> [T]he language of *Macbeth* is written in the idiom of the primitive imagination—the imagination stimulated by the fear of the unknown, of the unknowable . . . no longer a dividing line between the literal and the metaphorical, between the objective and the subjective; it is at once vague and precise, real and unreal; what is connoted is more important than what is denoted. It is seminal and it germinates into terror. (66)

The Weird Sisters, then, reflect anxiety about language and its relationship to an object. Shakespeare goes back to a past time to make the confusion more plausible for his audience. To see the Weird Sisters as objective—Banquo sees them and questions them—is not to rule out the subjectivity of dagger and ghost. They need "dead body parts, and especially dead bodies outside consecrated ground," asserts Gary Wills (1995, 38), for their concoctions. It may also be that they kidnap Banquo for use at Macbeth's dinner. King James I says that they "can put his own spirit in a dead body, which the *necromancers* commonly practice . . . when the devil carries it out of the grave to serve his turn for a space" (1597, 28–29, 41). Part of a Parliamentary law quoted by Dr. Samuel Johnson made it a capital crime to "take up any dead man, woman or child out of the grave—or the skin, bone, or any part of the dead person, to be employed or used in any manner of witchcraft, sorcery, charm, or enchantment" (1951, 599). Lear perhaps believes himself a victim of grave robbers when he complains, "You do me wrong to take me out of the grave."

D. J. Enright refutes the ideas of G. Wilson Knight:

He stresses [in *Wheel of Fire*] the notion of "the objectivity of evil": evil "comes from without," and thus it is, he maintains, that "the Weird Sisters are objectively conceived." Evil comes from without—as if it were some species of radioactivity emanating from another planet and unamenable to scientific investigation. The consequences of applying this conception of evil is that Macbeth can only be seen as the innocent victim of an epidemic or a traffic accident or, better a collision with a meteorite . . . in the good cause of bringing out the play's momentousness, [Knight] has simply reduced its significance. (1970, 122)

Shakespeare tends to have it both ways, and perhaps he employed James's sense of the versatility of evil spirits. James distinguishes between a spirit "that outwardlie troubles and followes some persons" and one that "inwardlie possesses them" (1597, 62). While it is unnecessary to argue, as Wills does, that the "witches are [not] just emanations of Macbeth's inner state" (1995, 37), not just products of "Macbeth's psychological makeup" (43), the play does not inhabit one plane of objectivity. According to Peter Hall, "Different levels of reality are used deliberately in the play. . . . There is the bloody dagger which Macbeth sees and we don't," and, at the banquet: "he imagines so concretely that he sees [the ghost of Banquo] and we see it, but nobody else on stage sees it" (1982, 245). The play becomes a series of Henry Jamesian exercises in point of view, as the variety of critical responses suggests.

Margaret Webster deals with what *we* should see of the Weird Sisters:

I believe that we should see as little as possible of the Witches in the flesh of actors or actresses. The unseen voice of evil, its imminence, its very facelessness, these things have a chilling power; we can use shadows, or twisting silhouettes, the glimpse of hands, the outline of a head, shifting, hovering, formless; their voices should echo from the hollow rocks and stream away against the wind. We should see them by reflection, through the human beings who come so terrifyingly close to the unknowable. (1957, 174)

Whatever they are, they are inferior to the larger order: They "melted, as breath into the Winde," and they may have winds to lend, but "teares shall drowne the winde." The power of compassion is greater than anything the Weird Sisters can muster. C. E. Whitmore gives them more independence than Banquo does. For Banquo they are "Instruments of Darknesse." Whitmore claims that the "Sisters do not derive their might from any covenant with the powers of evil, but are themselves such powers, owing their sinister capacities only to themselves" (1915, 256). Willard Farnham argues that the Sisters are "demons of the fairy order such as the Elizabethans also called hags or furies. They are fiends in the shape of old women who do evil wherever and however they can." But, adds Farnham, their power can only be realized through a human agency: "the word 'weird' as applied to them cannot mean that they have con-

trol over Macbeth's destiny and compel him to do all that he does'' (1950, 80).
"They tempt Macbeth to do evil, and they tempt him with great subtlety. They
cannot force him to do it'' (80). "By their imperfect speaking they tempt him
to commit crimes for which he is to assume full moral responsibility, a responsibility so complete that it will be not only for doing but also for forming the
thought of doing, each criminal deed'' (81). Their power stems partly from the
"apparent objectivity,'' as Wilbur Sanders says, with which they match Macbeth's "inmost consciousness . . . with a heart-stopping fidelity'' (1968, 278).
That "apparent objectivity'' is crucial to their success. The Weird Sisters hover
neutrally over the issues that divide mere mortals—"When the Battaile's lost,
and wonne.'' Their interest is in the way in which eternity is divided. They are,
according to Stephen Siddall, jesters sent from the court of Satan to humankind:
"Their language is contrived in the form of rhyming couplets that can express
both riddling uncertainties that confuse and mislead their victim, and also the
banal naivety of children's games'' (1988, 89).

McGee suggests that they are "additions to Christian demonology [from the
classics] . . . felt to be necessary perhaps because there is comparatively little
demonic symbolism in the Bible'' (1966, 55). McGee says that "witches, Furies,
devils and fairies were virtually synonymous'' (57).

Jean Seznec cites the medieval tendency exemplified by the allegorizing of
Ovid's *Metamorphoses* by an anonymous commentator, who sees

> the whole of Christian morality in the poem, and even the Bible itself. The
> Argus eyes that Juno scatters over the tail of the peacock are the vanities
> of this world; the peacock is the vainglorious mortal who flaunts them;
> Diana is the Trinity; Actaeon, Jesus Christ. Phaethon represents Lucifer and
> his revolt against God. Ceres looking for Proserpina is the Church seeking
> to recover the souls of the faithful who have strayed from the fold. Her two
> torches are the Old and New Testaments; the child who insults her and
> whom she transforms into a lizard is the Synagogue. (1961, 92–93)

It is probably a more direct path that takes the furies to initiation as witches
and devils. Crucially for the Church, the furies, witches, and the Devil himself
were doing the work of the gods or God, howsoever in the negative shadowlands
of the Kingdom.

A skeptical view of the late sixteenth century is provided by G. Giffard: "I
am afraid, for I see now and then a Hare; which my conscience giveth me is a
witch, or some witches spirite'' (1593, B I). The rational Theseus says something similar:

> in the night, imagining some fear,
> How easy is a bush suppos'd a bear!

But while he may be right in the general instance, Theseus is wrong here, as Hippolyta quietly insists:

> But all the story of the night told over,
> And all their minds transfigur'd so together,
> More witnesseth than fancy's images,
> And grows to something of great constancy;
> But, howsoever, strange and admirable.

George Puttenham discusses the abuse of language that is "occupied of purpose to deceive the eare and also the minde, drawing it from plainnesse and simplicitie to a certaine doublenesse, whereby our talke is the more guilefull & abusing" (1936, 154). The Weird Sisters, of course, operate with "a certaine doublenesse." According to an anonymous late Jacobean, "The *devils*, we know, did *equivocate* in their oracles, but only by a *verbal equivocation*, consisting of words of double and doubtful signification: wherein although there were deceit, yet it was not by a flat lie, but by an indirect truth" (quoted in Dent 1969, xiii, emphasis in original).

Robert West argues that

> both Macbeth's fall and the Weird Sisters' part in it [are] awesome mysteries which we may feel and in part observe, but for which we have no sort of formula. Shakespeare does not look behind these mysteries, and he does not suggest that we may do so. Rather he looks *into* them, shows us the phenomena in a piercing way that conveys a sense of their ghastly significance without bringing us much the nearer to a rational account of them or of it. (1956, 24)

Thus the play *involves* us in the unnameable plight of the victims.

D. J. Palmer calls the long line of Banquo's issue "a diabolical parody of the emblematic pageants and allegorical masques with which royalty was greeted and honoured in Shakespeare's day, often at a banquet" (1982, 56). The Weird Sisters deliver "a complimentary allusion from the point of view of a Jacobean audience ... in keeping with the usual function of this kind of spectacle" (56). Palmer points at the economy and audacious development of the demonic pageant: "[W]hat to [Macbeth] is a 'horrible sight' is to us a congratulatory pageant" (61). Hall agrees: "The line of kings is a nightmare to Macbeth," but to others, "[i]t means security ... peace, succession, continuity" (1982, 244). Hall's interpretation, of course, runs counter to the destabilizing aspects of the script discerned there by postmodernist critics.

Hecate, Palmer argues, is "a goddess, not a grotesque hag, and a spectral counter-part to that other Queen of Night, Lady Macbeth" (1982, 57). "Shakespeare clearly specifies [in the Weird Sisters] the traditional figures of English folk-lore" (58). All the apparitions, Palmer notes, are male. They "come like shadows, then depart" as if Macbeth's shadow, that is what he has repressed and what he shallowly interprets. Certainly Hecate in Jonson's *Masque of Queens* attributes cosmic powers to herself and her followers:

> When we have set the elements at wars,
> Made midnight see the sun, and day the stars;
> When the winged lightning in its course hath stay'd,
> And swiftest rivers have run back, afraid
> To see the corn remove, the graves to range
> Where places alter and the seas do change;
> When the pale moon, at the first voice, down fell
> Poison'd and durst not stay the second spell. (213–220)

Macbeth's response to the two sets of prophecies emerges from different aspects of his "free will" (see Sanders 1968, 280–81, on Macbeth's reaction). His free will is greatly diminished by the time he chooses to seek out the Weird Sisters at the end of the banquet scene, so whatever the formula might have been, it has changed. The two sets of prophecies have an inverse relationship to each other. Macbeth acts in response to the first set and is passive as he (mis)interprets the second. Each response is the wrong one, but once he acts on the basis of the first, no action can save him from the predictions of the second. Action is fatal. Inaction is also fatal, but the latter is preordained. His moral reservations in light of the first prophecies drive him to understand the depth of his deed and all its implications—except the experiential—but he goes ahead. He accepts the surface of the second set, partly because it serves his purpose to do so, but also because he has surrendered depth. He can no longer read "deeper" meanings. He has exhausted them for himself, with the exception of "deepe damnation." In the case of Lady Macbeth, her depth reads *her*.

William O. Scott argues that

> The double nature of the prophecies (as merely descriptive and so powerless
> to effect what they predict, and yet binding upon Macbeth as a kind of Fate)
> is reflected in his equivocal attitude to them: in so far as he acts, he takes
> the future on his shoulders and undertakes to create it, thus becoming the
> accomplice, or even the master, of his fate; yet he persists in regarding the
> future as pre-ordained and Fate as his master. (1986, 172)

Once he does choose to master the future, it becomes his master. "Though he had once been honest with himself about the consequences of evil," Scott writes, "while self-deceiving about his motives for thinking of them, he now is fully aware of his purposes but unwilling to give the foretelling of consequences a proper scrutiny" (170).

Scott says of the second set of prophecies, "The very proliferation of conflicting or doubtful messages and symbols should itself hint that there may be traps of interpretation" (1986, 172)—to us, yes, as we detach ourselves from a frantic Macbeth and sense that second meanings do pertain, even if we as audience members do not know what they will turn out to be.

The second set of prophecies represents a disjunctive analogue to Christ's parables, disjunctive because the truths beneath Christ's allegories are positive. In Matthew 14:13–14, Christ says, "Therefore speake I to them in parables, because they seing, do no se: and hearing, they heare not, nether understand. / So in them is fulfilled the prophecie of Esaias, which *prophecie* faith, By hearing ye shal heare, and shal not understand, and seing ye shal se, and not perceive." He continues in 14:15 to say that "with their eyes they have winked, lest they shulde se with their eyes." The winking of the eyes becomes a moral blinding, a willful avoidance of the truth in which both the early Macbeth and Lady Macbeth indulge. There follows in Matthew the Parable of the Sower.

NOTE

1. See also R. M. Frye 1963, 147–48, 157–65; Bernard McElroy 1973, 211–14; and Robert Reed 1965, 168–71.

Works Cited

Bulman, James. 1985. *The Heroic Idiom of Shakespearean Tragedy*. Cranbury, N.J.: Associated University Presses.

Burton, Robert. 1628. *Anatomy of Melancholy*. Edited by Floyd Dell and Paul Jordan. Reprint. London: Tudor, 1927.

Coursen, H. R. 1967. "In Deepest Consequence: *Macbeth*." *Shakespeare Quarterly* 18, no. 4 (Autumn): 375–88.

Curry, Walter C. 1937. *Shakespeare's Philosophical Patterns*. Baton Rouge: Louisiana University Press.

Dent, R. W., ed. 1969. Introduction. In *Macbeth*. Dubuque, Iowa: W. C. Brown.

Enright, D. J. 1970. *Shakespeare and the Students*. London: Chatton and Windus.

Farnham, Willard. 1950. *Shakespeare's Tragic Frontier*. Berkeley: University of California Press.

Fawkner, H. W. 1990. *Deconstructing 'Macbeth': The Hyperontological View*. Cranbury, N.J.: Associated University Presses.

Frye, R. M. 1963. *Shakespeare and Christian Doctrine*. Princeton, N.J.: Princeton University Press.

Giffard, G. 1593. *A Dialogue concerning Witches*. London.

Homan, Sidney. 1986. *Shakespeare's Theater of Presence: Language, Spectacle, and the Audience*. Lewisburg, Pa.: Bucknell University Press.

James I. 1597. *Daemonologie*. Edinburgh.

Jewel, Bishop John. 1847. "Defense of the Apology." In *Works*. Edited by John Ayre. London: Parker Society.

Johnson, Samuel. 1951. *Johnson*. Edited by Mona Wilson. Cambridge, Mass.: Harvard University Press.

Knight, G. Wilson. 1957. *The Wheel of Fire*. New York: Meridian.

McElroy, Bernard. 1973. *Shakespeare's Mature Tragedies*. Princeton, N.J.: Princeton University Press.

McGee, Arthur R. 1966. "*Macbeth* and the Furies." *Shakespeare Survey* 19:55–67.

Moseley, Charles. 1988. "Macbeth's Free Fall." In *Macbeth*. Edited by Linda Cookson and Bryan Loughrey. London: Longman.

Palmer, D. J. 1982. " 'A New Gorgon': Visual Effects in *Macbeth*." In *Focus on 'Macbeth.'* Edited by John Russell Brown. London: Routledge and Kegan Paul.

Puttenham, George. 1936. *The Art of English Posie*. Translated by Alice Walker and G. D. Willcock. Cambridge: Cambridge University Press.

Reed, Robert. 1965. *The Occult on the Tudor and Stuart Stage*. Boston: Christopher.

Robinson, Ian. 1968. "The Witches and Macbeth." *Critical Review* 9 (Fall): 99–104.

Sanders, Wilbur. 1968. *The Dramatist and the Received Idea*. Cambridge: Cambridge University Press.

Scot, Reginald. 1886. *The Discoverie of Witchcraft*. Edited by B. Nicholson. London.

Scott, William O. 1986. "Macbeth's—and Our—Self-Equivocations." *Shakespeare Quarterly* 37 (Summer): 160–74.

Seznec, Jean. 1961. *The Survival of the Pagan Gods: The Mythological and Its Place in Renaissance Humanism and Art*. Translated by Barbara F. Sessions. New York: Harper.

Siddall, Stephen. 1988. "Ceremony in *Macbeth*." In *Macbeth*. Edited by Linda Cookson and Bryan Loughrey. London: Longman.

Stallybrass, Peter. 1982. "*Macbeth* and Witchcraft." In *Focus on 'Macbeth.'* Edited by John Russell Brown. London: Routledge and Kegan Paul.

Turner, John. 1992. *Macbeth*. Buckingham: Open University Press.

Webster, Margaret. 1957. *Shakespeare without Tears*. New York: Fawcett Premier.

West, Robert. 1956. "Night's Black Agents in *Macbeth*." *Renaissance Papers* 1, no. 1: 1–23.

Whitmore, C. E. 1915. *The Supernatural in Tragedy*. Cambridge: Cambridge University Press.

Wills, Gary. 1995. *Witches and Jesuits*. Oxford: Oxford University Press.

PSYCHOLOGICAL APPROACHES

Psychological approaches to *Macbeth* would tend to apply a particular theory to the characters: Elizabethan humor theory, Freud's theory of repression, Jung's descriptions of psychological types and his analysis of the male and female psychic structure, Adler's will to power, Horney's definitions of defense mechanisms, and so on. Such criticism tends to be anachronistic when it applies modern theories to seventeenth-century characters, and it tends to treat fictional creatures as real people. In defense of these approaches, however, it is claimed that Shakespeare anticipates modern approaches, as Freud constantly recognized, and that the characters *do* display psychic activity which can be phrased in metaphors not necessarily available to Shakespeare. The most useful and persuasive category of psychological criticism since the early 1980s has been the feminist approach, which looks at the women in the plays, particularly as they are marginalized by patriarchy and male attitudes ("The repetition in a Womans eare / Would murther as it fell"), at gender relationships, and at characters marginalized by their sexual orientations.

The play has long attracted responses to the psychology of its characters, which seem as susceptible to modern theory as to earlier concepts of demonic possession. It is worth pointing out to those who insist that criticism be "historical" in its terms, that Elizabethan humor theory is neatly consistent with Jung's positing of the extroverted and introverted personality types. The sanguine and the choleric are extroverts, the melancholic and phlegmatic are introverts. Furthermore, Christian psychology, particularly as articulated by Saint Augustine, Saint Jerome, and Saint Bernard, can be said to incorporate much more than a trace of a theory of repression. Saint Jerome's prayer was, "O Lord, keep me from becoming what I am at night." A good example of this debate between body and soul is Richard III's dream and dream analysis in the early morning of his last day on earth. It is worth noting that Jung borrows the word "archetype" and its concept from Augustine. The relationship between Macbeth and Lady Macbeth is an obvious site for the analysis of gender relationships on which feminist approaches so usefully focus.

Jung has not been popular with critics of Shakespeare. For one thing, psychological approaches to the plays based on twentieth-century theory are "not historical." For another, Freud's lucidity in outlining metaphors of the psyche based on sexual repression seems preferable to Jung's metaphysical murkiness in developing mythologies that apply to all souls and single souls. Jung is seen as generating "totalizing" theories in a context of splintered visions based on sexual orientation and vividly demarcated cultural boundaries. Jungian approaches demand a response based on a perceived self-hood as opposed to a formula that absolves the critic from "being there." Jung, like Freud, has been accused of tailoring facts to fit theories. Furthermore, Jung, a product of a phallocentric society, could and did make comments that can be called "sexist" today, and therefore he is to be generally discredited. Jung's distinction between "feeling" (an evaluative function) and "sensation" (a perceptive function) can be confusing to those who have not done some basic work in the area. Add to that the objection to "jargon" in a jargon-ridden profession and the tendency of Jungian approaches to produce Jungian allegories, and Jung is easily dismissed.

Paul J. Stern outlines Jung's limitations:

> In the intellectual realm, Jung's great synthesis remained very much at the level of verbal operations whose superficialities were concealed by an impressive array of erudition. Jung's often-noted lack of lucidity, his turgid style, the leakiness of his logic, his inability to distinguish between hypotheses and facts [show that h]is syntheses did not eventuate in genuine union. (1976, 256–57)

Jung's description of psychological types, however, can be useful in examining *conflict*. Hamlet, introverted thinking, can find nothing right about his mother's remarriage. But Gertrude, extroverted sensation, can sense only that it

was "o'rehasty." Furthermore, Jung's emphasis on the limitations of consciousness helps show how characters can err in depending on consciousness. Henry
V, for example, is hit with a powerful tide of introverted feeling coming from
his repressed orientation and function on the eve of Agincourt. Given the extroverted thinking that has gotten him to this point, the presentation of this
opposing material is almost inevitable. "Ego," for Jung, equates to "consciousness." The problem with ego is that it can be taken to be "all"—a "hubris of
consciousness" (Singer 1973, 408) like that Othello exhibits on landing at Cy-
prus and seeing Desdemona or Lear on his going off to prison with Cordelia,
where the woman becomes a victim of the male's projections. In each case the
male believes he has "arrived" ("my soul's joy," "Have I caught thee?") just
as he commits a tragic error. Jung helps us describe the *enantiodromia*, or
reversal, that characters suffer into extreme introversion and out again—as in
Henry V at Agincourt, or Lear, who goes mad and then comes "out of the
grave," or into an extreme introversion that becomes the "hell" Lady Macbeth
experiences. Jung's approach carries with it the theological implications that
were very much alive on Shakespeare's stage. Since we, as spectators, also have
a psychological orientation (and may even know it, thanks to a Myers-Briggs
test), Jung helps us understand our own reaction to characters on stage and to
the complex negotiations that Shakespeare depicts within the psyches of his
major characters. Jung's concept of individuation comes from Aristotle, for
whom "soul" equated to "capacity" and included a teleological imperative.
When Freud came upon material that could not be accounted for in his patients'
biological backgrounds, he assigned it to "the archaic heritage" (1969, 167).
Jung's theories have encouraged scientific explorations of otherwise unexplained
phenomena—for example, the controversial findings of Rupert Sheldrake, which
means that scientists must now dismiss Sheldrake as literary critics must dismiss
Jung (see Sheldrake 1981, 1995; Coursen 1988). Jung's theories tend to incorporate Freud's. The Oedipal issue, for example, is not merely a problem to be
resolved but also, at the archetypal level, a liberating source of energy, a contact
with the maternal.

Harvey Birenbaum argues that *Macbeth* forces us into an intense relationship
with it: "[We] develop . . . a sense of responsibility for the symbolic consciousness of the play, as though it were our own projection" (1982, 22). One reason
is that it presents in its main characters psychological types likely to capture
our own orientations. At the outset, Macbeth tends to be introverted sensation;
Lady Macbeth, extroverted thinking. Macbeth ends up as an almost absolute
extrovert; she is helplessly introverted and controlled by her subjective response
to her senses—the knocking at the gate, the smell of blood on her hands. Robert
Lordi (1982) argues that our response is to a single personality represented by
Macbeth *and* Lady Macbeth, each an opposite side of the other. From a Jungian
standpoint, that "division of experience" and psyche accounts for their love
and their crucial inability to understand each other.

If we relate to the hero, it may be because he embodies the classic Oedipal conflict. He is, as Terry Eagleton remarks, "a Macbeth who incarnates the infantile desire to kill the father and possess the mother" (1967, 90).

Gender Criticism

One of the problems facing feminist critics is that the play provides in Lady Macbeth one of the strongest female characters in the canon, one who dominates the opening scenes of the play, regarding Macbeth's "humane scrupulosity as merely ineffectual weakness" (Moelwyn 1966, 77). According to H. W. Fawkner, "Lady Macbeth comes to assume all the obnoxious aspects of patriarchal thinking. She patronizes Macbeth, seeks to bring him back into the logical system of masculine dialectic and male dominance in the name of order" (1990, 92). In the classic anima/animus conflict, the woman takes on the stereotypical aspects of the male for the moment; and he, of the female. Neither is in touch with real sources of contrasexual power at that moment. He thinks of *birth*, she of killing children. She predicts *his* future, not he hers. Merchant Moelwyn suggests that "we experience a sharp sexual affront" in her "Come you Spirits" soliloquy. The "demand that her sex be destroyed carries a shocking force" (1966, 75).

In one "rewriting" of the script, her sex *is* destroyed. She represents an energy that must be erased, so that whatever masculinity may be is elevated at the end to a superior position. Certainly a feminist of the militant strain must reject the "Sermon of the State of Matrimonie": "Now as concerning the wives duety. What shall become her: shall she abuse the gentlenesse and humanity of her husband and, at her pleasure, turne all things upside downe? No surely, for that is far repugnant against Gods commandement" (Rickey and Stroup 1966, 242). Even while granting Macbeth's wish to become king, it can be argued that Lady Macbeth does "abuse" his "gentlenesse and humanity."

Joan Larsen Klein remarks that "Lady Macbeth, despite her attempt to unsex herself, is never able to separate herself completely from womankind" (1980, 241)—and, one might add, in spite of her efforts to become a Weird Sister. "She seems to have forgotten or repudiated the dictates of reason or her own conscience. Shakespeare may even intend us to conclude that she had renounced her God" (242). Klein suggests that "the virtues which Lady Macbeth sees as defects in Macbeth's character and obstacles to his success are in fact the better parts of her own being" (245).

Husband and wife do share a common humanity, but it does not emerge simultaneously. Each loves in the other a perceived lack in him or herself—not recognizing it. Her animus makes him a stereotype—or would. He cannot become one without hardening his heart (see Cunningham 1963). If Klein is right, Lady Macbeth transfers her psyche to him. But that does not work. It remains intact, even if hidden. Macbeth is an introvert. He puts a subjective screen in front of an object. That screen is at once his own conscience and the cosmos which is coded into that conscience. She is an extrovert. She has no subjective screen. She acts and *then* considers. Of her damnation Klein says that "medieval definitions of eternal time as the everlasting 'now,' the present during which all things that have happened or will happen are happening" (1980, 249). Not exactly—it is a "now" in which the terrible past must be endlessly repeated. There is no future for her except for the few moments structured into the sequence of the past that are endlessly recapitulated for her. She can get beyond the night of the murder only to ask where her counterpart, Lady Macduff, may be "now."

Her madness makes "Memory, the Warder of the Braine" much more than a "Fume," as she had boasted she would induce in Duncan's guards. She can "now neither forget her guilt nor sleep the sleep of oblivion . . . the fallen unblessed nature 'gives way' to 'cursed thoughts' " (Klein 1980, 250). The repetition in a woman's ear keeps murdering as it falls, as her groans and sighs attest. She "ignorantly and perversely identified with male strength," asserts Klein, and "is able to unsex herself only through the act of self-murder—in contrast to her husband, whose single attribute now is the 'direst cruelty' she begged for" (251).

Coppelia Kahn adds that, at the banquet, Lady Macbeth "implicitly defines manhood as unblinking resolution, untouched by pity or fear, and he defines it as the courage to confront his own evil [which, by his definition, if this is the case, he lacks] . . . And once again, she taunts him with effeminacy" (1981, 181). Kahn shrewdly links the Weird Sisters with Lady Macbeth as props of Macbeth's conscious intentions: "[T]he witches take Lady Macbeth's role as feminine powers on whom Macbeth can rely for inspiration and reassurance" (186). That follows, of course, only after Macbeth's resistance to both the Weird Sisters and Lady Macbeth in Act One. As Lady Macbeth's human agency dwindles and as Macbeth's evil tendencies grow, the Weird Sisters' power also grows, encouraging Macbeth's overconfident evil in a terrible fission that concludes only when he glimpses their paltering and is then dispatched by Macduff.

Even though she has a sense of who Macbeth is (or was) under the male persona, she herself has access only to the male stereotype. It does not strengthen her; it blocks her humanity and fatally weakens her.

Marilyn French sees the ending as the establishment of the "masculine" over the "feminine." The play concludes "in a totally masculine world . . . with Macduff's entrance bearing [Macbeth's] bloody severed head. . . . [S]ome balance is restored to the kingdom, there is no change in its value structure. . . . What is reasserted is moral schizophrenia" (1983, 51).

Peter Erickson agrees. The "restoration of order is contingent on the conspicuous exclusion of women," premised on an "escapist belief in an entirely masculine social order," emerging from a "general pattern of distorted masculinity" (1985, 121–22). Of the ending, Carolyn Asp argues that "the manly stereotype . . . exceeds the limits of soldierly valor and embraces the extreme of retaliatory violence" (1981, 168).

Richard Levin (1989, 8) responds to French's ideas by pointing out that "decapitation . . . was a legal punishment at the time, and that the heads of criminals were often displayed to the public (a practice that is referred to in the play itself at I.2.23).'' Furthermore, the bringing of a head to a ruler was proof that the criminal was indeed dead, as at the end of *Richard II* and in *Measure for Measure*.

Levin states further that ''these feminist readings are all ahistorical or even antihistorical . . . there is no evidence that anyone believed [revenge] was wrong because it was masculine'' (1989, 7). They ''impose upon the play a standard of judgement . . . that is quite different from and (in their own view) much higher than the standard actually operating in the play'' (8).

Furthermore, such feminist ''divisions of experience'' divide along the lines of stereotype. Jung resolves the problem by placing masculine and feminine potentiality within the single psyche. Macbeth is ''full of the milk of human [or humane] kindness,'' that is, in touch with his *anima*. Lady Macbeth is a classic case of an animus-possessed woman, and, in the anima-animus conflict, as Jung describes it, the woman invariably wins even though the man's position is morally and spiritually superior. Furthermore, the introvert and the extrovert exchange places as a result of her victory. I have dealt with the Jungian approach at length elsewhere (1985 and 1986).

Susan Snyder argues cogently that ''[t]he natural universe revealed in the play is essentially attuned to the good'' (1992, 200); however,

> to see in the play's human and physical nature only a straightforward pattern of sin and punishment is to gloss over the questions it raises obliquely, the moral complexities it opens up. . . . What is [the Weird Sisters'] place in a moral universe that ostensibly recoils against sin and punishes it? Are they human witches or supernatural beings? (201–3)

Duncan, who is ''the mild paternal king is nevertheless implicated here in his society's violent warrior ethic, its predicating of manly worth on prowess in killing. But isn't that just what we condemn in Lady Macbeth?'' (204). There I disagree and will develop that point below in discussing Macbeth as murderer.

> Lady Macbeth's actions and outlook thoroughly subvert this ideology, as she forcefully takes the lead in planning the murder and shames her husband into joining in by her willingness to slaughter her own nurseling . . . the label [evil] tends to close down analysis exactly where we ought to probe more deeply. Macbeth's wife is restless in a social role that in spite of her formidable courage and energy offers no chance of independent action and heroic achievement. (204)

She must ''turn to achievement at second hand, through and for her husband'' (205). ''The obedient wife [Lady Macduff] dies, with her cherished son, just as the rebellious, murderous lady will die who consigned her own nursing baby to death'' (205). The play dramatizes the ''contest between public and private commitments that can rack conventional marriages, with the wife confined to a private role while the husband is supposed to balance obligations in both spheres'' (206).

In perhaps the most influential psychoanalytic analysis of the play, Janet Adelman argues that the all-male ending, with Malcolm elevating his followers to earldoms, shows that

> The play that begins by unleashing the terrible threat of destructive maternal power and demonstrates the helplessness of its central male figure before that power thus ends by consolidating male power, in effect solving the problem of masculinity by eliminating the female. In the psychological fantasies that I am tracing, the play portrays the failure of the androgynous parent to protect his son, that son's consequent fall into the dominion of the bad mothers, and the final victory of a masculine order in which mothers no longer threaten because they no longer exist. In that sense, *Macbeth* is a recuperative consolidation of male power, a consolidation in the face of the threat unleased in *Hamlet* and especially in *King Lear* and never fully contained in these plays. In *Macbeth*, maternal power is given its most virulent sway and then abolished; at the end of the play we are in a purely male realm. We will not be in so absolute a male realm again until we are in Prospero's island kingdom, similarly based firmly on the exiling of the witch Sycorax. (1987, 117)

Macbeth, according to Adelman, is ''terrifyingly pawn to female figures'' (1987, 93). They influence him, no doubt, but do they make him a *pawn?* He is alienated from his anima, or contrasexual androgynous energy, but if he is just a puppet in the hands of terrifying female figures and a victim of his inability to construct a self independent of their manipulations, he is subtragic, a figure more like Theodore Dreiser's Clyde Griffiths than the heroic figure of myth that early descriptions make of him. Adelman makes him human enough but subtragic.

The play seems to present a reestablishment of a natural healthy cosmos, but ''bases that order upon the radical exclusion of the female'' that stems from ''the fantasy of a bloody masculine escape from the female,'' that, in turn, reflects Shakespeare's ''ambivalence'' and ''equivocation'' (Adelman 1987, 107–9). Branches are *not* nature rising against Macbeth, as in a popular ''symbolic'' interpretation, but a destruction of ''generative possibility.'' They may ''seem to allude to the rising of the natural order against Macbeth, [but] they obscure the operations of male power, disguising them as a natural force'' (109–10). The cutting of the branches is, of course, a Biblical subject, as Job 14:7–9 suggests: ''For there is hope of a tre, if it be cut downe, that it will yet sproute, and the branches thereof will not cease. / Though the rote of it waxe olde in the earth & and the stocke thereof be dead in the grounde, / *Yet* by the sent of water it wil bud, and bring forthe bowes like a plant.'' Job 14:16 reiterates: ''His rotes shalbe dryed up beneth, and above shall his branche be cut downe.''

The latter fate points at the abuser of God who, like Macbeth, ''shal nether have sonne nor nephewe among his people, nor any posteritie in his dwellings'' (Job 14:19). *There* is generative force cut off and, if the allusion serves, it is not destroyed in Scotland, only in Macbeth, as he himself complains: ''the Seedes of *Banquo* Kings.'' The line of kings shows irrefutably that Scotland is not denied generative possibility. Adelman's brilliant work demonstrates one problem with ahistorical readings that ultimately develop the critic's metaphor, not necessarily the play's.

Harry Berger, Jr., in discussing the ''dialectic of gender conflict'' (1982, 73), makes a similar point about the perceived feminine, in a society controlled by men, and the masculine stereotypes. Lady Macbeth exhibits a ''mimetic desire to join the male ranks'' (72), even as the thanes demonstrate a ''pathologically protective *machismo*'' (68). The thanes worry about ''female contamination'' (71) and try to ''drive out women'' (74). Macbeth is their ''dark double who followed the logic of their own desire to its ultimate conclusion'' (64). By indicating him they elide ''deeper consideration of their own motives or complicity'' (73). By exorcising the woman, they exercise the controls that allow a society to function even as it reflects their deepest fears.

The conclusion of this critical tendency is that Macbeth entertains simultaneous fantasies—of absolute, destructive maternal power and of absolute escape from that power, which Macbeth believes he has accomplished. He has achieved the status of self-generation: ''What's he / That was not born of woman?'' He believes he has escaped from the nature of things, from nature itself. The elimination of all female presence assuages the fears of male identity. The play allows him to hold this belief for a time, then abolishes it. Jung would argue that an ego as isolated as Macbeth's is psychically doomed because it is exiled from its generative, feminine resources.

If Walter Clyde Curry is correct in arguing Lady Macbeth's *actual* demonic possession, of course, the exorcism of the specific she (as fiend, not merely ''Fiend-like Queene'') would be understandable. She, asserts Curry, ''is possessed of demons . . . she calls on precisely the metaphysical forces which have seemed to crown Macbeth . . . sightless substances, *i.e.*, not evil thoughts and 'grim imaginings' but objective substantial forms, invisible bad angels to whose activities may be attributed all the unnatural occurrences of nature. Whatever in the natural world becomes beautiful in the exercise of its normal function is to them foul, and *vice versa*'' (1937, 86). Lady Macbeth consciously wills that evil spirits ''invade her body and so control it that the natural inclinations of the spirit toward goodness and compassion may be completely extirpated'' (87).

> [T]his possession of spirit [does not involve] the infusion of the demonic substance [into] the substance of the soul—only the spirit of God may be fused in this manner with the spirit of man. Rather the unclean spirits overwhelm the intellectual nature of man only when they are permitted to seize upon those members in which the vitality of the soul resides. (88)

As John Donne proclaims in Holy Sonnet 14, "Reason, your viceroy in mee, mee should defend, / But is captiv'd, or proves weak and untrue" (Coffin 1952, 252).

Gary Wills, however, asserts that Lady Macbeth "never commits the formal crime of conjuring and necromancy" (1995, 74) and is not a witch "in any technically legal or theological sense" (83).

Norman Holland links the Weird Sisters to the issue of the feminine in the play: "In many ways *Macbeth* would seem to be the purest statement of Shakespeare's masculine ideal. . . . Once Macduff's wife and babies have been killed, Macduff and Malcolm are completely separated from women, whereas Macbeth, still tied to his mad and sinister wife, despairs and dies." But, because Shakespeare

> presents the witches apart from their prophecies to Banquo and Macbeth, they seem to have powers above and beyond their tempting Macbeth and fulfilling their prophecies through him. Banquo's sons *will* be kings, even though Banquo does nothing about it. An ambiguously female supernature surrounds the main (male) events, influencing them surely, but perhaps also governing and dominating them. Being womanly but also partly male, the witches are for Shakespeare doubly duplicitous. We cannot tell the extent of their dangerous power, both male and female, but the visions they conjure up have to do with birth and death and the cycling of generations, as well as with the traditional Shakespearean concern, kingship. (1989, 80–81)

The supernature may well be feminine, as Holland suggests, but it is compassionate—tears shall drown the wind. That is the superior principle or force, since principle is the force in this play, even if temporarily suspended or delayed.

The issue of the masculine and the feminine has attracted other critics. Stevie Davies argues that Lady Macbeth recreates for Macbeth the

> remembered helplessness of babyhood dependent on the all-powerful, hunger-filling love of a mother who may offer or abstain from offering the means of life; who lifts the infant to soar through vertiginous heights and leans it back as if to drop in infinite space, impressing it with fear of having its brains "dashed out." Macbeth works through the male experience of his continuing bond with the feminine as a condition of dependency threatening to his autonomy. (1986, 169)

Michael Davis suggests that Edward and his support of Malcolm indicate "an alternate understanding of man as not confronted with a hostile nature, but as living within a beneficent nature . . . the alternative to manliness is womanliness, and . . . the two need not be understood as incompatible" (1979, 25)—as the play has made clear early. Macbeth can be a soldier of the king and still full of humane kindness—the latter reading (F1) a reinforcement of "kindness" in its ethical dimension (see Horowitz 1965). David B. Barron asks whether Macbeth make a choice to submit to female influence, whether he unconsciously identifies with his mother, or whether his problem is a combination of choice and unconscious impulse? (1970, 253–79). There we have a set of alternatives that *might* inform an actor's choices or a director's decision. Too much psychoanalytic criticism is atheatrical as well as ahistorical.

Anthony Dawson's discussion of the actor's body would seem to fit under the category of performance, but is perhaps best placed within the discussion of the play's psychology. The Elizabethan theater, according to Dawson, "insist[ed] on both presence and representation" (1996, 38), as did the Anglican compromise, in which "the 'substance' of Christ's body *co-exists* with the sanctified bread" (38). It is also true that the Tudor claim was hardly absolute, although *allegiance* as a result of what Dawson calls a "rifted" (38) society was meant to be. "The actor's body is obviously present, but the 'presence' of the *character's* body is more ambiguous because it depends on representation in the person of the actor" (38; emphasis in original). Anxiety riddled late Elizabethan England and found its focus in *Hamlet*. The "body of the actor is primarily a *rhetorical* instrument, and the exchange in which he is engaged can best be construed as a kind of socially efficacious ritual enabled by the act of participation" (39; emphasis in original). The ritual can be violated, of course, as in Hamlet's apparently angry command to Lucianus and subsequent interruption of the play-within, at the moment that Lucianus mimes an antisacramental poisoning.

What is the effect, Dawson asks, of the boy actor's rubbing his hands as Lady Macbeth?:

> Here we get into ideological questions. For one way of looking at the scene would be to see it as an instance of recuperation, a move to establish an essentialist notion of the "good woman" underneath the monster. In such a reading, the production of interiorization, of conscience, becomes an instrument of ideology, female nature reconstituted as non-monstrous, and hence the female threat to male power is neutralized by referral to a benevolent nature according to which order and patriarchy are maintained. Even this threatening dominant, *monstrous* woman, the text might be made to say, must rub the stain of blood from her guilty hands and therefore be gathered back into the hierarchical system which she has so outrageously challenged earlier in the play. (1996, 41; emphasis in original)

But "by setting the scene metatheatrically,"—a play within a play, very like the opening scene of *Anthony and Cleopatra*, except that Cleopatra knows she is performing—giving the audience thereby "an ironic consciousness . . . the text puts the ideological reading into play and at the same time engages it with a theatrical one. The space between the two kinds of reading is both contested and negotiated" (41). The "feeling, personated body . . . contends against the discursive one, not thereby knocking the latter out of commission but perhaps

allowing for a ritual of participation'' (41). Our awareness of the discrepancy—
the irony—opens a space for participation. ''What is staged is a contest between
alternative ways of making meaning, of turning theatrical experience into meaning'' (41)—external authority—recuperation—and present authority of impersonation, which is the impersonation of authority. ''In her final scene, the
histrionic element is entirely missing: she is asleep'' (42). Yes, but she reenacts
acting—her looking like the innocent flower and being the serpent under it.
''[N]owhere in the play is Lady Macbeth more ineluctably *present*—she is now
herself'' (42; emphasis in original). ''[T]he Shakespearean theatre may be said
to seek the primacy of its art *over* criticism, and, in the present instance, the
medium it uses is the (boy) actor's body'' (42; emphasis in original). ''Engaged
in *watching* is for Shakespeare the most potent way of releasing [representa-
tional] power, so he points to it not simply to subvert it, but to embody it''
(43).

Margaret Webster contrasts Lady Macbeth and Macbeth. He has a ''dual . . .
nature . . . war is his trade. . . . Yet he has a sensitivity of soul which makes him
a prey to every trick of the imagination. His senses are preternaturally sharp;
sights and sounds translate themselves into images, vivid, surrealist images of
a dream, or a nightmare.'' His poetry ''is the expression of a man who is almost
psychically receptive to every vibration of the atmosphere around him. It is
absurd to suppose that such a temperament is incompatible with military valor''
(1957, 170). ''Lady Macbeth, on the other hand, is completely devoid of imagination; and there is almost no music in the writing of her part'' (170). Webster
agrees with Curry: ''[T]hese sightless substances . . . use her, possess her, just
exactly as she had prayed them to do'' (172).

It has long been noted that what Macbeth expresses at the outset gets repressed at the end. A sensitive man, in touch with his ''feminine'' side, he ends
by accepting the stereotypes of bloodiness, boldness, and resoluteness. A man
initially certain of who he is ends by frantically seeking external guarantees of
security. He may be a powerful warrior, but he hesitates to shed the blood of a
kinsman king. At the end, he is out for ''lives'' because his ''gashes / Do better
upon them,'' rather than upon himself. What Lady Macbeth represses at the
outset gets expressed in her sleepwalking and possible suicide. She exchanges
her violent extroversion for a vivid introversion, the horrifying image making
of the early Macbeth, who ''yield[s] to that suggestion'' and others early on.
He feels the future as horror, as he considers how his hand will turn the sea to
red. Lady Macbeth feels the past as horror, as she considers how her hands will
never be clean. The Weird Sisters control time sufficiently to confuse mortals
who believe in them about what time it is. ''The future in the instant'' becomes
a tormenting past for her, a sequence of empty syllables for him.

R. A. Foakes contrasts the attitudes of Macbeth and Lady Macbeth toward
the murder. ''Macbeth is shown creating his own hell . . . in Marlowe's play hell
as deprivation remains merely a concept. It remained for Shakespeare to realise
on stage what this means in terms of character'' (1982, 8). This realization

would exemplify what Snyder calls the emphasis of Luther and Calvin, who believed that "hell is a state of mind, the condition rather than the location of those doomed by God to destruction" (1965, 27). The "common moralistic accounts of the play," asserts Foakes, "are torn between condemning him as a criminal and rescuing a grandeur, integrity, even virtue for him at the end" (1982, 10). Lady Macbeth's "unfamiliarity with images of death perhaps makes it easy for her to contemplate the murder of Duncan without anxiety" (14). But there is a *lot* of anxiety there, isn't there? Furthermore, familiarity with death in battle does not insulate Macbeth from the "horrid Image" of the murdered Duncan. Her "words evade the deed, as if she cannot bear to see the weapon, or the wound it makes, or the actual shape of the man to be murdered" (15)— but she is primarily anxious about *prevention*.

William Hazlitt vividly captures the early states of Macbeth, who is "driven along by the violence of his fate like a vessel drifting before a storm. . . . His blindly rushing forward on the objects of his ambition, or his recoiling from them, equally betrays the harassed state of his feelings," and Lady Macbeth, "whose obdurate strength of will and masculine firmness give her the ascendancy over her husband's faltering virtue" (1930, 187–88).

A. C. Bradley suggests that "the development of her character—perhaps it would be more strictly accurate to say, the change in her state of mind—is both inevitable and the opposite of the development we traced in Macbeth" (1904, 298). G. Wilson Knight concurs: "As her husband grows rich in crime, her significance dwindles" (1957, 152). Klein remarks that "Macbeth wades deeper and deeper in blood in order to stifle the tortures of a mind which fears only the future . . . Lady Macbeth, her husband's 'sweet remembrancer' . . . does little but think of horrors past" (1980, 248). William Scott notices one of the ironic effects of their never inhabiting the same psychological space at the same time: Macbeth's "secrecy from his wife is a kind of openness with himself" (1986, 168). Scott sees this as suggested by and of "amphibology," that is, the "principle of latent double meaning" (170). She earlier did all the dirty work: "Leave all the rest to me." He tells her later, "Be innocent of the knowledge." Their "crossing pattern" is not a straight line, of course. At the banquet, they revert to their early roles, but this time in public—depending on how much a production suggests that their frantic conversations are overheard by the dinner guests. They represent a kind of single psyche, horribly split and unable to integrate but capable only of developing into a parody of healthy spirit as each assumes an opposite orientation. "[W]hat [she] did so freely" later "looks so green and pale" to her. She moves from "singleness"—an unconsidering firmness of purpose—to depth. He moves from awareness of a dual nature to an inertness in which, as Edward Dowden writes, his "sensibility has grown so dull that even the intelligence of his wife's death—the death of her who had been bound to him by such close communication in crime—hardly touches him, and seems little more than one additional incident in the weary, meaningless tale of human life" (1872, 255). He achieves finally an almost mad and unconsidering firmness of purpose. "Lady Macbeth," adds Dowden, "gains for the time sufficient strength by throwing herself into a single purpose, and by resolutely repressing all that is inconsistent with that purpose . . . she cuts off from herself her better nature, she yields to no weak paltering with conscience" (251–52). But as she pauses because Duncan reminds her of her father, Macbeth later pauses in front of Macduff because Macbeth's "soule is too much charg'd / With blood of [his] already." José Benardete points at the parallel between the early Lady Macbeth and the later Macbeth: "[I]f Lady Macbeth unsexes herself, Macbeth may be said to dehumanize himself" (1970, 71). He must eradicate the anima which she thought so strong in him earlier. "[W]hen she dies," remarks Eugene Waith, "tortured by the conscience she despised, Macbeth is so perfectly hardened, so perfectly the soldier that she had wanted him to be, that he is neither frightened by the 'night-shriek' nor greatly moved by the news of her death" (1950, 268). John Russell Brown suggests that Lady Macbeth can be seen as providing "an analogical sub-plot, in the manner of a history play, to illuminate the course of her husband" (1963, 27).

Peter Hall "could make a case for the sleep-walking scene being a liberation of her imagination, so that she is almost like the early Macbeth when he roams imaginatively over the consequences of every action" (1982, 246). She recapitulates then, in an ex post facto consideration what *his* imagination had done before. Now she finds (or something in her finds) the answer to her earlier question when Macbeth had talked of murdering sleep: "What doe you meane?" "You" is no longer Macbeth, but God.

Alice Fox discusses two aspects of Lady Macbeth and Macbeth that bring them before us as husband and wife, in spite of her threat of infanticide and his commission of it: "[W]e become aware of the protagonists as human beings who want to have children [which awareness] elicits that fellow-feeling which is essential to tragedy . . . we [also] become aware of the protagonists as human beings whose desire for living children has been frustrated" (1979, 138).

Hardin Craig concludes that "*Macbeth* is thus a tragedy of the marriage relation as well as of the state. The joint guilt of Macbeth and Lady Macbeth ultimately separates them, and they perish as individuals, each alone" (1948, 256).

Richard Wheeler (1980) argues that Macbeth's reliance on Lady Macbeth results from the undercutting of his efforts to achieve autonomy. Her certainty, though, dooms them both. *Macbeth*, like the other tragedies, demonstrates a irreconcilable conflict between ways of understanding the self.

According to Foakes, Macbeth and Lady Macbeth by the end of the play

> have moved in opposite directions mentally, and she is now in a condition not unlike that of Macbeth before the murder of Duncan; when he saw visionary daggers and imagined nothing could wash away his blood-guilt, she had no apparent sense of horror; but as he has moved from a state of emotional turmoil and moral anxiety to one of blank indifference, so her

cool self-command has given way, and the disturbance of her mind is now
expressed in nightmare images. (1982, 22–23)

Foakes puts it mildly when he says, "The play reveals . . . the inadequacies of
self-fulfillment as a goal" (26).

Macbeth moves from tension to resignation and from a hallucinatory state to
one in which he commissions his murders with the calculation of a Richard III.
Even then, however, he recognizes that his "soule is . . . charg'd / With blood,"
that is, accused by and infused with. Lady Macbeth moves from certainty to a
resignation which is damnation. Both are damned. One accepts it, the other has
it thrust upon her. Damnation, as Dante suggests, varies with the nature of the
crime. Lady Macbeth is a victim of *unresolved* tension. Her wish to be "unsexed," asserts Robin Grove, ends with "a triumphant *sexual* outcry" (1982,
131). Her repeated "Come . . . Come . . . Come . . ." that Grove cites is reiterated in the mad scene: "come, come, come, come." Her efforts to isolate the
act from who *she* is will not work. She can say that " 'Tis the Eye of Child-
hood, / That feares a painted Devill," forgetting that she has looked with that
eye only moments before, when Duncan reminded her of her sleeping father in
a scene recalled from long ago.

In an essay dealing with time and its effect on the psyche, Freud remarks that
it is "impossible to guess" how in so short a period "the hesitating ambitious
man" can become "an unbridled tyrant and his steely-hearted instigator into a
sick woman gnawed by remorse." Freud posits "two disunited parts of a single
psychical individuality." *Macbeth* is "concerned with . . . childlessness." Holinshed's ten-year reign gave Macbeth and Lady Macbeth time in which this
issue could develop. Shakespeare's much shorter time span obscures the issue.
Lady Macbeth's transition from "callousness to penitence" is a reaction to her
childlessness. Macbeth is "punished by barrenness for his crimes against gen-
iture" and, appropriately, is killed by a victim of those crimes (1957, 316–24).
The play suggests that Lady Macbeth and Macbeth have no living son, but there
might have been one, or time for one before Macbeth became king. Once he
becomes king, of course, his reign seems to last for a brutal few months.[1]

In another study of the two major characters, Bernard Paris, argues that Macbeth and Lady Macbeth make a Horneyean bargain in hopes of achieving his/
her goals. But as bargains with God are quickly forgotten once the emergency
is over, bargains with fate cannot work, since fate is superior to human intention
but inferior to, or another name for, God's intention (1982, 7–20).

In a humanistic approach to the play that does not posit the false gender
dichotomies typical of much psychoanalytic criticism, Robert Kimbrough argues
that

Shakespeare sensed that humanhood embraces manhood and womanhood
[and] that so long as one remains exclusively male or exclusively female,
that person will be restricted and confined, denied human growth. Each will

> become a prisoner of gender, not its keeper. . . . Gender liberation appears
> in Shakespeare when a character of one sex experiences thoughts and emo-
> tions beyond those traditionally associated with the gender values of that
> sex. Because a woman dressed as a man has simultaneously two genders,
> the theatrical device of girl-into-boy disguise provided Shakespeare with a
> kind of laboratory testing where he could isolate such moments of height-
> ened, broadened awareness. (1983, 175–76)

"Women" (boy actors playing women playing men) "are liberated from the
confines of socially appropriate gender behavior" (176). Lady Macbeth and
Macbeth "are prevented from attaining and maintaining a full range of human
character traits because of cultural attempts to render some exclusively feminine
and some exclusively masculine" (176). "[W]e are moved through pity to understand and to fear the personal and social destructiveness of polarized masculinity and femininity" (177). Kimbrough maintains that "to be 'manly' is to
be aggressive, daring, bold, resolute, and strong" (177). The Weird Sisters get
him to buy into that stereotype later. "To be 'womanly' is to be gentle, fearful,
pitying, wavering, and soft, a condition often signified by tears" (177). When
Macduff "feele[s] it as a man," he "expresses a fuller range of his being: his
humanhood" (178). "One of a witch's most pronounced and commonly evoked
powers was to destroy normal sexuality" (179). " 'Human kindness' was still
a redundancy in Shakespeare's day, because to be kind was to be human."
"Macbeth has succumbed to the gender definitions of male and female of his
society as they have been expressed by Lady Macbeth—divided, separated definitions which reject the bonding nurture of the milk of human kindness" (183).

I should add that in an anima/animus conflict, each person is controlled by
the stereotypical contrary gender. Shakespeare's remarkable psychological economy gets conflict into the same words ("faile?" for example). At the banquet,
Macbeth is "not a girl baby, but one of Lady Macbeth's 'men-children' " (Kimbrough 1983, 185). "Shakespeare appeals to our shared humanity, our potential
for a human fulfillment which rises above gender division" (186). The concept
of shared humanity and shared gender characteristics is very unpopular, of
course, in today's politics of division. "The speech ['troops of friends'] allows
us to pity Macbeth because it shows he retains a vision of a fuller, healthier,
'wholier' life, even though he has narrowed his life, repressed his nature, choked
his human kindness" (187). It follows that "[w]hile Shakespeare in *Macbeth*
criticises the destructive polarity of masculine versus feminine, consistently informing the play is his recognition of a fuller, healthier way of life, his vision
of potential human wholeness, his androgynous vision" (188). This is a vision
which a comedy like *As You Like It* achieves. It is a vision against which
tragedy, in this case self-imposed alienation *from* selfhood, is played.

NOTE

1. For other Freudian approaches, see Norman Holland's massive study (1966). See also Maurice Charney's review of Holland's book (1968).

Works Cited

Adelman, Janet. 1987. " 'Born of Woman': Fantasies of Maternal Power in *Macbeth*." In *Cannibals, Witches, and Divorce: Estranging the Renaissance*. Edited by Marjorie Garber. Baltimore: Johns Hopkins University Press.

Asp, Carolyn. 1981. "Be Bloody, Bold, and Resolute: Tragic Action and Sexual Stereotyping in *Macbeth*." *Studies in Philology* 78 (Spring): 68–76.

Barron, David B. 1970. "The Babe That Milks: An Organic Study of *Macbeth*." In *The Design Within: Psychoanalytic Approaches to Shakespeare*. Edited by Melvin D. Faber. New York: Science House.

Berger, Harry, Jr. 1982. "Text against Performance in Shakespeare." In *The Forms of Power and the Power of Forms*. Edited by Stephen Greenblatt. *Genre* 15: 49–79.

Bernardete, José. 1970. "Macbeth's Last Words." *Interpretations* 1 (Spring): 63–74.

Birenbaum, Harvey. 1982. "Consciousness and Responsibility in *Macbeth*." *Mosaic* 15 (June): 17–32.

Bradley, A. C. 1904. *Shakespearean Tragedy*. London: Macmillan.

Brown, John Russell, ed. 1963. *Macbeth*. Great Neck, N.Y.: Barron's.

Charney, Maurice. 1968. Review of Norman Holland's *Psychoanalysis and Shakespeare*. *Shakespeare Quarterly* 19 (Autumn): 401–03.

Coffin, Charles M., ed. *The Complete Poetry and Selected Prose of John Donne*. New York: Random House.

Coursen, H. R. 1985. "A Jungian Approach to *Macbeth*." In *Shakespeare's Rough Magic: Renaissance Essays in Honor of C. L. Barber*. Edited by Peter Erickson and Coppelia Kahn. Cranbury, N.J.: Associated University Presses.

———. 1986. *The Compensatory Psyche: A Jungian Approach to Shakespeare*. Lanham, Md.: University Press of America.

———. 1988. " 'Morphic Resonance' in Shakespeare's Plays." *Shakespeare Bulletin* 6, no. 2 (March-April): 3–8.

Craig, Hardin. 1948. *An Interpretation of Shakespeare*. New York: Dryden Press.

Cunningham, Dolora. 1963. "*Macbeth* and the Tragedy of the Hardened Heart." *Shakespeare Quarterly* 14, no. 1 (Winter): 39–48.

Curry, Walter C. 1933. *The Demonic Metaphysic of 'Macbeth.'* Chapel Hill: University of North Carolina Press.

———. 1937. *Shakespeare's Philosophical Patterns*. Baton Rouge: Louisiana University Press.

Davies, Stevie. 1986. *The Idea of Women in Renaissance Literature: The Feminine Reclaimed*. Brighton, England: Harvester.

Davis, Michael. 1979. "Courage and Impotence in Shakespeare's *Macbeth*." *Sarah Lawrence Essays* 4 (February): 7–29.

Dawson, Anthony. 1996. "Performance and Participation: Desdemona, Foucault, and the Actor's Body." In *Shakespeare, Theory, and Performance*. Edited by James Bulman. London: Metheun.

Dowden, Edward. 1872. *Shakespeare: A Critical Study of His Mind and Art*. Reprint. New York: Capricorn, 1962.

Eagleton, Terry. 1967. *Shakespeare and Society*. New York: Schocken Books.

Erickson, Peter. 1985. *Patriarchal Structures in Shakespeare's Drama*. Berkeley: University of California Press.

Fawkner, H. W. 1990. *Deconstructing 'Macbeth': The Hyperontological View*. Cranbury, N.J.: Associated University Presses.

Foakes, R. A. 1969. *Macbeth*. Indianapolis: Educational Press.

———. 1982. "Images of Death." In *Focus on 'Macbeth.'* Edited by John Russell Brown. London: Routledge and Kegan Paul.

Fox, Alice. 1979. "Obstetrics and Gynecology in *Macbeth*." *Shakespeare Studies* 12: 127–41.

French, Marilyn. 1983. *Shakespeare's Division of Experience*. New York: Ballentine Books.

Freud, Sigmund. 1957. *Some Character Types Met with in Psychoanalytic Work*. In *Complete Works*. Edited by James Strachey. London: Hogarth Press.

———. 1969. *An Outline of Psychoanalysis*. Edited by James Strachey. Vol. 23. New York: Norton.

Grove, Robin. 1982. " 'Multiplying Villainies of Nature.' " In *Focus on 'Macbeth.'* Edited by John Russell Brown. London: Routledge and Kegan Paul.

Hazlitt, William. 1930. *Complete Works*. Edited by P. P. Howe. London: Scott.

Holland, Norman. 1966. *Psychoanalysis and Shakespeare*. New York: McGraw-Hill.

———. 1989. "Sons and Substitutions: Shakespeare's Phallic Fantasy." In *Shakespeare's Personality*. Edited by Norman Holland, Sidney Homan, and Bernard Paris. Berkeley: University of California Press.

Horowitz, David. 1965. *An Existential Approach to Shakespeare*. New York: McGraw-Hill.

Kahn, Coppelia. 1981. *Man's Estate: Masculine Identity in Shakespeare*. Berkeley: University of California Press.

Kimbrough, Robert. 1983. "Macbeth as Prisoner of Gender." *Shakespeare Studies* 16: 175–90.

Klein, Joan Larsen. 1980. "Lady Macbeth: 'Infirm of Purpose.' " In *The Woman's Part: Feminist Criticism of Shakespeare*. Edited by Carol Ruth Swift Lenz, Gayle Greene, and Carol Thomas Neely. Urbana: University of Illinois Press.

Knight, G. Wilson. 1957. *The Wheel of Fire*. New York: Meridian.

Levin, Richard. 1989. "The New Attack on Shakespeare's Tragic Revengers." Paper presented at the Shakespeare Association of America, Boston, March.

Lordi, Robert. 1982. "Macbeth and His 'dearest partner of greatness,' Lady Macbeth." *Upstart Crow* 4 (Fall): 94–106.

Moelwyn, Merchant W. 1966. "His Fiend-Like Queen." *Shakespeare Survey* 19: 75–81.

Paris, Bernard. 1982. "Bargains with Fate: The Case of *Macbeth*." *American Journal of Psychiatry* 42: 79–91.

Rickey, Mary Ellen, and Thomas B. Stroup, eds. 1966. *Certaine Sermons and Homilies*. Gainesville, Fla.: Scholars' Facsimiles.

Scott, William O. 1986. "Macbeth's—and Our—Self-Equivocations." *Shakespeare Quarterly* 37, no. 2 (Summer): 167–74.

Sheldrake, Rupert. 1981. *A New Science of Life*. London: Blond and Briggs.

———. 1995. "Dogmas and Pet Theories." *Times Higher Education Supplement* 1174 (5 May): 378.

Singer, June. 1973. *Boundaries of the Soul*. New York: Doubleday.

Snyder, Susan. 1965. "The Left Hand of God: Despair in Medieval and Renaissance Tradition." *Studies in the Renaissance* 12: 198–208.

———. 1992. "*Macbeth*: A Modern Perspective." In *Macbeth*. Edited by Barbara Mowat and Paul Werstein. New York: Washington Square Press.

Stern, Paul J. 1976. *C. G. Jung: The Haunted Prophet*. New York: Dell.

Waith, Eugene. 1950. "Manhood and Valor in Two Shakespearean Tragedies." *ELH* 17 (Fall): 265–68.

Webster, Margaret. 1957. *Shakespeare without Tears*. New York: Premier.

Wheeler, Richard. 1980. " 'Since first we were dissevered': Trust and Autonomy in Shakespearean Tragedy and Romance." In *Representing Shakespeare: New Psychoanalytic Essays*. Edited by Coppelia Kahn and Murray Schwartz. Baltimore: Johns Hopkins University Press.

Wills, Gary. 1995. *Witches and Jesuits*. Oxford: Oxford University Press.

Macbeth as Murderer

A number of commentators have looked at the character of Macbeth, particularly in his role as a murderer. Peter Hall says that Macbeth's "actual self is introverted, with a deep imagination and sense of fantasy, with a rapid, feverish ability to proceed from consequence to consequence, like someone in a dream or a nightmare" (1982, 236). In "modern terms one would say he was introverted and mentally effeminate" (236). In Jungian terms, Macbeth has a strong contact with his anima, or contrasexual psychological orientation.

Some critics see Macbeth as a character within an immutable cosmos that incorporates his own nature, a microcosm of the cosmic design. "The confusion in the political world," suggests Theodore Spencer, "is not merely reflected in the world of Nature and the individual; it is ... *identified* with it" (1961, 154). As Derek Traversi remarks, "Macbeth's murder of Duncan is ... in the first place a crime against the natural foundations of social and moral harmony" (1956, 152).

Although he leans to a historicist reading, Peter Quennell offers that Duncan

> may be a prosy, talkative old fellow mortal. At the same time, he is the Lord's Anointed; and his murder ... threatens the law of proportion and degree. Shakespeare must emphasize the sovereign's sanctity—James I, Duncan's descendant, lived in perpetual terror of assassination—and endow the spectacle of the butchered monarch with a solemnly impressive colouring. (1963, 329)

Robert Ornstein argues that

> Shakespeare explores in *Macbeth* the mystery of man's will to self-destruction—his capacity to commit the acts which violate his essential

being. . . . [He] kills because his wife makes him admit that he wishes to kill; and because he condemns himself before he kills Duncan, the act of murder is fraught with a hatred of self which eventually and inevitably becomes a hatred of all of life. . . . Unable to admit that he has made the world a hell, Macbeth attempts to project the horror of his life as the pattern of all existence. For if consciousness is nothing more than a cosmic joke, then the senseless fury of his acts is no worse than the peaceful lives of those who are led quietly to oblivion. (1965, 222, 223, 225)

The play asks about the meaning of consciousness, that is, our awareness of our being. Ours must be Cartesian, but that orientation is there *pre facto* in the play, often, for Macbeth, as a barrier to the consciousness that would free itself of the inhibitions of the "humane Statute" and "gentle Weale" and the "terrible Dreames" sent to him by what lies under consciousness. Both Macbeth and Lady Macbeth show that we cannot outrun our awareness of our being.

R. S. Crane looks at the positive and negative aspects of Macbeth and claims that

> both of the views we are given of the hero are true . . . the form of the play is really the interaction of the two views in our opinions and emotions— what we ourselves see him to be as we witness the workings of his mind before the murder of Duncan, then after the murder, and finally when, at the end, all his illusions and hopes gone, he faces Macduff. (1953, 172)

Macbeth, writes Crane, is a man

> not naturally depraved, who has fallen under the compulsive power of an imagined better state for himself which he can attain only by acting contrary to his normal habits and feelings; who attains this state and then finds that he must continue to act thus, and even worse, in order to hold on to what he has got; who persists and becomes progressively hardened morally in the process. (173)

Paul Jorgensen points at an element of Macbeth that may account for our continuing contact with, if not sympathy for, him:

> Macbeth's real tragedy consists in the meaning of all he has lost. . . . For him there can be no more communion with his human kind at banquets. He will lose the one person whom he truly loves. . . . He has lost the innocent sleep which he murdered and the solace of labor used for the King. More terrible are the spiritual losses . . . and above all the resultant pain of loss, carrying with it the death of renown and grace, and, ultimately, of human feeling. (1971, 214–15).

J. Middleton Murry points out that "Macbeth makes no bargain with the emissaries of the powers of darkness: nor are they bargainable" (1936, 326).

Murry argues that "nothing . . . compels him to be assistant and accomplice to the working" of the Weird Sisters' predictions (326). He begins the process, however, and "[c]onscience once drugged, murder becomes but a matter of convenience" (327). The process that overwhelms Macbeth and Lady Macbeth is a "new madness . . . the outcome of their effort to hold self and not-self together in one consciousness" (328). But Macbeth "has murdered . . . that daily death of Time which makes Time human" (329). "He is the victim of uninterrupted and unending Time, chained to the wheel of an everlasting Now" (330). His "hereafter"

> does not mean "later"; but in a different mode of time from that in which Macbeth is imprisoned now. . . . Life in this time is meaningless—a tale told by an idiot—and death also. For his wife's death to have meaning there needs some total change—a plunge across a new abyss into a Hereafter. (332)

If so, Lady Macbeth will not be there. She is trapped in the past. Macbeth may get a last glimpse of her from the far bank of whatever *his* Hereafter may be.

J.I.M. Stewart, master (as Michael Innes) of the "great house" genre of murder mysteries and a keen prober of motivation, contends that "Macbeth's rational motives are made insufficient, elusive, contradictory, in order to bring home to us not the mere thrill of evil but its tortuousness and terrifying reach; its becoming presence just over the threshold of certain more than common natures" (1949, 88). Stewart points at one of the aspects of the character that makes him *unlike* us.

Matthew Proser deals with Macbeth's strategies for avoiding conscious responsibility for his actions—but does Macbeth see the murder of Duncan as valorous, as Proser argues? Lady Macbeth, no soldier (and no murderer) may, but Macbeth is clearer sighted than that. "The 'black and deep desires' are acknowledged by Macbeth, but 'the eye' and 'the hand' seem detached from him, while the nameless deed 'is done.' It appears to do itself or is done by an act of prestidigitation" (1965, 64). Macbeth seeks the ability to "enact . . . without moral reservation—the ethic of pure desire" (74).

For Michael P. Davis, Macbeth becomes a Nietzschean superman: "To cross those limits means to become something non-human, meaning either sub-human or super-human" (1979, 9). "Nietzsche described nihilism as the resolution rather to will nothing than not to will at all" (24), as Macbeth does when he cries that he wishes "that th'estate o'th'world were now undon."

The modern liberal abhorrence to war ignores the wars that do occur and the young people, mostly men, who are sent by their governments to participate. That participation may be encouraged by a dehumanization of the enemy—they are "gooks" to Americans who kill Vietnamese—but in most cases participation in war is involuntary, a matter of being the wrong age at the wrong time or, as so often occurred during the war in Vietnam, of being of the wrong social class or race. I do not believe that Macbeth's feats in battle are to be seen as a bloodthirsty prelude to later violence. There is a difference between unseaming an enemy "from the Nave to th' Chops" and demanding to be filled "from the Crowne to the Toe, top-full / Of direst Crueltie." Henry V, admittedly while giving a locker-room speech, says, "In peace there's nothing so becomes a man / As modest stillness and humility. / But when the blast of war blows in our ears, / Then imitate the action of the tiger." *Macbeth* makes the distinction between lawful combat in defense of one's king and the murder of that king-kinsman-guest.

Shakespeare is at pains to distance us from Macbeth at the outset, indeed to make Macbeth an epic hero. An epic usually involves a hero who represents more than himself—"Bellona's bridegroom" or "valor's minion"—and who defends a country or king, as Roland does for *Carles li reis* in the Old French eleventh-century epic, *Chanson de Roland*, and as El Cid does in the twelfth-century Spanish epic, *Poema del Cid*. The emphasis is on battle, particularly on face-to-face confrontations and their gruesome results. Consider Roland's defeat of Grandonie at Ronsevals: "With one stroke of Durendal he slit the helmet of Toledo steel as far as the nose, then cut through the teeth and lips, unthreaded the chain mail, ripped through the silver pommel, and crushed the horse's spine" (Goodrich 1961, 83). Among many examples in *The Iliad*, consider Patroclus's dispatch of Thestor and Eryalaus:

> The reins flew from Thestor's frantic hand.
> His chariot swerved across the churning sand
> of Troy. The spear of Patroclus, beneath
> the jaw of Enops's son, between the teeth,
> became a pole with which Thestor was pulled,
> a sacred fish on a hook of bronze. Blood pooled
> in the place to which his face fell. Then came
> Erylaus, whose skull was smashed by the same
> gray stone to which his useless helmet dropped,
> his eyes filled with death, his breathing stopped.
> Nor did Patroclus refrain from toil
> till blood rivered within that kindly soil. (Chadwick 1742, 16, 470–81)

The Bleeding Sergeant begins in medias res ("Doubtfull it stood"), employs epic similes ("As two spent Swimmers"), and describes a final feat of arms, in which the hero confronts the villain and, in this case, "unseam[s] him from the Nave to th' Chops." The full epic machinery distances the hero from the "reality" of the battle, making both him and the war part of an allegorical struggle which is not to be confused with a literal battle. Furthermore, the battle is usually being waged for the "good" side against treason or foreign invasion, indeed often for the "Christian" polity, as in *Chanson de Roland*.

Terry Eagleton argues, "Every action done to attain security mars itself: every act has a built in flaw, a consequence which escapes, like Fleance, from the control of the actor and returns to plague him'' (1967, 131). Eagleton begins with a fallacy: ''By leaving us without an explicit reason for the battle, Shakespeare strips violence of its rational pretenses and obliges us to confront it as a stark primitive fact, a kind of primal given, like Chaos'' (80–81). *Treason*—no matter how conveniently configured by the party that does the defining—is an explicit reason, particularly when it is combined with an attack launched by a foreign power.

''Violence and death,'' Eagleton writes, ''have been Macbeth's matrices of meaning'' (89). To ''transcend death by inflicting it on others and surviving is a sacred achievement within Scotland's religion of violence'' (88–89). Eagleton claims that Macbeth ''does not fear death because in the intoxication of battle he *is* death . . . a killer, a battlefield survivor who takes definition from the deaths of others'' (79). But this ignores his struggle before the murder. ''Macbeth wishes it were . . . a simple shift of violence from battlefield to bedchamber'' (89). Where does he say so? ''I would it were as easy kill this man, / My king, as it has been his enemies, / To save my king, that I have killed in war.'' Is not E. E. Stoll accurate in calling Macbeth ''an ambitious man with his thoughts both before and after the crime, set, not upon the reasons which would impel or justify him, but upon those which would deter him'' (1933, 77)?

Michael Long adds, ''This 'bloody execution' sounds brutal; but the epic rhetoric almost makes it sound magnificent'' (1989, 31). A statement as supremely silly as ''the doers of good sound either like or worse than the evildoers'' (Booth 1983, 97) insists that we ignore the epic treatment of Macbeth in battle and the uncontested fact that the ''evildoers'' are either foreign invaders or treasonous allies of those invaders. The basic fact is that, right or wrong, battle involves killing, and that is never done daintily.

R. A. Foakes asks whether the image of ''turning the battlefield into another place of a skull, or dead bones [is to be] likened to the soldiers who crucified Christ'' (1982, 12). At best, says Foakes, the linkage between duty and ambivalence is one of contrast not similitude: ''Macbeth's horror at, and fascination with, a new vision of death—not the brutal and casual slaughter of the battlefield, but the calculated murder of a king'' (13).

In talking to his Soldiers incognito before Agincourt, Henry V definitely makes war a moral institution (IV. 1. 155–71). James Calderwood suggests that Shakespeare's treatment of the battle at the beginning of *Macbeth* links that battle with the killing of Duncan. It may do so, but it should *not* do so for Macbeth, as Calderwood implies:

> The black mass aspect of Duncan's murder is a radical extension of the sacralizing of violence on the battlefield, where Macbeth was supposed to bathe in reeking wounds and memorize another Golgotha. He now literalizes the symbolism of the Mass, which does memorize Golgotha, by killing the Christ-figure in fact. (1986, 99–100)

What Calderwood describes *is* depicted in *Julius Caesar*, when the conspirators try to create a memorable ceremony after killing Caesar (III. 1. 105–118). The play refutes the effort at instant ritual.

Killing in battle licenses neither killing in other contexts nor the killing of Christ. Killing in war does not necessarily make men bloodthirsty in peacetime. What seems like a facile rhetorical step for the critics is *not* an easy one for Macbeth, as the play makes abundantly clear. One might ask whether Macduff at the end is any less brutal than Macbeth as he was described in the opening battle.

Alan Sinfield argues that a conventional reading of the play endorses the use of violence in order to keep a political system in place and, in fact, that persons participating in it and condoning it do not see violence on behalf of their own political system *as* violence (1986, 63–77). Violence is an essential component of the growth of the modern state. It is, of course, euphemized as, for example, "in defense of democracy," even as the enemy is demonized as "hun" or dehumanized as "gook." The traditional reading of the play has to be qualified, as I suggest, by Shakespeare's use of the epic conventions to describe Macbeth's actions in the initial battle. One might ask: What state, modern or premodern, *has* grown without a reliance on warfare as an instrument of policy?

Frank Chapman Sharp establishes the criteria for the anti-Macbeth position:

> Macbeth is a man without real scruples although faint images of restraining voices sometimes chime upon his inner ear. What moral sensitiveness he possesses is only sufficient to enable him to enjoy coddling himself for his regret at his unfortunate conduct, to make of him a sentimentalizing dealer in fine phrases. (quoted in Burgess 1903, 91, note 2)

Bertrand Evans comes down hard against Macbeth, opposing those who excuse his murder or, perhaps, who see it as inevitable because it happens in the play, and over and over again in production: "Macbeth himself makes the choice, and it is a particularly heinous one" (1973, 600). One point of view, asserts Evans, holds that Macbeth "is essentially a *good* man who is corrupted despite a strong moral sense and inner struggle against corruption, by the overwhelming combination of Fate, his wife, sudden and unexpected opportunity, and swelling ambition" (600).

> [T]he majority view among critics of nearly three centuries [holds that] the progress of Macbeth [is] from a basically good man, a moral man, through stages of corruption, revulsion, and increasing pangs of conscience, to remorseless tyrant and wanton killer, and at last to an unfeeling lump, surfeited alike with murder and sorrow. (600)

Evans says, however, that

Macbeth is not basically a good man at all, but a man of criminal mentality, either already corrupted or in any event corruptible, because he possesses a severely defective moral mechanism, or no moral sense at all. Fate, Witches, Lady Macbeth, opportunity, overreaching ambition, all combined, would never corrupt a Brutus or a Hamlet. (600)

That is to imply, of course, that Brutus and Hamlet remain untainted.

Wayne Booth, however, argues Shakespeare's placement of material and the dramatic emphasis of that placement. Macbeth's discussion of the "double trust" speech, asserts Booth, "which shows just how bad the contemplated act is builds sympathy for the planner" (1963, 183). "What would be an intolerable act if depicted with any vividness becomes relatively forgivable when seen only afterward in the light of Macbeth's remorse" (185). The act is vivid to perpetrators after the fact, not in the murder but in its effects on them and in their guilt: "the suffering of these criminals is worse than their crimes" (187). Shakespeare "insure[s] that each step in [his] protagonist's degeneration will be counter-acted by mounting pity" (187). Surely Booth is wrong to say that Macbeth "does not understand the difference between 'bloody execution' in civilian life and in military life" (189). The difference is a segment of his struggle. He is not just Malcolm's dead butcher—at least not at first.

John Bayley argues that it "is essential to the hypnotic tension of the play that Macbeth should not seem in any ordinary way 'responsible' for his actions" (1981, 191). H. W. Fawkner, however, claims that Macbeth "has absolute insight into the immorality of the deed. If [Bertrand] Evan's notion of Macbeth as a moral idiot were true, we would have no tragedy at all" (1990, 85). Right, nor would we have the struggle to cancel his own humanity—that great bond that keeps him pale because being blanched with fear is part of his humanity. He questions those who keep their natural color!

Much of the critical debate, of course, is up to the *actor* to adjudicate, and he will do so in different ways, as the discussion of production below will show. Evans argues that "finally, Macbeth never does repent on moral grounds, never recognizes that he has done wrong—never, indeed, learns what 'wrong' means. Rather, he learns only to regret that he could not 'get away with it,' and spitefully blames the Witches for having misinformed him" (1973, 601). Certainly that is true later, once the second set of prophecies begins to materialize. It is also true, however, as Crane argues, that Macbeth "acts in the end as the Macbeth whose praises we have heard in the second scene of the play" (1953, 212). He is a soldier of the king again, even if that king is himself and a regicide.

Macbeth exhibits simultaneously a clear understanding of why it is wrong to kill Duncan and an equally clear wish to avoid the consequences of the killing. He would like to be an existentialist in an essentialist world. That is one reason why Shakespeare provides the world he does for *Macbeth*, among the many options available.

On Macbeth's early soliloquies, Michael Goldman argues, "Shakespeare gives these images a powerful histrionic setting by having Macbeth use them, much like an actor rehearsing a role, to explore and indeed to discover his new emotions'' (1982, 146), to discover "what it is like to *commit* evil'' (151; emphasis in original). "My Thought, whose murther yet is but fantasticall,'' for example, means not the thought of murder, but the murder of thought. He must *kill* the thought of murder, must murder its concept, to do it. I must obliterate my understanding of the deed so that I may accomplish it. This is a version of Francis Fergusson's emphasis on Macbeth's stress on outrunning "the pawser, Reason'' (1957, 115–25). Goldman suggests that "what holds Macbeth rapt through the whole play [is] that the evil he grapples with is *his*'' (1982, 152; emphasis in original). What paralyzes him is that he cannot establish an independent stance for the evil he embodies.

William O. Scott writes, "Strange too is the prospect that a horror can be a temptation'' (1986, 164). I would suggest that anyone who has tried to give up a strong addiction has some sense of the linkage of horror and temptation. In dealing with two iniquities that inform *Macbeth*—the Gunpowder Plot and the willingness of priests to lie, Thomas Morton asked and answered his own question: "And can any by an wilfull lie deceive his owne selfe, as thereby be made ignorant of his owne meaning? This were to distract a man from himselfe'' (1606). "Yet,'' continues Scott, "not only does Macbeth seek to describe such distraction, he tries to induce it. Macbeth wants consciously to deceive himself'' (1986, 164). And some critics claim that he does so. Even as he tries to convince himself, points out Scott, referring to the "If it were done'' speech, "Fully to imagine the crime with its attendant breach of trust is to see how its success becomes its failure'' (165).

Colin Manlove makes a similar argument regarding the ways in which Macbeth permits his consciousness and his unconscious to be divided. In the language of Shakespeare's psychology, both levels of human mental and spiritual activity would have been called "conscience.'' Macbeth

> can pretend that everything he says of Duncan's visit is perfectly natural, can seek to divide himself from his evil purpose so that his wife will be the prompter [but] [i]n the very act of envisaging so fully the ghastliness of the deed to others, he has imagined himself as having done it. (1981, 144)

Edith Sitwell quotes Stephen Spender on what Macbeth fears:

> Macbeth certainly has good reason to fear even-handed justice. . . . The real fear is far more terrible. It is a fear of the extension into infinity of the instant in which he commits the murder. The bank and shoal of time is time that has stood still; beyond it lies the abyss of a timeless moment. (quoted in Sitwell 1961, 26)

That, Spender suggests, is Macbeth's damnation.

Macbeth walks through the murder, letting his "corporal agents" do the work as if they were on an independent patrol, a roving commission. The dagger with gouts of blood gives him the necessary afterimage—"it is done." Scott suggests that the "murderous thoughts are truly his own yet (he would like to think) seem somehow to be put upon him as if by unknown forces" (1986, 167). The upshot of a surrender to hallucinations or an effort to narcotize inward knowledge even as the body acts by a kind of proxy (or later, in murdering Banquo, by hiring cutthroats) will be the ghost of Banquo. As he moves to murder Duncan, adds Scott, "His imaginings impel him onward, yet he must refuse their actuality as they lead him" (167).

"A murderer," Derek Russell Davis argues, "usually says that he felt detached or that it was unreal or happening in a dream. Some loss of the sense of reality is the rule" (1982, 217). Macbeth, as he goes to murder Duncan, may, as Quiller Couch suggests, "proceed to his crime *under some fatal hallucination*" (quoted in Lerner 1964, 178; emphasis in original). Certainly he is strangely detached, but not oblivious as Lady Macbeth is. His breakdown after the murder is extreme, but temporary. It keeps him sane or at least ensures that further breakdowns, like the one he experiences at the banquet, are also temporary.

Theodore Reik looks at the interruption of the human system of communication and interaction that can occur and can result in murder:

> It is still not sufficiently realised that the criminal at the moment of the act is a different man from what he is after it—so much so that one would think them different beings. . . . Our psychological judgment, our instinct as well as our experience, seem to tell us sometimes that the deed does not belong to the doer nor the doer to the deed. Nevertheless the act must be an expression of the criminal's mental tension, must spring from his mental condition, must have promised gratification to his psychological needs. We are faced by a riddle as long as we do not know what motive actuated him. In many cases, and especially in the most serious crimes, he can, with the best will in the world, give us but inadequate information; he is unable to establish a connection between his deed and his personality. (1936, 42–43)

Multiple murderer John Wayne Gacy once said, "The body probably did it, but the mind doesn't know it" (1980).

Macbeth's "fit" and Banquo's Ghost may have some affinity with the modern disorder known as manic-depression described by Kay Redfield Jamison:

> [P]eriods of total despair would be made even worse by terrible agitation. My mind would race from subject to subject, but instead of being filled with the exuberant and cosmic thoughts that had been associated with earlier periods of rapid thinking, it would be drenched in awful sounds and images of decay and dying: dead bodies on the beach, charred remains of animals,

toe-tagged corpses in morgues. . . . I became exceedingly restless, angry, and irritable, and the only way I could dilute the agitation was to run along the beach or pace back and forth across my room like a polar bear at the zoo. (quoted in Walker 1995)

Works Cited

Bayley, John. 1981. *Shakespeare and Tragedy*. London: Routledge and Kegan Paul.

Booth, Stephen. 1983. *'King Lear,' 'Macbeth,' Indefinition and Tragedy*. New Haven, Conn.: Yale University Press.

Booth, Wayne. 1963. "Shakespeare's Tragic Villain." In *Shakespeare's Tragedies*. Edited by Laurence Lerner. Baltimore: Penguin.

Burgess, William. 1903. *The Bible in Shakespeare*. New York: Thomas Y. Crowell.

Calderwood, James L. 1986. *If It Were Done: 'Macbeth' and Tragic Action*. Amherst: University of Massachusetts Press.

Chadwick, E., trans. 1742. *The Iliad*. London: Bulls Head.

Crane, R. S. 1953. *The Languages of Criticism and the Structure of Poetry*. Toronto: University of Toronto Press.

Davis, Derek R. 1982. "Hurt Minds." In *Focus on 'Macbeth.'* Edited by John Russell Brown. London: Routledge and Kegan Paul.

Davis, Michael. 1979. "Courage and Impotence in Shakespeare's *Macbeth*." *Sarah Lawrence Essays* 4 (February): 7–29.

Eagleton, Terry. 1967. *Shakespeare and Society*. New York: Schocken Books.

Evans, Bertrand. 1973. *The College Shakespeare*. New York: Macmillan.

Fawkner, H. W. 1990. *Deconstructing 'Macbeth': The Hyperontological View*. Cranbury, N.J.: Associated University Presses.

Fergusson, Francis. 1957. *The Human Image in Dramatic Literature*. Garden City, N.Y.: Doubleday.

Foakes, R. A. 1982. "Images of Death: Ambition in *Macbeth*." In *Focus on 'Macbeth.'* Edited by John Russell Brown. London: Routledge and Kegan Paul.

Gacy, John W. 1980. Quoted in *Portland Press-Herald* (Portland, Maine), 31 December, p. 31.

Goldman, Michael. 1982. "Language and Action in *Macbeth*." In *Focus on 'Macbeth.'* Edited by John Russell Brown. London: Routledge and Kegan Paul.

Goodrich, Norma L. 1961. *Medieval Myths*. New York: Mentor.

Jorgensen, Paul A. 1971. *Our Naked Frailties*. Berkeley: University of California Press.

Lerner, Laurence, ed. 1964. *Shakespeare's Tragedies*. Baltimore: Penguin.

Long, Michael, ed. 1989. *Macbeth*. Boston: Twayne.

Manlove, Colin. 1981. *The Gap in Shakespeare*. London: Vision.

Morton, Thomas. 1606. *A Full Satisfaction concerning a Double Romish Iniquitie: Hainous Revellion, and more than heathenish Aequivocation*. London.

Murry, J. M. 1936. *Shakespeare*. London: Society of Authors.

Ornstein, Robert. 1965. *Shakespeare: The Tragedies*. Edited by Clifford Leech. Chicago: University of Chicago Gemini.

Proser, Matthew. 1965. *The Heroic Idiom in Five Shakespearean Tragedies*. Princeton, N.J.: Princeton University Press.

Quennell, Peter. 1963. *Shakespeare: A Biography*. New York: Avon.

Reik, Theodore. 1936. *The Unknown Murderer*. London: Hogarth Press.

Scott, William O. 1986. "Macbeth's—and Our—Self-Equivocations." *Shakespeare Quarterly* 37, no. 2 (Summer): 167–74.

Sinfield, Alan. 1986. "*Macbeth:* History, Ideology and Intellectuals." *Critical Quarterly* 28 (Spring): 63–77.

Sitwell Edith. 1961. *A Notebook on William Shakespeare.* Boston: Beacon.

Spencer, Theodore. 1961. *Shakespeare and the Nature of Man.* New York: Macmillan.

Stewart, J.I.M. 1949. "Steep Tragic Contrast in *Macbeth.*" In *Character and Motive in Shakespeare: Some Recent Appraisals.* London: Longman, Green.

Stoll, E. E. 1933. *Art and Artifice in Shakespeare.* Cambridge: Cambridge University Press.

Traversi, Derek. 1956. *An Approach to Shakespeare.* Garden City, N.Y.: Doubleday Anchor.

Walker, Susan. 1995. "Mind Disorder Expert Writes a Disturbing Memoir." *Toronto Star,* 21 October, p. D7.

MATERIALIST CRITICISM

Materialist criticism looks at literature with a Marxist eye. Western literature tends to be a rationalization of capitalism and of the lucrative status quo that the few in authority would maintain. "Essentialist" readings suggest that a rational and benevolent order underlies all events. Materialist readings look for the fissures and interstices that subvert authority. The evidence adduced by the materialist critique is not necessarily a conscious product of the writer, but it problematizes what in previous generations of critics had been accepted as "givens" and as the "author's intention." The materialist approach has an affinity with New Historicism, which sees a work of literature as part of a context of other documents and influences circulating within a given culture. A work of literature, then, must be "contextualized." It cannot be understood in isolation from the discourses of its zeitgeist.

Materialist critiques must be attended to because they contradict the essentialist thesis on which much of this book is based. I offer them at some length, so that the cogency of the counterthesis can be felt and evaluated.

The materialist argument can be traced to the revisionism of John Dover Wilson: "[F]rom the eleventh-century standpoint Duncan was the usurper, and Macbeth the vindicator of the true line of succession" (1947, ix). That assertion is itself dubious, but it is also irrelevant. H. W. Fawkner is correct, I think, when he suggests, "If Macbeth really has a grievance, then the whole play called *Macbeth,* far from being one of the most brilliant dramas ever devised, would sink into mediocrity and indifference" (1990, 78).

The argument tends to take two directions. The first, exemplified by John Turner, Graham Holderness, and Michael Hawkins, is that *Macbeth* is a history play and thus Duncan's political system is subject to the same imperfections, self-deceptions, and rationalizing justifications as any other. The second, a corollary, as put by Brian Morris and James O'Rourke, argues against the "world of the play" as sacramental.

Turner chooses to treat the play not as "a fable about human nature," but as a "historical drama" (1992, 5). He claims that the Weird Sisters "baffle the very categories they invite" (14), a tendency typical of a play "much preoccupied with problematical ways of seeing, with hallucination, fantasy and dream, with disturbances of vision caused by desire and horror" (20). Its "audience is perhaps as troubled as its characters" (20). The Sisters "represent everything that cannot be accommodated within Duncan's religious patriarchy" (21). They are "deviants who disclose the norms of the larger society in its ceaseless struggle for power against its own oppositional forces" (21). Duncan's is "a guilty society unable to contain its own internal contradictions" (59), and thus "Macbeth's murder of Duncan is not an unnatural attack upon an innocent society" (59). The rebellion of MacDonwald, after all, shows that "murderous thoughts . . . already belong to Scotland as part of the national culture that Macbeth shares" (61). This approach, then, rejects Terry Hawkes's argument that Macbeth chooses to exile himself from "an accepted scheme of things, an established world-view, an achieved and authenticated community" (1973, 146).

Here, of course, is the heart of the materialist argument. Duncan's society is "tragically vulnerable to its own inner contradictions" (Turner 1992, 62). Duncan's strategy is to build up a series of obligations from his thanes so that kingship can seem like a God-derived office as opposed to one merely supported by consensus and the feudal contract. Service to the king, however, can breed the need for a greater reward than the king wishes to offer—the throne itself. The world of the play, however, seems to support Duncan's conception. Unlike *Othello*, clenching down to that "close-shut, murderous room," as A. C. Bradley calls it (1904, 145)—where no cosmic response or intervention occurs—and unlike *King Lear*, where we are not sure what the cosmic facts are, as Robert West points out (1968)—the Scottish Play seems to emerge from E.M.W. Tillyard. The materialists argue, however, that much of the "world picture" material is simile ("*like* angels trumpet-tongued," "*like* a naked new-born babe"), that Duncan's is "a whole harmonious *conception* of man, nature, and God" (Turner 1992, 83; emphasis added) that has been reified by conservative critics, and, as Turner argues, that the Old Man's report of the aberrations that Shakespeare borrows from Holinshed may just be "superstitious gossip such as attaches itself to events that erupt violently into community" (97). One could wish that Turner debated more with received opinion on *this* script. Why, for example, does Macbeth phrase the destiny of his victims within the terms of the inherited tradition—"to Heaven, or to Hell"? Is that just a convenient fiction, or is the cosmic fact embedded even in a Macbeth who would cancel the bond? Turner's "answer" is to agree with philosophers like Robert Rorty, "I do not think there is such a thing as human nature" (6). "[C]oncepts of human nature are only ever-changing responses to ever-changing historical situations" (28). While that statement may be true (certain aspects of Jungian psychology would argue otherwise), one "historical situation" from which Shakespeare may have derived his sense of human nature in *this* play is the medieval tradition of

Saint Augustine and Saint Bernard. If so, for "fallen mankind," Duncan's is more than a flawed political concept. The issue is not *its* inherent contradictions but the *nature* of human nature as depicted in this play.

Turner argues that the endings of *Macbeth* and *King Lear* "engage most subversively with the official culture of their time" (1992, 122). If Turner means that *Macbeth* does not, finally, support the static hierarchy of "the Elizabethan World Picture," that is true. If, however, as he also says, that as the play ends it gives us "the world that . . . the audience inherits as its own" (120), that is not subversive. James, after all, "was determined to . . . build . . . up the central power of the monarchy" (118). Certainly Malcolm does that. His thanes and kinsmen reenunciate the interrupted principle that permits the king of Scots to name his successor. The collaudatio—or voice vote—hails Malcolm as "King of *Scotland*," an addition that goes beyond mere election. Do the thanes so shouting really believe that they "celebrate the return of justice and the natural order to a reintegrated Scotland" (110)? Is it not more likely that they participate knowingly in an "evolutionary [process], imaging the birth of a recognizably modern world" (113)? Malcolm, at least, knows that Scotland has not merely "return[ed] to the order out of which violence first broke" (100). As J. K. Walton points out, "Malcolm was in fact the first of a line of kings who established the principle of primogeniture" (1964, 121, n. 2). Having dismissed Duncan's world as just a flawed concept, Turner seems to yearn for it as he contemplates "loss—loss not only for the thanes but also for ourselves as we watch from the diminished world which Malcolm bequeaths to us" (107). Turner makes of *Macbeth* a version of *Richard II*, where Gaunt mourns the fading sanctions and continuities, where a poetic murderer inhabits the vast middle reaches of the play, and where an exponent of realpolitik takes over at the end, lamenting what he has lost in gaining the throne. Malcolm is much less hindered by guilt than Bolingbroke and much freer of "history" as well—as Turner grants in general terms.

Holderness argues that "[m]ost criticism of the play [involves] a process of naturalisation, wherein what is strange becomes familiarized, what is disturbing becomes reassuring, what is subversive becomes a confirmation of orthodox political, moral, and aesthetic values" (1988, 62). He argues "that the political world of the play presents no such celebration or confirmation of royal sovereignty, either in feudal Scotland or in Jacobean England" (63). "An orthodox moralistic reading of the play has to assume a fixed moral framework from which Macbeth's action can be seen as a deviation; and to further assume that the play can guarantee from its audience a preconditioned response to its ethical propositions" (63).

If that is the case, however, and it may be, how does Holderness account for what we used to call our ambivalent response to the play?—which he nicely phrases. The play's "effect is to render heroic what it criminalises, to lend glamour and excitement to the very things it warns against, and to induce a strange kind of respect in us for those impulses and actions we are taught by the play's morality-fable to fear, reject and shun'' (63). Tragedy does that, doesn't it? Having roused that response in us, a production then finds us ''leav[ing] the theatre with all its immoral, antisocial and politically dissident impulses safely cauterised or quelled'' (64). Does it?

Holderness asserts that ''the very language with which the King seeks to unify his kingdom involves a systematic denial of its constitutive reality'' (66). That may be. But language, even in an early seventeenth century which could still believe that words were linked magically to objects named, was still limited, as was man's power to understand the deeper mysteries of God and His universe. Holderness contrasts ''savage butchery'' against the ''decorously chivalric gesture of courtly compliment,'' a contrast that ''testifies to a radical uncertainty at the heart of the play'' (66). But that is to say that Duncan should have avoided battle and surrendered to the traitors. It is doubtful that, had he done so, ''savage butchery'' would then have been avoided.

Holderness objects to the moralistic reading of the play, but he can do so only by waxing moralistic about the battle fought to preserve Duncan's kingship. Holderness indicts a ''contradictory historical society which cherishes at its heart the violence and uncertainty which will eventually destroy it'' (67). He ignores the epic treatment given Macbeth at the outset and the central fact that Macbeth's fighting as a soldier of the king was manifesting *loyalty*, not brutality, even if brutality in battle was one of the necessary components of the defense of the king. Holderness is on shaky ground when he suggests, ''The objections Macbeth considers are not universal moral principles but ethical scruples derived from the values of feudal society'' (67–68). ''Thou shalt not kill'' is not merely medieval. It may be that ''the play [does not] ultimately dispel, moderate or purge the violent delights it dramatises: criminal desire is aroused and accounted for, but not pacified'' (69). But it *is* criminal, nonetheless, and both Macbeth and Lady Macbeth perceive themselves to be damned as a result of their deeds. Holderness does not account for *assassination*. That evil continues to be fascinating, even after we have seen the play, accounts for the play's power to affect our imaginations. We may remember Lady Macbeth wandering back in time to a never-ending nightmare and Macbeth's head fixed on a pole as Macdonwald's had been, even if the director, a Welles or a Polanski, has imposed a *de capo* coda showing that evil seeps into the future under Malcolm's feet as it were.

At the end, says Holderness, ''Duncan's system of trust and loyalty is replaced by a remote and vigilant cautiousness, exercised with the defensive calculation of a king who will not expose himself to the protection of those whose power he relies on'' (70). Here is a case of Malcolm's being blamed for *not* being like his vulnerable father. ''His personal retainers (thanes) become administrative officers (earls),'' states Holderness (70). The system does change. It has to. At the end, we have ''measure'' according to the more precise calibrations of a modern world. Malcolm is cautious, even calculated. Who would expect or argue otherwise? When Malcolm promises to ''performe . . . This, and what needfull else . . . in measure, time, and place,'' it is as if he had listened to James

Calderwood: "[A]ction in *Macbeth* seems almost relentlessly to subvert the aristotelian principles of wholeness, completeness, and limited magnitude" (1986, x). "Humane statute purg'd the gentle Weal" once, but that did not deter Macbeth.

In the notes for the 1992 Bogdanov production, which is discussed in chapter 6, Holderness asserts that *Macbeth* "never . . . presents . . . a moral order" to us; therefore, none can have been violated. Macbeth, then, misperceives the world he is in, and does so *in soliloquy*. If so, we must reexamine the soliloquy convention, in which, up until now, we have accepted that the character speaking believes what he or she is saying. Moreover, we must reexamine everything in the play that alludes to "a moral order" and conclude that Lady Macbeth is faking her sleepwalking, for some obscure motive of personal gratification, as she may have faked her faint to somehow get Macbeth to stop talking. We are left to second-guess the error Macbeth admits he is making in killing Duncan. That error is defined in the dimensions of a moral order, even if he is only playing at similes (*"like* angels" *"like* a naked new-born babe"). Macbeth would not agree with Holderness that "Macbeth is not in any sense 'evil,' " nor would Macbeth defend himself by claiming, "The individual cannot be blamed for the self-destructive contradictions of a divided society" (1992, 4). Macbeth may lack modern psychological and sociological language; indeed he expresses himself with metaphors with which Dante would have no difficulty. He may confuse himself, but he is not confused about his role in society or about the role of society within a purposive cosmos. The play does not allow us to see him as a "victim" of contradictions other than those he creates for himself. If used as a rationale for production, this thesis will destroy the inherited script, as I will suggest.

Michael Hawkins argues that "no one has history as a background . . . everyone is part of it" (1982, 155). Bradley and G. Wilson Knight, he remarks, "have a certain timelessness and ahistorical quality" (155). What, he asks, "was particularly evil to the Jacobeans about the murder of Duncan as portrayed in the play?" (156). He argues against the reification of "evil" by Knight, L. C. Knights, L. B. Campbell, and Irving Ribner. Hawkins asserts that the "loss of historical individuality is . . . a perversion of historical scholarship" (156), meaning, one assumes, that the critical stance of "objectivity" encourages the proliferation of received opinion. Received opinion in this instance is that Shakespeare espouses "a fully-fledged political and religious philosophy or even eschatology, so that his plays become *exempla* of the lessons that history teaches" (157). Such a stance produces readings that do not "go much beyond commonplace" (157). Instead, historical scholarship should "raise the questions which concerned contemporaries and see how Shakespeare dealt with them" (159). "Here," continues Hawkins, "should be stressed that amendment of Holinshed which makes the *whole* of Macbeth's reign one of terror in Scotland, a disruption of nature and the 'chain of being,' and equates his overthrow with the restoration of order and concord to the whole of society" (160).

The prefeudal system was based on "blood and kinship relationships," the feudal on "[c]ontractual relations . . . a hierarchy of ties," within which the king was obliged to "protect and consult his leading vassals." When the king elevates *his* status, he reduces "contractual obligations." The "elite felt itself threatened" (and that is certainly true of Worcester in the first part of *Henry IV* and of the Archbishop of York in the second part). What Duncan does is to introduce "institutional politics" and a resultant "gap between the probable fallibility of the actual king and the infallibility of his office" (i.e., the concept of "the king's two bodies"). The result of this assumption of institution *to* the king is that "fiscal, judicial, military monopolies become established in the Crown [and] bureaucratic forms [are established] to administer them" (Hawkins 1982, 161). The "tension between the varying forms of existing political relationships . . . caught the attention of Tudor England and provided Shakespeare with the topics he explored" (162). "*Schema* [like] 'the Elizabethan world picture' were propounded . . . by those, from the king downwards, with an interest in the *status quo*" (162). "Such views could be sustained only as long as they avoided specifics, talking about the king as sun but not dealing with the question of his power to tax at will" (163). The issues of king as sun and crown as taxing agency are raised vividly in *Richard II. Macbeth*'s "lack of institutional ways of resolving issues gives prominence to the variety of personal links" (163). The personalization gives motive to characters and enhances their hold on us. *King Lear* has a "court"—a strange vision of a full-scale Jacobean system of justice projected onto a joint-stool, but no real way to resolve grievances except by summary sentence, brutality, trial by combat, or full-scale battle. According to Hawkins, "[O]ne political issue is resolved at the end because Macbeth has no son to perpetuate the blood feud" (165)—his line is extinct, a good thing for Scotland, as it is not for Denmark. Otherwise, Hawkins states, the "feudal values shown are deeply flawed" (165). "The greater the need to curb men of violence, the greater the emphasis on oaths of loyalty" (166).

Macbeth's effort to shore up his contractual system falls apart, of course: "[T]he banquet . . . is the most significant affirmation of feudal unity in the play." It "is also an affirmation and recognition of superiority and a demonstration of power" (Hawkins 1982, 166). One can agree, of course, with the general premise and point out that Macbeth has broken previous contractual obligations violently and that therefore his banquet shows what is *not* in Macbeth's power. He has tried to cancel a greater "Bond" than the feudal contract. Emphasis *just* on the deep flaws of feudalism makes for a flawed and superficial argument. "Machiavelli's work," continues Hawkins, is "the product of the particular pressures and needs of courtly politics in the early modern period" (171). And it may be that Malcolm *needs* Macbeth so that Malcolm can set up a new regime more responsive to those needs and pressures than was his father's system, based on the *trust* essential to any contract. Macbeth becomes for Scotland what Richard III was for England—a scourge. "The pieties of an unchanging social order could be used as a reference point, but it was change—the rise and fall of great men—which held the attention'' (172). One could say, further, that the falls of great men also were responsible for or coincident with shifts in modes of governance. Marxists might say that the politics of assassination do not alter the inevitable processes of historical movement. That may be so. And it may also be so that the official view of the Gunpower Plot was sycophantically reflected back to the crown from all articulate quarters. Still, without taking a Carlylean view of history, one wonders why it was John F. Kennedy who was assassinated and not Richard Nixon; Robert Kennedy and not Edmund Meese; or Martin Luther King, Jr., and not Pat Robertson.

Richard II dramatizes a transition from a ceremonial to a pragmatic mode of kingship. Bolingbroke enacts a neofeudal system. It is the only model available to him. Malcolm's new order involves ''administration,'' not just ''trust.''

''The fact that Macbeth has to pay himself makes his crime, as has been neatly put, 'strongly if not justly motivated.' We may perhaps ask . . . 'who has more substance as king, Duncan or Macbeth?' '' (Hawkins 1982, 175). Even Macbeth answers in favor of Duncan; that is, if we can accept ''clarity in office'' as ''substance.'' Malcolm promises at the end to ''make us even with you.'' He expresses an awareness of balance, even *tenuous* balance, against his father's overflow earlier and Duncan's inability to reward adequately: ''More is thy due, than more than all can pay.''

To make *Macbeth* a history play, Hawkins is forced into untenable or contradictory positions. ''Duncan attempts to impose not a hereditary succession by primogeniture, but a *nominated* one: these are not identical, even if the eldest son is nominated, since the whole point of nomination is that he need not be'' (1982, 175). The point of heredity is that future crown princes need not be *nominated*, only formally invested as Prince of Cumberland.

''As in *Lear*,'' Hawkins continues, ''Shakespeare is more concerned with the conduct of existing kings [and] with their provision for the succession as an aspect of their competence—than with abstract rights, though the management of the latter is an aspect of monarchy'' (1982, 176). One could argue that Duncan, after a successful battle against both traitors and invaders, attempts to solidify his dynasty *and* Scotland's future. No one in the play, particularly including Macbeth, argues that *Duncan* is not the rightful king. Lear divides his kingdom, making an effort to ''prevent . . . future strife'' but ensuring that it will come. Only an invasion from France brings hostile factions together in Britain.

Shakespeare has already given Bolingbroke the reign that Holinshed gives both Macbeth *and* Bolingbroke but that Shakespeare denies Macbeth. The fragility of a feudal system and, in Bolingbroke's case, the necessity of centralizing power in the crown are vividly shown in the Second Henriad. But there, it was the *king* who violated the sacred and the legal premises of his own kingship (see Coursen 1982).

Macbeth is not a good king, Hawkins is forced to admit (1982, 178), as if it is merely his ineptitude that makes his reign difficult for Scotland, as if this were a political play without cosmic surroundings, and as if his *success* as king would have justified his murder of Duncan. He cannot help but be a failure, given the example of kingship set and the premises of the world. Even a skillful king—Claudius of Denmark—is brought down by some of the same larger-than-political forces that doom Macbeth. In the instances of *Hamlet* and *Macbeth*, history or politics is not the ultimate dimension within which the actions of the play occur.

Shakespeare does not "make Macbeth's death literally bestial," states Hawkins (1982, 168), trying to normalize Macbeth *in* history. He does fight, giving us a glimpse of his former heroism (even if the New Historicist approach brutalizes that heroism). But he is "tied . . . to a stake," is "bruited" (a pun on "brute"), and is a "Hell-hound." The play does what New Historicism can neither countenance nor incorporate. It takes Macbeth beyond history; it essentializes him within a worldview that only yields to history, assuming that it does, through the transitional figure, Macbeth. Macbeth drops down the chain of being, even if he keeps his lost humanity before us and even if the chain of being is just a metaphor by play's end.

Morris notes the absence of *organized* religion in the play: "There is no church, there are no priests" (1982, 30). The play makes a very Reformationist point; the issue, as Martin Luther would have it, is the "inward man," and Shakespeare makes that issue vivid. One could ask, how much organized religion appears in *Beowulf*? In that Christianized eighth-century Anglo-Saxon court, a complete reconciliation between Wyrd and Christianity has not been achieved. Beowulf exemplifies both Germanic values and Christian virtues. Shakespeare gives Macbeth both epic strength and a Christian conscience. Morris claims that "sin, repentance, forgiveness, salvation and grace [are] . . . no more seen than the dark side of the moon" (30). Such a reading makes the play "more like Marlowe's *Tamberlaine* than his *Faustus*" (30). One must ask where Tamberlaine says that *he* is damned. Macbeth accepts that stoically; Faustus thinks he can still repent at some later time. "*Macbeth* is not sharply and continuously aware of the religious dimension in human life" (30). This reiterates the Kottian view that *Macbeth* is just "History as . . . nightmare" (Kott 1964, 75), that "[h]istory in *Macbeth* is sticky and thick like a brew or blood" (76) and that the blood has no sacramental resonance.

In his speech, "If it were done," contends Morris, "Macbeth is content to dismiss death, heaven, hell and judgement" (1982, 31). This is true, *if* we ignore his "If," which qualifies all that follows and refutes Morris's assertion. "The angels and the cherubim, God's ministers," he writes, "are no more than similes and illustrations of the immediate political problem" (31). This inverts the value scheme of the play, much as both Lady Macbeth and Macbeth try to do. We should ask—*what* problem? There is none, unless Macbeth creates one. Macbeth acts "without one whit of concern for his immortal soul" (32). No—he knows it is lost. He tells us so. He "never envisages that by Sin he has grieved God's heart of love" (51), Morris claims. That would be to sentimentalize what does happen. Morris proves that the play is neither heavily political nor geographical. Nor is it freighted with heavy allusions to actual religious practice. So what? Macbeth's line to the Weird Sisters about the "Windes" fighting "against the Churches" is an amplification into malign nature of Faustus's line: "And make my spirits pull his churches down" (VI, 123). Neither Macbeth nor the play dismisses judgment. The scene after the murder is discovered is configured as Judgment Day. The play is not to be understood in its references but felt on the level of its allusions.

One might quote *Faustus* to Lady Macbeth:

> *Faustus*: I think hell's a fable.
> *Mephisto*: Ay, think so, till experience change thy mind. (v. 164–65)

One might quote Macbeth to Morris: "And mine eternall Jewell / Given to the common Enemie of Man"; "an eternall Curse fall on you": "Let this pernitious hour, / Stand aye accursed in the Kalendar!"; "And damn'd all those that trust them!"; "Accursed be that tongue that tels mee so."

O'Rourke attacks the essentialist reading and shifts the ground of debate about the play from an emphasis on character. O'Rourke explores Stephen Booth's suggestion that Aristotle's *Poetics* has become "a sign of the covenant between literature and the ultimate values of the universe" (1983, 94). Specifically, O'Rourke follows Harry Levin (1961) in attacking "Bradley's usual description of a Shakespearean tragedy as a process leading from the temporary disruption of cosmic order to its restoration [which] displaced the idea of catharsis from an account of the experience of the playgoer to a description of the world of the play" (O'Rourke 1993, 213). Levin suggests that "the analysis of Shakespearean drama has taken a somewhat casuistic turn, and has combined neo-Hegelian rationalization with quasi-Aristotelian terminology" (1961, 134). I do not believe that the sense of the universe as providential and an experience of catharsis are incompatible or mutually exclusive. The play *does* show a restoration of order. We can debate the nature of that order and the character of its restorer, Malcolm, but the *dis*order caused by Macbeth is at least imaged in the play in metaphors of a violation of a Tillyardian "world picture." It is true that Bradley's opening chapter, "The Substance of Tragedy," puts more emphasis on a character's *decision* than does Levin, who says that

> encounters with mere contingency may be as inevitable as they are unpredictable; and tragedy is at least a forewarning against them, a warning lest our blessings be turned into curses. Moreover, it is an attempt to indicate limits which we may overstep at our peril, to locate the point where our wills converge with our fates, to discern the odds that confront and confound our best-laid plans. (1961, 104)

Bradley, however, is very clear about the intersection between act and destiny: "That men may start a course of events but can neither calculate nor control is a *tragic* fact" (1904, 15)—and often a political fact as well. Macbeth *wishes* he could control consequences but knows he cannot, even if he does not know precisely what the consequences of his murders will be.

O'Rourke says that Wyrd rules *Macbeth*, a simultaneity of past/present/future that erases causation and human motivation and certainly any purposive cosmos. For O'Rourke, the play is "profoundly subversive of Christian metaphysics that structured the symbolic order of the society" (1993, 214). To make his case, he relies on Macbeth's "Tomorrow" speech and Lady Macbeth's seeing "beyond this ignorant present," feeling the future in the instant, which is something only God can do. "Seeing the 'future' as the present is, in a Christian metaphysics, an attribute of God. The subversive metaphysics of *Macbeth* depersonifies this perspective which sees all time, all tomorrows and yesterdays as simultaneous—that is, it removes the figure of 'God,' or the *logos*, from that position" (217). But Macbeth's speech is his own and cannot be accepted as defining the play. Lady Macbeth's usurpation of God's synthesis is hers; again, it is not applicable to the play around her. Certainly the large contexts of the play refute both Macbeths when they ask that "Starres hide [their] fires" or that "thick Night . . . Come." Job (14:7–8) speaks of God: "He commandeth the sunne, and it riseth not: he closeth up the starres, as under a signet. He him self alone spreadeth out the heavens." Their willful defiance of God's prerogative and the retribution that visits them are profoundly *supportive* of Christian metaphysics.

Do the Weird Sisters "cause Macbeth to kill Duncan?" Although O'Rourke asserts that the question is "unanswerable" (1993, 218), he suggests that the answer is yes, "as neither Providence nor divine volition can account for the action of the play. The idea of free will is dissipated in the failure of naturalistic questions to produce a causal chain that runs from motivation to action to consequence" (218). "[T]he prophecies, rather than inciting Macbeth towards the killing of Duncan, should have led him to view Malcolm's nomination with an equanimity born of his certainty of his own eventual succession" (219). Of course, that is something that sets Macbeth apart from most of us. It is also another play, a misreading of human reaction even if *not* acted upon, and of Macbeth's reactive mechanism as dramatized. He is *not* equanimous. Macbeth sees the murder as, at best, an "appalling duty" (Bradley 1904, 284). Lady Macbeth, remarks O'Rourke, "had sought to live entirely on the naturalistic plane, only borrowing from the witches the expediency of a 'fair is foul' mentality" (1993, 220). Macbeth murders "*in absentia*, his guilt is like that experienced in dreams . . . the actual transgression which inspires . . . retribution has only a shadowy, ambiguous existence" (221). This ignores too much, including Duncan's blood and the nature of the experience. Who has not had this kind of experience?—one in which we absented ourselves from full consciousness as we endured it the better to keep the retribution we were suffering *in* the shadows? The results for Lady Macbeth, of course, are that full consciousness absents itself from *her* for good.

After the murder of Duncan, it may be true of the "World of *Macbeth*" that it is "the playing out of a tale from which there is no possibility of deviation [and that] erodes any sense of morality; if there is no choice, there is no responsibility, and if there is no responsibility, there is no point to moral distinctions" (O'Rourke 1993, 222–23). Macbeth's "bend up each *corporall* Agent to this terrible Feat" tells us what he is doing, or trying to do. Anyone who has not done that—that is, walk through something he does not want to do—will not understand that distinction *and* its destructive effect on the human psyche.

Macbeth, continues O'Rourke, is "the story of the dominion of Wyrd" (1993, 223), "a determinism without temporal development or causality" (225). Choice *is* difficult at the outset, distinctions are blurred (see Coursen 1967), but the largest distinctions are all too clear to Macbeth. Lady Macbeth may not *know* what she is doing—though the vehemence with which she tries to exorcise her humanity might argue otherwise—but in the world of the play ignorance does not excuse her. O'Rourke must ignore Macbeth's "If it were done" speech, which with an absoluteness rare in tragedy outlines the case against the decision he is simultaneously making. The speech does blur cause and effect, as Booth would argue (1983), but it makes responsibility indelible.

"Macbeth has, for most of the play," argues O'Rourke, "attempted to live under the naturalistic assumption that he could race against time. Eliminating the space between imagining and doing seemed to him the necessary means of his own success" (1993, 216–17). And, as Francis Fergusson has argued, Macbeth races *against* a pursuing "Reason" (1957, 115–25). But if naturalistic assumptions are incorrect, what other assumptions govern people? The postmodernist approach ignores the world in which the play exists, or dismisses it for, in this case, what Macbeth says about it once it has condemned him from within his own value system, one built into his psyche whether he likes it or not. His is not the final statement; nor is Malcolm's.

A very specific placement of Macbeth in a historical context is that of Christopher Caudwell, who says that Macbeth exhibits an "intemperate will, 'bloody, bold, and resolute' without norm or measure, is the spirit of the era of primitive accumulation. The absolute-individual will overriding all other wills is therefore the principle of life for the Elizabethan age. Marlowe's Faust and Tamburlaine express this principle in its naivest form" (quoted in Walton 1964, 122, n. 2). "Macbeth," says Walton, "may be seen to have some affiliations with the early 'heroic' days of capitalism, tragically conceived" (1964, 122).

Works Cited

Booth, Stephen. 1983. *'King Lear,' 'Macbeth,' Indefinition in Tragedy*. New Haven, Conn.: Yale University Press.

Bradley, A. C. 1904. *Shakespearean Tragedy*. London: Macmillan.

Calderwood, James L. 1986. *If It Were Done: 'Macbeth' and Tragic Action*. Amherst: University of Massachusetts Press.

Campbell, L. B. 1930. *Shakespeare's Tragic Heroes*. Cambridge: Cambridge University Press.

Coursen, H. R. 1967. "In Deepest Consequence: *MacBeth*." *Shakespeare Quarterly* 18, no. 4 (Autumn): 375–88.

———. 1982. *The Leasing out of England: Shakespeare's Second Henriad*. Lanham, Md.: University Press of America.

Fawkner, H. W. 1990. *Deconstructing 'Macbeth': The Hyperontological View*. Cranbury, N.J.: Associated University Presses.

Fergusson, Francis. 1957. "*Macbeth* as the Imitation of an Action." *The Human Image in Dramatic Literature*. Garden City, N.Y.: Doubleday Anchor.

Hawkes, Terrence. 1973. *Shakespeare's Talking Animals*. London: Edward Arnold.

Hawkins, Michael. 1982. "History, Politics, and *Macbeth*." In *Focus on 'Macbeth.'* Edited by John Russell Brown. London: Routledge and Kegan Paul.

Holderness, Graham. 1988. "Come in Equivocator: Tragic Ambivalence in *Macbeth*." In *Macbeth*. Edited by Linda Cookson and Bryan Loughrey. London: Longman.

———. 1992. Note. Program for *Macbeth*. London: English Shakespeare Company.

Kott, Jan. 1964. *Shakespeare: Our Contemporary*. Garden City, N.Y.: Doubleday.

Levin, Harry. 1961. *The Question of 'Hamlet.'* New York: Viking.

Marlowe, Christopher. 1604. *The Tragical History of Dr. Faustus*. Edited by Louis B. Wright and Virginia A. LaMar. New York: Washington Square, 1959.

Morris, Brian. 1982. "The Kingdom, the Power and the Glory in *Macbeth*." In *Focus on 'Macbeth.'* Edited by John Russell Brown. London: Routledge and Kegan Paul.

O'Rourke, James L. 1993. "The Subversive Metaphysics of *Macbeth*." *Shakespeare Studies* 21: 213–27.

Tillyard, E.M.W. 1948. *The Elizabethan World Picture*. New York: Macmillan.

Turner, John. 1992. *Macbeth*. Buckingham: Open University Press.

Walton, J. K. 1964. "*Macbeth*." In *Shakespeare in a Changing World*. Edited by Arnold Kettle. New York: New World.

West, Robert. 1968. *Shakespeare and the Outer Mystery*. Lexington: University of Kentucky Press.

Wilson, J. Dover, ed. 1947. *Macbeth*. Cambridge: Cambridge University Press.

6

THE PLAY IN PERFORMANCE

The "value or importance" of studying Shakespeare is to learn that he wrote *scripts*, that scripts are not literature, and that a script is not a play but merely part of a process that leads to a play. And then to *begin* to learn how to read a script (for which *all* literary strategies are disastrously misleading).

—Homer Swander

MACBETH ON STAGE

I would qualify Professor Swander's assertion by saying that literary strategies can be useful when we ask how they inform the play as a *script*—that is, as a set of signals meant to be deciphered by actors and an audience.

Gary Waller states, "It is useful to think of acting, like reading and criticism, as a mode of *producing*, not merely *reproducing*, meanings, and to think of the Shakespearean script making the meaning only as it is loosed into the world as production, within changing signifying systems and historical formations." Waller opposes to this dynamic process a dependence on "apparently fixed textual meanings waiting to be read atemporally from the text by the attentive reader armed with the appropriate [critical] vocabulary" (1992, 102). Waller argues for communication between the critical camps. I would suggest that what is needed is communication *from* critics to the energies of production. More and more, theory and the plays that theory treats are diverging. And that is true particularly of those theoreticians who write about production. According to W. H. Worthen, "Shakespearean production is perhaps peripheral to the most challenging and exploratory work in contemporary performance and performance theory" (1996, 13). The process of production, from read-through to rehearsal to performance uncovers "*stage* realities present in the text" (Hodgdon, 1979; emphasis added).

We are learning a lot about Shakespeare's stage during the reconstruction of

Shakespeare Repertory *Macbeth*. Photo credit: Jennifer Girard

the Globe on Bankside. In this configuration, the actors were surrounded by the audience. The platform opened out into the space where part of the audience stood. Above the groundlings were the galleries. Behind the actors was the lords gallery. The effect of spectators behind the stage, argues Frank Hildy (1996), is to bring the action forward toward the audience on the ground and in the galleries.

Macbeth, of course, may not have appeared originally at the Globe. As R. M. Frye suggests, "In other instances, most notably *Macbeth*, we may safely assume that an unusually short play represents a version prepared either for acting during the winter months when sunset closed the plays earlier, or for use at court or under special circumstances where other activities might impinge" (1982, 31–32). Michael Long agrees,

> It may well be that *Macbeth* was written for performance at court. . . . King James, first monarch of the newly united England and Scotland, supposed descendant of Banquo, a stickler for the Divine Right of Kings, an expert on witches and a fan of plays which were not too long, is an obvious candidate for the attentions of the author of *Macbeth*. (1989, xii)

In responding to any Shakespeare play, it is helpful to remember what R. M. Frye calls "Shakespeare's practice of providing all the materials for comparison and contrast, and leaving it to members of the audience to draw their own conclusions" (1982, 245–46). Frye's example is the contrast between Edward the Confessor, a physician who can cure, and Macbeth's Doctor, who finds Lady Macbeth's malady "beyond my practice." We must complete any of Shakespeare's plays in performance for ourselves.

It is also true, however, that the response to Shakespeare in production is not primarily cognitive or rational. Robin Grove argues that we do not experience the play in the theater in "terms which direct us specifically into modes of *thought* . . . as 'themes' and 'values' and 'aspects' and 'ideas' . . . drama like this is capable of taking the place of 'thought' . . . great drama prompts us to be sensuously intelligent: bodily, intuitively" (1982, 114). As we respond to a play in performance, we will be reminded inevitably that, as Sheldon Zitner says, Shakespeare's "is a relational not an essentializing or ideologizing stage," looking at "the open middle-distance of social relation, [at] humanity seen not in the all-defining close-up of psychology or at the far and narrowed distance of sociology" (1981, 8). While Shakespeare *can* close up to psychology—in soliloquy or mad scene—and while he can open out to larger vistas, as when characters in history plays predict or *mis*predict the future, Zitner is largely accurate and helps explain why the plays have been so susceptible to gender criticism since the recent inception of that approach.

William Scott says of Shakespearean production that "it is the function of the player to lie like truth and of the audience to believe what it knows to be equivocation" (1986, 174). We participate in the fiction by *believing* it during its few hours upon the stage. *Macbeth*, more than most other scripts, calls for an involvement that goes beyond a willing suspension of disbelief. It implicates the spectator in "self-fulfilling prophecies which undermine the self and . . . lies which performatively become truths—we confront the metadramatic illusions with which the play both forbids and compels us to delude ourselves" (174).

It has taken time itself to prove the point made by Leah S. Marcus:

> Insofar as we have attempted to define the shadowy historical person behind the giant name, we have identified a playwright who used topicality not to limit, select, and shape his audiences in ideological terms but to disperse ideology prismatically so that his plays . . . would take on different colorations in different settings and times. (1988, 218).

In previous epochs, critics believed that *they* had discovered the "real" Shakespeare—an undisciplined genius who required the structures of measure, time, and place for the late seventeenth and eighteenth centuries, a visionary holding a lamp into the darkness for the Romantics, a solid moral beacon for the Victorians. Now we recognize that Shakespeare holds a mirror up to zeitgeist. As Ann Thompson remarks, "In some sense all future readings could be said to be 'there' in the text, but we have to wait for the historical circumstances which will make them visible" (1988, 81).

Thus Harold C. Goddard can remark on *Macbeth*'s modernity:

> If the fragmentary passages describing Scotland under Macbeth are assembled they read like a documented account of life in the countries subjugated by the "strong" men of the twentieth century. With its remote setting and ancient superstitions, *Macbeth* to a superficial mind may seem dated. On the contrary few of Shakespeare's plays speak more directly to our time. (1951, 2:109)

Ironically, however, it is usually a mistake for a director to place a production precisely in a modern context. The script tends to hollow out to *only* the contemporary metaphor, which makes nonsense of everything from individual words and lines to entire battles. Sylvan Barnet argues that "modern-dress productions make the play too local, too bound to the present, and rob the play— any play—of its archetypal dimension" (1987, 263). In Barry Jackson's modern-dress 1928 production, for example, the "witches were a problem, since witches are not a part of modern society" (263–64). In the Theodore Komisarjevsky production at Stratford-on-Avon in 1933, "The witches . . . were hags plundering corpses on the battlefield; they told the fortunes of Macbeth and Banquo by palmistry. . . . Banquo's ghost . . . was Macbeth's own immense shadow, and Macbeth's second encounter with the witches was conceived as Macbeth's dream" (264). Modernizations tend to insist on the "normalization" of the supernatural, as does a modernist medium like television. I will deal with the Bogdanov production below, which unfortunately proved the point about the superficiality of explicitly modern settings, and with the apparent exception, the Welles "Voodoo" *Macbeth* of 1936, a "fable about the evil king of an evil island" (Kennedy 1993, 148) that allowed for, indeed emphasized, the witch-craft in the script.

The early twentieth-century advocate of a return to Shakespeare's dramaturgy, William Poel argued that "if the plays were done on a Shakespeare-like stage ... they would not have to be cut, their scenes would not have to be rearranged, and there would not have to be long pauses when new scenery was being set up" (quoted in Barnet 1987, 262). The play, J. C. Trewin offers, "on an un-cluttered stage, can move with the speed the Jacobeans expected" (1978, 214). According to Peter Hall, "*Macbeth* with scenery that changes in any sense— even something going up and down—is impossible. The stage has to be a space which becomes what the characters say it is" (1982, 248). I have argued else-where that rapid pacing is still basic to a successful Shakespeare production, as opposed, for example, to the excruciating slowness of Lepage's infamous "Mud Dream" of 1992 (Coursen 1995, 194–201).

Shakespeare probably permitted a collaborative effort *within* the process of making his plays—as opposed to being a lone person scraping with a goose quill by candlelight in a solitary room. Stephen Orgel asserts that "Shakespeare habitually began with more than he needed ... his scripts offered the company a range of possibilities ... the process of production was one of selection as well as of realization and interpretation" (1988, 7). The Folio *Macbeth*, then, represents the honing down process of a company at work, with the exception of Hecate, who, as G. K. Hunter suggests, "must have been inserted into *Macbeth* at some point between 1609 and the publication of the first Folio (1623), presumably as part of an expanded version, used as a revival" (1994, 820). The process of shaping the script is described by Humphrey Mosely in 1647: "[T]he actors omitted some scenes and passages (with the author's consent [the authors being Beaumont and Fletcher]) as occasion led them; and when private friends desired a copy, they then (and justly too) transcribed what they had acted" (quoted in Frye 1982, 32). The concept of collaboration is a necessary one for contemporary companies, like ACTER (A Center for Theater Research) whose 1996 production is treated below, and for classes asked to deliver scenes to their cohorts. From the standpoint of both criticism and production, the emphasis on collaboration avoids the fallacy that Foucault calls "the author function," which Harry Berger, Jr., says imposes the "principle of closure, of semiotic inhibition ... to privilege certain readings and control 'unruly meanings' " by appealing to the authority of the "author's intention" (1987, 153).

In 1982 John Russell Brown conducted an interview with Peter Hall. From Hall, we get an approach to the play that is scholarly, but which subordinates scholarship to the purpose of the script, which is an instrument of performance. According to Hall,

> Amazingly Shakespearean drama still deals with feudal societies in which
> conflict between Scotland and England, or France and England, can be re-
> duced to single-hand combat. Theatrically this is a wonderful thing to be

able to do; but it is also a true expression of the idea of Renaissance man as an individual. (1982, 233)

It is also true, of course, that single-handed combat can be accommodated to the stage and made dramatic, as in the Hal-Hotspur, Edgar-Edmund, and Macbeth-Macduff mano-a-manos, in which the individuals also stand for more than just themselves.

Of Duncan's elevation of Malcolm, Hall argues, "Duncan is deliberately challenging the thanes [in promoting Malcolm] by taking this political initiative abruptly" (1982, 233). On staging royalty, Hall suggests, "The king . . . is shown to be king by the way everybody else reacts to *him*" (234). "As far as the other thanes are concerned, no power-base is building up against [Duncan]" (234). That is probably true, but the staging can also show that Malcolm has no following. That may be a reason for his promotion to crown prince, but it can also show his vulnerability.

Ross's greeting to Macbeth, bringing word of the addition of Thane of Cawdor to Macbeth's titles is, states Hall, "almost an extension of Duncan's own part, almost an imitation of Duncan, and it shows how the state ought to work" (1982, 235). Hall sees Duncan as a politician who understands the system he operates: "I don't think [Duncan is] any kind of super religious figure" (234).

Hall contends that "[o]ne of the basic strengths of Shakespearian drama is that the audience is shown what a character is actually motivated by, and we then see them wearing a mask" (1982, 240). We see the other characters often, then, unaware of the masking and thus stepping into traps—benevolent in *Much Ado about Nothing*, malevolent when Edmund manipulates Gloucester and perhaps almost as bad when Edgar subjects Gloucester to a painful allegory, and contrasting, as when Henry V traps the traitors and later wanders incognito into the soldiers' campfire and quarrels with Williams. Our superior position is almost invariable, with the possible exception of Hermione's "death" in *Winter's Tale*, and is what was once called "dramatic irony."

Hall wisely argues that "we make a great mistake if we ever take Shakespeare away from the idea of the theatre as the globe, the actor as man, man as actor, and life as play. I think whole areas of the play get unlocked by remembering that" (1982, 241).

> Our post-Restoration theatrical tradition—I suppose we're still suffering from the nineteenth century—leads us to see emblems on stage as decorative and inferior, not as good as words. . . . One of the miracles of Renaissance theatre is the concept of the theatre as a metaphor of the world. That evil and hell is underneath, that man struts his life as a player on the stage, and that God and the gods exist above metaphorically. (244)

We should not forget as our theaters wallow in postmodernist eclecticism and anachronism that the early seventeenth-century audience knew that they were, as Alvin Kernan points out, "simply another group of players in a larger play, and that the physical theater is not final reality but simply another stage on which a longer play is being enacted before an unseen audience" (1974, 1).

We cannot recreate Shakespeare's conditions of performance and should not even if we could, since drama works in its society within the expectations of a specific zeitgeist and not in some reconstituted past. The effort to return to Shakespeare's staging results in a parody, as we realize when we look at old photographs of Poel's productions—useful and necessary as was his fighting free of the ponderous designs that dominated the Victorian stage. That does not mean, of course, that we ignore such factors as the religious background of this play, even if most theatergoers live in a secular age, or that we forget that "desert" had not differentiated to mean a sandy expanse but meant a wild and uninhabited place, or that we ignore how the plays continue to work as scripts. John Styan, for example, describes the imaginative space between Macbeth's exit from Duncan and Lady Macbeth's receipt of his letter:

> When in *Macbeth*, I. v, Shakespeare's audience saw Lady Macbeth reading the letter from her husband, they did not pause to consider that now, suddenly, the scene had changed from Forres to Inverness. . . . The change had been accomplished before Lady Macbeth made her entrance. The audience had heard Macbeth say to the King, "I'll be myself the harbinger, and make joyful / The hearing of my wife with your approach" . . . and the playwright would have upset them had the first lady to enter reading a letter *not* been Macbeth's wife, although they would justly have been surprised at the kind of joy they saw her exhibit. Speech and context of situation were imaginatively one whole. [Shakespeare] wrote a drama that created its own atmosphere and identified its own locality, if it needed to. (1967, 28–29)

Similarly, when Macduff and Malcolm enter for 4.3, we know that Macduff's wife and children have been killed. We know that he does not. We anticipate the coming of the terrible news. If Ross does not bring that news our anticipation will have been thwarted.

Since stage productions of *Macbeth* have been so well chronicled by Dennis Bartholomeusz, Arthur Colby Sprague, Richard David, Roland Watkins and Jeremy Lemmon, Marvin Rosenberg, Gareth Lloyd Evans, and Gordon Williams, I will consider them only briefly, and particularly at certain potentially troublesome moments in the script, like the Porter, Lady Macbeth's "feint," the ghost of Banquo, and the issue of Malcolm, and at very recent productions. I am indebted also to Arthur C. L. Brown (1913), Trewin (1978), and Carol Carlisle (1983), to Barnet's excellent summary (1987, 254–67), Hunter's "The Play in Performance" (in 1994, 807–14), and Long's "The Stage History" (in 1989, xi–xvi). See the line drawings of a Globe-style performance in the Watkins-Lemmon Harrow edition of the play (1964). See also the splendid pictorial evidence in Dennis Kennedy's book (1993), including a photograph of the final scene of the Welles-Houseman "Voodoo" *Macbeth* (p. 146), and Keith Parsons and Pamela Mason (1995, 124–29).

The history of production of *Macbeth*, like that of so many of Shakespeare's scripts, is marked by the effort to restore Shakespeare's text; that is, to "rescue ... the uncouth Shakespeare from the hands of his tasteful improvers," as Long remarks (1989, xiii), to liberate the script from stage traditions that had grown up around the text, and, particularly in this century, to recreate something like Shakespeare's original staging, even, as in the Globe project, his original production values.

D'Avenant's Witches (1673) sounded like this:

> Let's have a dance upon the Heath;
> We gain more life by *Duncan's* death.
> Sometimes like brinded Cats we shew,
> Having no music but our mew.
> Sometimes we dance in some old mill,
> Upon the hopper, stones, and wheel.
> To some old saw, or Bardish Rhime,
> Where still the Mill-clack does keep time. (in Furness 1873, 519)

D'Avenant's Macduff and Lady Macduff encounter witches, but they avoid temptation.

Macduff: He that believes ill news from such as these,
              Deserves to find it true. Their words are like
              Their shape; nothing but fiction.
              Let's hasten to our journey.

Lady Macd.: I'll take your counsel; for to permit
              Such thoughts upon our memories to dwell,
              Will make our minds the registers of hell. (520)

Macbeth's "My eye shall at my hand connive, the Sun / himself should wink when such a deed is done" normalizes both world and psyche.

D'Avenant's changes have not been retained, even in eclectic productions:

> Will all great *Neptunes* Ocean wash this blood
> Cleane from my Hand? no: this my Hand will rather
> The multitudinous Seas incarnardine,
> Making the Greene one, Red.

> My hands are of your colour: but I shame
> To weare a Heart so white.

> The divell damne thee blacke, though cream-fac'd Loone:
> Where got'st thou that Goose-looke.

These become

> Can the sea afford
> Water enough to wash away the stains?
> No, they would sooner add a tincture to
> The sea, and turn the green into a red.
>
> Thou has Hands
> Of Blood, But looks of Milk.
>
> Now friend, what means thy change of countenance? (in Furness 1873,
>   507ff)

In 1744 David Garrick wrote a dying speech for Macbeth:

> 'Tis done! The scene of life will quickly close.
> Ambitions vain, delusive dreams are fled,
> And now I wake to darkness, guilt and horror.
> I cannot bear it! Let me shake it off—
> ['Tis] not to be; my soul is clogged with blood—
> I cannot rise! I dare not ask for mercy—
> It is too late, hell drags me down. I sink,
> I sink—Oh!—my soul is lost forever.
> Oh!
> (Barnet 1987, 257–58)

This alteration was commended by Francis Gentleman: The idea of having Macbeth's head brought in by Macduff ''is either ludicrous or horrid [and is] therefore commendably changed to visible punishment—a dying speech and a very good one has been furnished by Mr. Garrick, to give the actor more eclat'' (quoted in Barnet 1987, 258).

Arthur C. L. Brown suggests that ''Macklin in 1772 was the first actor to appear as Macbeth in tartan and kilt (unless indeed the Scottish dress had been used in Shakespeare's day, as IV.3.160 may possibly indicate [in Malcolm: 'My countryman.'])'' (1913, xvi).

According to Barnet, Simon Forman's visit to the theater in 1611 is ''of little or no help'' (1987, 255) in our understanding of the early staging of *Macbeth*, but stage directions, '' 'Banquet prepared' and 'Drum and colors' strengthen our impression that the Globe offered realism of a spectacular sort'' (255). Forman's lack of descriptive detail suggests that, by the time of the second decade of the seventeenth century, staging conventions like ''banquet'' and ''courtroom'' were easily communicated to an audience, as Alan Dessen argues (1993).

A special issue in performance is that of the Porter. John B. Harcourt claims that the episode places ''Macbeth unsentimentally in a moral scale where it may be seen in its intrinsic tawdriness'' (1961, 395). No, argues Frederic B. Tromly, it is wrong to ''self-indulgently brand [Macbeth] a villain different from [the audience] and beyond their sympathetic understanding" (1975, 152). The "first half of the scene . . . translates Macbeth's crime from the distant, larger-than-life world of chronicle to the familiar realm of diminished moral expectations" (152–53). It "lowers the horizon against which Macbeth's crimes are to be judged" (Zitner 1964). Tromly suggests that "drink provides the same pathetic impotence which Lady Macbeth throws in the teeth of her husband" (1975, 154) and that "sexual frustration is a perversion of the 'fruitless crown' and 'barren sceptre' for which Macbeth finally realizes he has given his eternal jewel" (154)—like those *un*harrowed in Hell. "By translating the horrible into the familiar, the Porter scene creates a complex perspective from which to review the remaining events of the play. . . . Shakespeare employs all the resources of his art to create in this murderer-usurper a recognizable image of ourselves" (156). I doubt that the latter interpretation can be applied successfully to the Porter scene. It can be said, however, to place the murder in a world we inhabit. It has probably been noticed that the Porter is a kin of the First Clown or Gravedigger in *Hamlet* who can send out a "quick lie" and who deals with his betters with a full sense of his own ready wit and no awe of their position.

In the great Trevor Nunn production for the Royal Shakespeare Company, the Porter's music-hall approach was felt by some to be an intrusion on the tense darkness of the production. Whatever the Porter does, he should *further* the momentum of this hurtling script, not inhibit it. The pause can be like that which De Quincy describes, a moment in which horror is suspended again. *We* know what awaits these knockers-at-the-gate in the king's bedchamber. The rhythm of the knocking and then of the pause before the discovery simulates Macbeth's stop-and-start action as he decides against and for the murder itself.

Lady Macbeth's "faint" ("Helpe me hence, hoa") is a moment that points back at the calculating woman we have seen so far, who could also improvise when necessary ("Give me the Daggers") *or* ahead at the mad woman of Act Five. Realizing that Macbeth is drawing suspicion to himself by (1) having killed the grooms and (2) being so articulate about it ("His Silver skinne, lac'd with his Golden Blood"), and recognizing that she is supposed to behave like a stereotypic female ("The repetition in a Womans eare / Would murther as it fell"), and perhaps that she must atone for her "What in our House?", she feigns a collapse. Surely, she who has done so much so far would not faint at the mere *mention* of blood. Macbeth's lack of concern for her suggests that *he* knows she is playacting.

On the other hand, her recognition of what the murder *means* may be reflected to her for the first time from the faces of the thanes assembling on the cold stone floor of the castle. She has been up all night—and drinking—and, now that the murder has been discovered by the world at large, her consciousness simply gives way. Furthermore, the blood of the old man who resembled her father had a terrible effect on her, as we will learn ("yet who would have thought the olde man to have had so much blood in him"), and so the faint may be an initial signal of her later madness.

The Variorum *Macbeth* has a good discussion of the question (Furness 1873, 161–64), and A. C. Bradley's edition has a note on the issue (1904, 394–95). Where once most critics and theater practitioners believed she feigned her faint, recently opinion has swung to her actually fainting. Hall offers these options:

> [S]he sees the consequences of the crime in Macbeth, the new ability with which he tells the lie. . . . Or she may see all that is unleashed in the dramatic action: all those "spirits that tend on mortal thoughts. . . ." She sees them now: there they are, right in the head of her husband. [He expresses what she now at last understands?] Or it may be that she actually faints under the general pressure of events . . . but that's rather a boring choice for an actress to make. . . . Or it may be that she pretends to faint to distract from Macbeth's phoney excuses. [His speech is capable of radically different interpretations.] How this moment is played must depend on the production, the Lady Macbeth and how it is all working. This is one of the acts of bringing a play alive. There are often key moments which you can rationalize and say must be that way or that way, but there is no absolute in these matters. (1982, 239)

Helen Faucit, who returned the actual faint to the stage, in the face of the "eighteenth century assumption that the audience would almost certainly laugh at her obvious hypocrisy" (Carlisle 1983, 218), argued that it occurs in response to Macbeth's speech:

> [H]e recites . . . with fearful minuteness of detail, how he had found Duncan lying gashed and gory in his chamber! She had just faced that without blenching, when it was essential to replace the daggers . . . but to have the whole scene thus vividly brought again before her eyes was too great a strain upon her nerves. No wonder that she faints. (Faucit, quoted in Carlisle 219)

Of Faucit's faint, Henry Morley said that "she faints at the recurrence of the image which recalled her father. It is at Macbeth's words, 'Here lay Duncan . . . ' that she swoons" (quoted in Carlisle, 219).

Joan L. Klein looks at the pros and cons of the faint/feint: "[I]t may be that her faint is genuine, a confirmation of her debility. On the other hand, if her faint is only pretended in order to shield Macbeth, it is still a particularly feminine ploy" (in that it plays into masculine stereotyping of women as in Macduff's "gentle lady"). "True or false," Klein points out, "it dramatically symbolizes *weakness*" (1980, 248; emphasis added).

Ruth Nevo says that Lady Macbeth's "violently repressed womanhood . . . rises from the inner depths of her emotional nature to overthrow the outer superrationality in which she has dressed herself" (1972, 237). In Glen Byam Shaw's production, according to Michael Mullin, she "cannot stand the strain & loses consciousness" (1976, 103). Vivien Leigh's was a "genuine faint, not some shrewd attempt to distract people from Macbeth's embarrassment'' (Wills 1995, 84). Leigh's faint was ''as inevitable a result of the dramatic process as is the spark when two charged wires are brought together'' (David 1978, 129). Evans remarks that Helen Mirren had an objective correlative for her faint. Duncan's body was brought in, and ''on seeing it Lady Macbeth collapsed: a neatly achieved visual justification for her fainting'' (1982, 107).

Dennis Bartholomeusz argues that the feigned faint can be ''patently contrived to distract attention from Macbeth'' (1969, 252). In the Katherina Thalbach production of 1992, discussed below, even the characters on stage laughed. They knew she was feigning humanity when the question was, How is power to be disposed now? Watkins and Lemmon claim that ''[o]n the deep stage of the Globe, it is possible, though not easy, for the player to suggest that the 'faint' is deliberate'' (1974, 162). One assumes that the feigned collapse is easier to suggest because it is consistent with the Lady Macbeth the play has depicted thus far. According to Derek Russell Davis, after the murder, she experiences ''the horror and suspicion evoked in others'' and thus can no longer deny the fact and nature of the deed. Her faint ''reflects the precariousness of denial as a defense. When this defense fails, intense feelings are released, from which swooning gives a short-lived relief'' (1982, 217). Does the faint signal ''her vulnerability—which is going to lead to madness'' or is it ''yet another dem-onstration of her social adroitness, that she can faint in a womanly way at exactly the right moment to deflect attention?'' (Hall 1982, 239–40). John Russell Brown contends that ''Lady Macbeth's faint is hard to judge; she may feign it as a means of deflecting interest from her husband or it may be a first sign of the price she is to pay'' (1963, 48).

Lady Macbeth's faint is a splendidly deconstructive moment. If she faints, she signals the presence of absence; that is, something in her erases conscious-ness: ''She'' is *not* there, and the absence of presence, in which consciousness disappears, though ''she'' is still there. If the faint is feigned, she demonstrates the presence of presence, that is a self-control that simulates a loss of control, and the absence of absence, that is, she does not *really* faint. Goddard neatly has it *both* ways: ''[T]he acting by her body of an assumed fear is the surest way of opening a channel to the genuine fear she is trying to hide'' (1951, 2: 120).

Of Banquo's Ghost, J. H. Siddons ''says that Lady Macbeth, like Macbeth, sees the ghost of Banquo, but none of the reports of her performances indicates that she conveyed this to the audience'' (quoted in Sprague 1953, 260). In Henry Irving's productions, the Ghost was ''in 1877 some sort of optical illusion . . . a transparent greenish silhouette; in 1888 the ghost was a real man, who rose from a trick chair, and who later emerged from the crowd; in 1895 the ghost was not an actor but simply a shaft of blue limelight'' (Barnet 1987, 260). Trewin explains that ''some have shirked by employing an empty stool and a quivering green light, but this is a cowardly way out. Other revivals have left it to the imagination, though Shakespeare is explicit: 'Enter the Ghost of Banquo and sits in Macbeth's place.' '' (1978, 219–20). The Ghost enters at the moment Macbeth is saying to his wife, ''Sweet Remembrancer.'' Hall remarks about the Ghost, ''I am sure he just walks on. The excitement for the audience is that they see him first, and *then* Macbeth sees him. . . . Time seems to stop in this scene, so that it is experienced only in Macbeth's mind'' (1982, 246).

Terry Eagleton argues that

> Shakespeare has us share Macbeth's sight of the Ghost as a reminder of our imaginative participation not merely in the invisible murder of Duncan but in all of Macbeth's dark deeds. Beyond this, he reminds us of our complicity in the continuous dark deed he is perpetrating, the play *Macbeth*. . . . This entire ghostly play, he implies, does not lie outside our imaginations, dismissibly alien to our lives, anymore than the Ghost lies outside Macbeth's. [The] ironic effect of [Lady Macbeth's] scorn is lost if we, like her, see . . . nothing. (1967, 130–31)

We *have* participated as observers in the killing of Banquo, but that does not make us guilty of it, anymore than we are guilty of Iago's deception of Othello.

''Shakespeare's own imagination,'' states Eagleton, ''is preoccupied with the dissolution of the usual boundaries between the mind and matter, imagination and reality, ghostly presence and ghostly absence. The imagination is not an alternative to reality but continuous with it'' (1967, 131). Daggers exist in the mind and in the hand.

The new king Malcolm and the end of the play have attracted some attention and certainly, as my discussion of performance below suggests, can be variously and validly interpreted, depending on the values of a specific production. Unquestioned by previous generations, the interrogation of Malcolm is a product of recent distrust in political systems and political leaders, a good example of how zeitgeist opens up areas of the scripts to scrutiny. What follows is a brief footnote to the explication of the materialist theories discussed in Chapter 5.

Gary Wills asserts that Olivier ''identified [the play's] real problem, the way it sputters towards anticlimax in most presentations of Acts Four and Five,'' where it ''substitutes the pallid moral struggle of Malcolm and Macduff for the crackling interplay of Macbeth and his Lady'' (1995, 5). H. W. Fawkner says of the long scene in England, ''[I]t seems here as if Shakespeare, uncomfortable with this entire stabilization of his complex conception, wanted to get it out of the way as soon as possible'' (1990, 148). He ''quickly withdraws the wicked shadow that momentarily darkens the play's heroes'' (148). While the withdrawal *is* quick—its ''at-once-ment'' confuses Macduff—the scene itself is long and includes the references to Macbeth's antithesis, Edward the Confessor. Critics do find the material ''tedious'' (E. K. Chambers, quoted in Wilson 1947, 155) and ''dull and forced'' (Herbert Grierson, quoted in Wilson 1947, 155). Bradley calls it a ''fall off'' (1904, 57). G. Wilson Knight assigns the material to ''choric commentary'' (1957, 122), which, if true, would indict Shakespeare

as a suddenly miserable crafter of plays. The discomfort with stabilization attributed to Shakespeare seems to be a product of critical response. What is
remarkable about the long scene in England is how well it works on stage.

According to Andrew Gibson, Malcolm looks "like a faintly tawdry, calculating figure." His deception of Macduff is "unnecessary from the start. Stolid
Macduff is quite obviously no Machiavel" (1988, 95). Malcolm, having been
approached, as he tells us, by Macbeth's agents, has no way of knowing that
Macduff is no Machiavel, or that, even if he is not, that Macduff can be trusted.
Macbeth was not much of a Machiavel either, until he began to plan Banquo's
assassination. Furthermore, Prince Hal's verbal jousts with Falstaff seem mere
fun and games until we watch King Henry with the Chief Justice, the Archbishop, and the Cambridge conspirators. *Macbeth*, says Gibson, "associates the
victorious forces of right with dullness, mediocrity, insensitivity and emotional
boorishness" (99). Of the RSC version (with McKellen and Dench) Gibson
writes, "[A]fter the loss of the tragic hero, peace is something of an anticlimax"
(100). And that was true. Macbeth took a great energy with him from the world
and the effort to remove him had been exhausting. Shakespeare "absolutely
refuses to let us reconcile the values of imagination, feeling and poetry with
those of the good and right. He leaves us with an insoluble paradox" (100). If
so, the difference is one of style only. The values of "feeling and poetry" are
hardly those of political astuteness, as witness Richard II.

Fawkner argues that Malcolm's "necessary distrust" shows the "purity of
Grace / Kingship as somehow dislodged and disrupted" (1990, 151). But one
could ask whether Malcolm's use of necessary Machiavellian tactics means that,
while he is in that world, he has created it. No. It means only that he recognizes
the need for caution. Malcolm "pay[s] lip service [to brightness] in the construction of a banal moral dialectic within the cultural code of signification"
(152). Malcolm, like the Porter's equivocator, "swears in both scales against
either scale . . . the end justifies the means" (153). But the means themselves
are *verbal* and can be unsaid. The *end* is regicide, but of a different kind, and
the means can be seen as exorcism for Malcolm and for Scotland. A false
"presencing" leads to an erasure. We might like to believe that Shakespeare
undercuts this cultural code, since *we* not only cannot believe in it but see it as
the rationalization of tyranny, hierarchy, and patriarchy, but the undercutting
evidence is the importation of the critic. The world of the play supports quite
simply the concept of salvation/damnation. Angels *are* bright still, whether Malcolm believes it or not, whether *we* believe it or not.

Malcolm's lengthy self-detractions in act 4, scene 3 are a testing of Macduff,
of course, a means of delivering the "Childe of integrity," of discovering what
his father could not: "the Mindes construction." Macbeth has changed the rules,
and it may be that we are no longer in the sacramental world of which Duncan
was the chief secular object and architect, but which he took for granted even
after the examples of MacDonwald and Cawdor. Malcolm shows himself to be
the *politician* his father was not. But the speech is not necessarily just political.

It can be played as an exorcism, as Roger Rees played it in the RSC production. Malcolm reverses Macbeth's stance, becoming the outward serpent hiding what the true heart knows. He is, as Wills says, "a great counter-witch" (1995, 124), for himself as well as for Macduff. The speech can be played as a grappling *with* the "King-becoming Graces," a kind of prelude to kingship similar to Hal's apostrophe to the crown in the second part of *Henry IV*. It is not true, as Wilbur Sanders asserts, that the "very act of envisaging the corruption of his own nature has tainted [Malcolm]" (1968, 262).

It is self-refuting to condemn Duncan as the "weak king" and then to condemn Malcolm for not being *like* his father, therefore for not having learned from what happened to his father. The assertions of some postmodern criticism collide with themselves.

Opinion is divided on Malcolm's final speech, and, as the discussion of productions will show, it can be interpreted in very different but valid ways. L. C. Knights writes that the speech

> is a fitting close for a play in which moral law has been made present to us not as convention or command but as the law of life itself, as that which makes for life, and through which alone man can ground himself on, and therefore in his measure, now, reality. (1959, 142)

John Russell Brown, in his interview with Peter Hall, says that "Malcolm founds a new state by the exercise of a new kind of political intelligence," and Hall agrees (1982, 235).

James Calderwood, however, in paraphrasing Rene Girard (1977) states,

> The first gesture of the new king, then, is the last gesture of the play, to create the differences of Degree that proclaim an ordered society. However, as we know, from just such differences contentious "differences" arise. In endless reciprocation violence is the birth and death of meaning, and order the womb and tomb of disorder. (1986, 78)

Maynard Mack, Jr., remarks that "*Macbeth* ends with a restoration of order that is unmatched in fullness and dramatic weight in the other tragedies . . . [but with a] hard, somber mood" [as in Roger Rees's RSC Malcolm]. The king can be killed, but the whole world, human, natural, and supernatural reacts to offer a new king. Regicide is finally in some strange way impossible" (1973, 184). That is true in the theory of body politic, which Shakespeare challenges in having Lear resign, but not here. The line of kings that we and Macbeth have witnessed reinforces Malcolm's final reassertion of "measure, time, and place."

John Holloway, however, points out,

> The element of ritual in the closing scenes, their almost imperceptible relapsing into the contours of a sacrificial fertility ceremony, the expulsion, hunting down and destruction of a man who has turned into a monster, give

the action its final shape. As the action is seen to be turning into this recognizable kind of thing, this activity which has repeatedly been part of social life, its significance cannot but emerge into final clarity. The suspense and unpredictability which have held the audience's attention so strongly mutate into the working out of a movement which now seems pre-appointed. (1961, 110)

Lawrence Danson asks, "Has the order of Nature really been destroyed by Macbeth, so that 'nothing is but what is not'? Or do 'measure, time, and place' . . . still encompass and control the apparent perversion of Macbeth's reign?" Do we return to the "normal nature of Nature and 'grace of Grace' ''? (1974, 125). The line of kings suggests that we at least return to the sequence that Macbeth interrupted. What the "nature of Nature" is from then on is indeterminable.

Hannah Pritchard and Sarah Siddons, in the eighteenth century, states Marvin Rosenberg, "with the aid of textual cuts and carefully shaped characterizations, lifted the power of Lady Macbeth over her husband to such dominance that the blame for his virgin venturing into murder became almost entirely hers" (1982, 74). The famous Fuseli painting in the Tate of a furious Pritchard and a timorous Garrick on "Why did you bring these Daggers from the place?" "emphasizes," says Rosenberg, "her ruthlessness as opposed to his humanity" (74). Pritchard did not faint. "Garrick was afraid audiences would laugh at the 'hypocrisy' of so formidable a figure pretending weakness" (75). Garrick cut the assault on Lady Macduff and the killing of Young Siward. Kemble wanted Weird Sisters, but the public would not allow it (79). His was a "gentlemanly Macbeth" (78). "Kemble in 1794 dared to break with tradition by not showing the ghost of Banquo, though in 1809 (against his better judgement), he restored the ghost at the request of the public" (Barnet 1987, 259). The elimination of a "visible specter [was] adopted by Macready, Booth, and Henry Irving, although not followed by Edwin Forrest [and] the Keans" (Arthur C. L. Brown 1913, xiv).

Siddons' Lady, according to William Hazlitt, was "a being from a darker world" (quoted in Rosenberg 1982, 78). Again her Lady Macbeth did not faint. In her mad scene, her "eyes glazed with the ever-burning fever of remorse" (quoted in Rosenberg 1982, 78). Siddons would have humanized her more, but the public would not permit it. Obviously, Siddons was a powerful performer.

> As she said, "He is about it," Mrs. Siddons was bending towards the door in the act of listening—her ear so close that I could absolutely feel her breath. The words, I have said were whispered—but what a whisper was hers! Distinctly audible in every part of the house, it served the purpose of the loudest tones. (J. H. Siddons, quoted in Bartholomeusz 1969, 112)

On the sleepwalking scene, W. A. Alger reports, "Knowles replied [to Edwin Forrest] with a sort of shudder. . . . 'Well, sir, I smelt blood! I swear that I smelt blood!' '' (quoted in Sprague 1953, 67).

"Then," asserts Long, "came Edmund Keen . . . with Kean we sense the power of Romanticism's recovery of Shakespearian depths and terrors, unmodulated into the polite and classical" (1989, xiii–xiv). "Macready in the mid-century and Irving a generation later explored the depths and complexities of the play's psychological life, trying to get inside the fears and fragilities of the hero and evoking the fierce forces in life which drove him helplessly along" (xiv). The Romantics, however, "tended to lose [the] public dimension" (xv).

Carlisle says of Sarah Siddons, "Audiences had come to expect a physically impressive Lady Macbeth, overbearing in her will, Lucifer-like in her ambition, awe-inspiring even in her later suffering—a woman who served (to quote Mrs. Siddons herself)—as her husband's 'evil genius' " (1983, 205). Faucit's "Lady Macbeth," states Carlisle, "was more feminine, more human" (205), "more ambitious on her husband's account than on her own" (207). When she said, 'dash'd the Braines out'—she "did not wish . . . to transform herself into a she-fiend; her fury was that of a desperate woman" (216). Her *"We fail"* was "a concession that failure is failure and ruin to them both" (Faucit's promptbook, quoted 216).

Helen Faucit, according to Rosenberg, ushered in the shift to "an affectionate wife, rising with resolution to partner her husband in his first crime, rather than to engineer it" (1982, 79). She "could carry off the 'faint' after Macbeth's description of the dead grooms without seeming hypocritical" (81). Macbeth becomes "bloodthirsty, selfish and callous. [The] lure of the supernatural was reinstated" (82). Macready "by mid-century, had absorbed . . . Macbeth's experience of the uncanny" (83). According to Wills, "Macready . . . deepened his sense of the damned soul's defiance by reading *Paradise Lost* while performing *Macbeth*" (1995, 74). "In 1847 Samuel Phelps restored the drunken porter" (Barnet 1987, 260). Ellen Terry was "the most famous of the softer Ladies" (Rosenberg 1982, 83).

Henry Irving's "spectacular scoundrel evidently satisfied some need of the time" (85). Irving depicted a "cowardly, ambitious blackguard, who had thought of murdering Duncan long before the play begins" (85). The mind of Irving's Macbeth "has already turned to evil thoughts" in his second (1888) production, and it was for that reason that the Weird Sisters met him (Barnet 1987, 261). The late nineteenth-century productions of Irving and Beerbohm Tree represented a "slow-moving pictorial amplification" (262). During a tepid final battle, as Edwin Forrest and his Macduff stroked rapiers, a spectator is reported to have shouted, "That's right, sharpen it!" (Hornblow 1919, 2:43).

Trewin provides a useful overview of productions in the twentieth century (1978, 212–20). He quotes John Masefield: The early Macbeth should be played "not like a moody traitor, but like Lucifer, star of the morning" and, in the later scenes, "not like a hangman who has taken to drink, but an angel who has fallen" (212–13). Lady Macbeth, "surprisingly brief (255 lines)," Trewin notes, "should not be over-gunned or—in another popular reading—turned to a seductive harpy" (213). He quotes Robert Speaight, who had "grown rather tired of subtle reasoning and sophisticated imagery sitting on heads that might have worn the antlers of Hengist and Horsa'' (214). Of the Weird Sisters, ''The less fantasticated the better, and the fewest cackling laughs'' (214).

A significant footnote to the production history of this play is the riot that occurred in New York City on 10 May 1849, when William C. Macready, the English actor, appeared in *Macbeth* at the Astor Place Opera House against Edwin Forrest, the American actor, in *The Gladiator* at the Broadway Theater. The attack by Forrest's supporters on the Opera House left twenty people dead. [On this unfortunate episode, see Alan Downer (1966) and *Royal Shakespeare Company Magazine* (1990, 4–5).]

Orson Welles's 1936 production in Harlem was, according to Kennedy, the

> first major production of Shakespeare in English to select a locale for the action that was overtly foreign to the spirit of the play. . . . The first two scenes were cut entirely, so that the opening showed Macbeth and Banquo flogging through dense vegetation to come upon a circle of voodoo cele-brants—not three witches—but an entire chorus—led by a male Hecate, who set the play in motion at the end of the scene with ''Peace! The charm's wound up.'' The main setting then appeared for Lady Macbeth's letter so-liloquy (I.5), eliminating Duncan's victory and the execution of Cawdor, making a strong connection between the witches and Macbeth's rapid rise. (1993, 145)

The concept, according to Welles, emerged from ''[t]he story career of Chris-tophe, who became 'The Negro King of Haiti' and ended by killing himself when his cruelty led to a revolt [and who] forms a striking parallel to the history of Macbeth'' (quoted in Houseman 1972, 197). ''The voodoo overtones were valued for their ability to exclude whites, for their suggestion of a power specific to blacks'' (Kennedy 1993, 147). Critic Roi Otley warned ''downtown visitors that the play is purely for Harlem consumption'' (quoted in Kennedy, 147). At the time, according to John Houseman, Harlem exhibited ''the typical minority pattern: united in misery, it remained fragmented in every other respect'' (1972, 176).

The photograph included in Kennedy's book shows Malcolm seated on the throne up right (1993, 146). The Weird Sisters hold Macbeth's head on a pole (stage left), and many subjects crouch in front of Malcolm. Macduff stands in the tower above Malcolm, pointing with his sword at the severed head. This would seem to be a normative ending, but then, says Kennedy, ''Hecate stepped forward to repeat the anthem 'Peace! The charm's wound up.' Welles provided a pessimistic *de capo* ending . . . the cycle of evil beginning again with a fresh victim, hopelessly repeating ignorance and oppression—and in a black context'' (147).

Welles's *Macbeth* featured, in Hecate, ''a composite figure of evil which

Welles had assembled out of fragments of witches' lines and to whose sinister equipment he presently added a twelve-foot bullwhip'' (Houseman 1972, 189–90). Houseman reports that another of Hecate's company, ''Abdul, an authentic witch doctor, seemed to know no language at all except magic.'' He requisitioned ''five live black goats [which were] sacrificed, hugger-mugger, according to approved tribal ritual, before being stretched into resonant drum skins'' (190). ''Later,'' relates Houseman,

> when we insisted, they did somewhat darken the tone of their incantations. For that reason, I was unnerved when, one night, in the first witch scene, I quite distinctly heard, amid the incomprehensible sounds of Abdul's unknown tongue, the words ''Meesta Welles'' and ''Meesta Houseman'' several times repeated. I never told Orson, for he was ridiculously superstitious. (193)

The banquet, says Houseman, featured ''nineteenth-century waltzes [interrupted by a] wild, high, inhuman sound that froze them all in their tracks, followed by Macbeth's terrible cry as the spirit of Banquo, in the shape of a huge luminous death mask, suddenly appeared on the battlements to taunt him in the hour of his triumph'' (200).

Critic Martha Gellhorn, who ignored Otley's advice to stay away, relates

> *Macbeth* will remain in this audience's mind from now on, as a play about people living in a Haitian jungle, believing in voodoo, frightened and driven and opulent people with shiny chocolate skins who moved about the stage superbly, wearing costumes that belonged to them and suddenly belonged to the play . . . the impression was of a hot richness that I have almost never seen in the theatre or anywhere else. (quoted in Houseman 1972, 201)

Someone who should have stayed away was Percy Hammond, who wrote a negative review in the *Herald-Tribune*, a Republican, vehemently anti–New Deal morning paper. The production, according to Hammond, was ''an exhibition of deluxe boondoggling'' (quoted in Houseman 1972, 202). Abdul performed a voodoo rite and Hammond died a few days later of what was called pneumonia (203).

Jack Carson, who played Macbeth, walked out in mid-show one night and was replaced by the stage manager, Tommy Anderson:

> No announcement was made and the audience, that night, had the strange experience of seeing the first half of Shakespeare's tragedy performed by a very pale, six-foot-four hero in a glittering bright yellow costume and the second by a dark, wiry, mustachioed five-foot-seven Macbeth in the dark-red uniform of one of Macduff's barefoot soldiers. (Houseman 1972, 204)

When Maurice Ellis, who took over for Carson as Macbeth, fell ill, Welles, who "had been waiting for just this chance . . . flew out [to Indianapolis] and played the role in blackface for the rest of the week" (205).

According to critic Brooks Atkinson:

> The witches' scenes . . . have always worried the life out of the polite, tragic stage: the grimaces of the hags and the garish make-believe of the flaming cauldron have bred more disenchantment than anything else that Shakespeare wrote. But ship the witches into the rank and fever-stricken jungle echoes, stuff a gleaming naked witch doctor into the cauldron, hold up Negro masks in the baleful light—and there you have a witches' scene that is logical and stunning and a triumph of the theatre art. (quoted in Houseman 1972, 199)

On the relationship between this production and Welles's subsequent film version, see Bernice W. Kliman (1992 and 1995).

Gareth Lloyd Evans offers a useful description of eight Royal Shakespeare Company productions from 1946 to 1980. "It is perhaps less difficult to exploit ironies of social, political and human behaviour between Then and Now than to file the Tragedies, with their complex temporal and psychological patterns, in the modern idiom" (Evans 1982, 88). The play was long a victim of a star system. The "post-restoration tradition" dictated "that whatever role the star played—good or evil—was not allowed, indeed conspicuously not allowed, to expunge a certain high directness, nobility, and a well-spoken, larger-than-life image of the idol" (1982, 90).

Godfrey Tearle "caressed the words as if their poetry were more important than their dramatic implications" (Evans 1982, 90). Ralph Richardson, a great Falstaff, was

> witty and intellectual . . . his voice, gestures and mien gave him no rendez-vous with high poetry. . . . Tearle created a Thane that was predictably grand and civilised, Richardson simply failed dismally, Scofield's was consistently out of sorts with its surrounding production, Porter's had the dullness of intellectual clarity, almost totally devoid of emotional vibrancy and Nicol Williamson, again predictably, confused eccentric behaviour with perceptive acting. (1982, 88–90)

"Robert Harris . . . lacked power. Evil was absent and was replaced by a head-shaking regret for a moral miscalculation which was deeply vexatious but not profoundly disturbing. 'His devil was a home-sick angel,' " according to Ruth Ellis (quoted in Evans, 89).

Valerie Taylor's "sleep-walking scene became a kind of penance for a bad social *gaffe* and completely neglected to depict the sickening reality of a mind turned and twisted to a memory which is a relentless shadow-version of her husband's imagination" (Evans 1982, 89–90). "Siobhan McKenna . . . refused to allow the sentimental aura generated by Shakespeare's hideous stage-child to fog her performance" as Lady MacDuff (92). While Vivien Leigh's Lady Macbeth opposite Olivier was "already curiously sexless" (96), Helen Mirren's "fall from normalcy is seen as a direct consequence of sexual deprivation" (106).

According to Evans, "Olivier's Macbeth marks the beginning of the end of a theatre-world that had persisted since the time of Shakespeare" (1982, 94). "[T]here is nothing philosophical about Macbeth. Images haunt him, not ideas" (97). "Olivier created an overwhelming sense of growing spiritual fatigue in a man haunted by some of the questions the play leaves us wondering about" (97). For "this actor," asserts Evans, "the tragic always walks within one theatrical ell of the absurd, the bizarre, the darkly foolish" (98). He synthesized "all elements . . . high and low verbal tension, poetry and prose, plain and decorated—to the end of intensifying the dramatic impact of character" (99).

According to Wills, Olivier's "Be innocent of the knowledge . . ." was "said with a kind of bemused tone of farewell" (1995, 83). Grove offers this about the Olivier-Leigh version: "[W]hat binds these two together is not ambition or bloodlust or fear alone, it is love: married love" (1982, 133). Their castle was quiet, the center of a vortex of storm and roughness. Lady Macbeth's lines about the "surfeited grooms" were "[w]ondering, heavy, lyrical, the voice sounds like that of the tenderness she used to know . . . [*not*] tigerish snarls" (135). Olivier depicted a triumph "over fear and conscience, only to have them rise again" (137). He charged the Ghost, chased it away, and was calm when he said, "Why so, being gone . . ." Grove contends that he "goes to his damnation open-eyed" (138).

According to Evans, Eric Porter's "Tomorrow" speech was "spoken with furious irritation: the idiot in charge had committed an irrational act in creating the universe, but this realisation offended Macbeth rather than drove him to despair" (1982, 101). Williamson's "speaking of dramatic verse conspicuously avoids the benedictions of rhythm and the other resources of poetry" (105). "There is a kind of stony-faced selfishness about it. . . . Its chief weakness is its total avoidance of everything that is meant, both in human and theatrical terms, by the word 'grace' " (106).

Of the 1976–1977 Trevor Nunn version, Evans remarks,

> The acting surrounding the Principals—Ian McKellen and Judi Dench—was, by far, the strongest of the period under review: notably John Woodvine's physically tough, slightly calculating, near flash-point Banquo; Roger Rees's intelligent, handsome, spiritually exhausted Malcolm, totally aware of the knife-edge he trod upon between Macbeth's murderous existence and Macduff's unknown motivation; and Griffith Jones's Duncan, saintly in look, grave and deliberate in speech—every inch the good king, yet in his first encounter with Macbeth seeming to be very vulnerable to age and to the obvious political eying and weighing of the court around him. (108)

Dench portrayed "a venomous but vulnerable and credible human being" (108). McKellen "hypnotise[d] the audience as they, in their turn, watched this man look with horror on what was happening inside and outside himself" (108). However, the "production lacked . . . a sense of chaos, both internal and external, and a sense of damnation—ritual and reflection seemed to insulate this Macbeth from the ultimate despair" (109). If Olivier showed Macbeth's "enormous undeveloped capabilities" (David 1978, 92) as Macbeth wanders through an increasingly limited world, McKellen showed how well Macbeth functions *in* that world, developing suave political skills that are finally irrelevant. I disagree with Evans about the production's emphasis on damnation, but McKellen's fascist Macbeth did involve a trade-off of the script's wilder outreach for a depiction of institutionalized evil.

A powerful production by the Haworth Shakespeare Festival at Clemson, South Carolina (15 March 1995) had a Lady Macduff (Irma Innis) who imagined her son's responses and spoke them for the infant. The production, set in Africa, obviously borrowed from Welles. Lady Macbeth's body lay downstage during much of the final action, and the final sword fight took place on the platform above the main stage. The imposition of a setting alien to the script vivified rather than blurred the issues of the play.

An earlier adaptation, *Umabatha* (1972), was based on the issue of Zulu identity in nineteenth-century South Africa, specifically the northeastern section of Natal along the Indian Ocean. The script "translates" inasmuch as traditional Zulu religion was based on ancestor worship, a creator, witchcraft, and sorcery. The king was responsible for rainmaking and other magic essential to the health of the tribe. According to Rex Gibson, "Chanting, drumming, and rhythmically beating shields, a huge cast created a tribal *Macbeth* of immense ritual power" (1993, 171).

Modern directors apparently no longer believe that the "holy-supernatural" element of *Macbeth* can be transmitted to an audience. One of the last efforts to do so was Nunn's, in which Griffith Jones (Duncan) prayed fervently in a futile effort to dispel a looming storm of evil and where, later, liturgical music washed ironically against the wreckage of Macbeth's "last supper." In that production, the discrepancy between the loving cup that Ian McKellen (Macbeth) passed around and the blood on the Murderer's face was made clear, and Judi Dench's Lady Macbeth was not *at* the table. Thus the production enforced the distinction that Shakespeare's script makes in basing the scene on the Eucharist—the "notorious evil liver must not presume to approach the Lord's Table until he [or she] hath amended his [or her] former naughty way of life" (*Book of Common Prayer* 1605) Nunn considered that the Christian heritage was still available to an audience of the late 1970s. If not, the production educated its audience about a world where even those who would "cancel" the world's order must express the possible destinations of their victims within the inevitable terms of inevitability, heaven and hell, and where the murderer is chief victim, rendering his "eternal jewel" to "deep damnation." All of that is there in the script. The Nunn production was spare and fast paced, playing through its two and a quarter hours without interval. Its "depth" came from great acting *and* the resonance of "deepest consequence" of the antique world-view vibrating under the vivid actions of characters striving to live in a different, "modern" world. Nicholas Brooke suggests, "The odd stress on religious rituals which had been tedious in the main theatre [in Nunn's 1974 production] was neutralized here because it seemed a convenient device to organize the play in what was very nearly a round space" (1990, 47). In fact, the stress seemed not "odd" but one which came from deeply inside the inherited script. Brooke suggests that "it was the narrative, not the characters of the protagonists, that prevailed, with extraordinary tension" (47).

None of the three productions of *Macbeth* in Great Britain in early 1992 made any effort to depict or to develop the sense of the positive supernature that the script details, and, it follows, none of these productions could make much of the "instruments of darkness" that the script also treats at length. These were not "tragedies of damnation," in which the fall of both Macbeth and Lady Macbeth can be charted against the huge dimension of an ethereal sky whose brows overlook the smolder of bottomless perdition, but narratives of political disaster and failed personal relationships. Yet the exploration of even a limited sector of this script shows how alive it still is, and produced radically different productions, two out of three of which were excellent: the Schiller Theatre production at the Mermaid and the Buttonhole Theatre Production at the New End Theatre in Hampstead. The English Shakespeare Company subjected its actors to a nightmare out of *Das Kapital*, overpowering their work quite literally with machinery—the rationale being, one assumes, that Marx's great work was written in England only about 250 years after *Macbeth*. That the latter is hardly a critique of even the Elizabethan world picture is of no matter. The script was reduced to banalities like equating Lady Macbeth's "violent delights" to "the most contemporary case of child-abuse" (Holderness 1992, 2). The search for explicit modernity can reduce the script to irrelevance and incoherence, and here the effort at "intertextuality" was an invitation to a nihilism that the theatre can *depict* but that it should not *represent*.

The Schiller *Tragodie des Macbeth* was in German (Dorothea Tieck's translation) and was "obviously not Shakespeare Stratford-style" (Billington 1992, 21). It received a standing ovation from a full house. Given the reverential treatment Shakespeare usually gets in England—Deborah Warner being a positive exception and Michael Bogdanov usually a negative one—it was not surprising that this production, full of Brechtian alienation devices, multimedia effects, and explicit sexuality should be greeted so enthusiastically.

The response, however, was not just to something new and strange. Director Katharina Thalbach's staging was brilliant. The set incorporated two basic playing areas: a large platform, with a staircase that could open down to it and fold up again, and the apron around the platform. This format threatened the actors

with the "Desdemona's Bed" syndrome, where a central object inhibits ma-
neuverability, but movement, both physical and chronological, was quick and
fluid, except where pauses were built intentionally into scenes. A third playing
area was a rope network, a horizontal spider's web, to which the Weird Sisters
climbed "into the air" and from which they chirped through a miked-up link
to a synthesizer. They sounded like 33-and-1/3 speeded up to 45 rpms but
contrasted effectively with the shrieks and moans that made up the "vocal or-
chestration" of this production. Thalbach (1992) said that the idea for this rope
network came from the alternative title for Kurosawa's great film, "Throne of
Blood," which is "The Castle of the Spider's Web."

The platform proved versatile. It served as heath, the site of the Bleeding
Captain's epic tale, the empty space around which the thanes sat in terrible
silence after the murder of Duncan—Banquo staring accusingly at Macbeth—
and the table at which Macbeth enticed the two Murderers, Macbeth motioning
that they come closer and closer to him in a wonderful mime of entrapment.
Marcus Vollenklee (Macbeth) explained that the primary function of the platform was to suggest that "Power is handled on tables" (1992). Deals fall apart
on tables as well. The platform was the table for the banquet, for which Lady
Macbeth spread a huge white cloth. The platform became the Macbeths' bed;
the tablecloth became the sheet with which they engaged in a tug-of-war as they
wrestled with uneasy slumber. As Macbeth struggled with the image of Banquo
for the red robe of kingship during the Apparitions Scene, the lights suddenly
came up, showing Macbeth tossing in nightmare, the red robe his "insecurity
blanket." Banquo had melted into the surrounding darkness within a sequence
that represented a splendid "special effect." The platform became Dunsinane,
buttressed by ten huge panels that were pulled up to face outward and "laugh
a siege to scorn." It became a wrestling ring in which Macbeth and Macduff
engaged in a parody combat that spilled, of course, into the space around the
ring.

The best integration of platform and outer stage occurred at the end. The
format allowed Siward and his soldiers to arrive outside Dunsinane even as
action continued within it. The sense of "surroundedness" was augmented by
the ropes that dropped down around the central platform—the ropes a metonymy
for Birnam Wood and a reminder that the Sisters' prophecies were even now
dropping around Macbeth. Young Siward challenged Macbeth by knocking
down one of the elevated panels. When Young Siward was killed, Macbeth
tipped the panel up again, sliding the body back into the space outside Dunsinane. Macduff launched his attack on Macbeth by knocking down another panel.
As Macbeth was about to deliver a prophecy-defeating deathblow, another panel
fell, catching Macbeth's sword on the upswing. Later, Macduff freed that sword
and used it to decapitate Macbeth. This final sequence was a brilliant, minia-
turized emblemization of action that pulled our imaginations forward even as
we marveled at the skill and timing of the stagecraft.

Yet another playing area was a small platform, stage right, on which the scene in England was played. This area—up right—associates itself with distant and romantic tonalities, and here Malcolm was an effete tea drinker, listening to songs from another play ("In the spring-time, the only pretty ring-time"). In the meantime, Macbeth had become the gross, fat-legged politician of German cartoons of the 1920s, so the rugged Macduff had no options but was, like many people of integrity in any system, faced with equally unacceptable choices for leader. Malcolm was a reluctant victor. He turned away from the bloody farce of combat and had to be forced by Macduff to accept the crown. Macduff lay red hands on Malcolm, making Malcolm's tunic of Macduff's "color." The new king bore, as Paul Taylor nicely put it, "the *stain* of succession" (1992, 30; emphasis added). Malcolm's final "We shall not spend a large expense of time," in which he "anglicizes . . . the thanes . . . as earls" (Brooke 1990, 49) was delivered in English, as if the change in language could somehow placate the hungry tiger of power facing him. His panicky words were tossed into a rising cacophony of sound and fury.

Thalbach's smaller platform also became *the* stage, as when Lady Macbeth came down the stairs, sweeping them in preparation for Duncan's visit. She recited Macbeth's letter, which she had almost learned by heart. She pulled it from her apron pocket to finish reading it and held it out to us for our verification. (The kingship, Thalbach said, is *their* baby.) She then tore up the letter. Its fragments, however, remained in view, at once a visual incrimination and a reminder of sundered expectations. One of the best moments on the smaller stage occurred when Macbeth descended from the murder room. After "I have done the deed," he and Lady Macbeth stood side by side in front of the red-lit stairs, absorbing the impact after all of their nerving up *for* the deed. They felt their own relationship crumbling into emptiness. Another good moment in this space was the lineup of three candles in darkness—Waiting Woman, Lady Macbeth, and Doctor—in the mad scene, an echo of the three flashlights the Weird Sisters had used earlier.

Two other excellent moments were Lady Macbeth's "faint" and Banquo's arrival at the banquet. Her collapse was fraudulent, and even she recognized that it had been a silly effort to appear but as a "gentle lady." The issue was political, not moral or legal. Everyone knew who had borne the knife. When Macbeth said of Banquo, "would he were here," Macbeth spread his cloak wide to suggest how complete things would be then. When he dropped his arms, Banquo stood at his left shoulder, here indeed! It was yet another of the stunning transitions in a production that splendidly suited word to action, action to word.

At the end, downstage of the freeze-framed "coronation," the Three Sisters flashed their lights over the audience, "We need not NEW masters, but NONE!" This effort to go beyond Caliban was gratuitous—the excessive verge on which this production trembled time after time as it made its subtextual commentaries on the actions the script dictates. It was, however, the end of the show and it suggested, as Polanski had done in his film, that evil is a separate entity. The script does not support Manicheism, but that is a quibble when poised against such a vibrant and inventive production—the kind of revivification of a script that we always hope for but seldom get.

A major problem with the production was a "rock" inset for Hecate, complete with a revolving globe that sprinkled reflections against the walls of the auditorium. The visual effect was splendid, incorporating the audience within the space of performance. But this was a performance quite apart from the pressures of drama, diverting us from the ways in which the Macbeth myth was being redelivered, yanking us from the sequential rhythms that were being so vividly recreated for us. The idea, of course, was to show that even the scripted world of the play is subject to attack by disintegrative forces. The interpretation per se showed that much, even within the narrowed focus of a purely political world that showed, as Michael Billington remarks about this production, "[P]ower stems not from the brain but from an area squarely below the belt" (1992, 21). This Duncan, for example, was no sainted king but a skull-faced old lecher who peered at Lady Macbeth's bosom (admittedly open for inspection) and, knowing that Macbeth was busy elsewhere, grabbed a final kiss that she could only half refuse. Little did he know that, as he planned assignation, she plotted assassination.

Thalbach said that she had reservations about the rock interpolation. She saw the moment as a kind of "time-tunnel—to our time and back again" (1992). She suggested that the music creates a break in a production without an interval. She said that the management in Dublin (where the production had been before its three-performance stop in London) had insisted on an interval, perhaps because the bar trade had been brisk before the performance or would be during the interval.

The rock interlude was a gratuitous imposition on a postmodernist production from which the Elizabethan world picture had been excised and replaced by a bleak, existential vision, as Thalbach's editing made clear. Duncan's "This castle has a pleasant seat" got a big laugh, it being so inconsistent with the shabby truth. Banquo's subsequent description of "procreant cradles" was cut—though Thalbach had bird sounds twittering fatuously during Duncan's speech—as was, inevitably, the apotheosis of Edward the Confessor in 4.3.

The scene that got the biggest laughs was the murder at Fife (4.2). Lady Macduff was a grotesquely pregnant hag who lugged her huge, idiot son from place to place and spoon-fed him. The audience's laughter was cruel—endorsed by Artaud—and uneasy. Lady Macduff scuttled with her youngster, piggy-back, away from the murderers, unaware that junior was dead. She was stabbed in the belly, so that the play's preoccupation with infanticide was visualized and, with the splendid duplicity of this production, Macduff's announcement of his own bloody entrance was anticipated.

The scene at Fife is, of course, a culmination—from much reported bloodshed to its presentation and, from there, to the counterpattern of nemesis and Macduff's revenge. It is easily the best scene in the BBC-TV version, and it is powerful even in the Polanski film, which by then has splashed a lot of gratuitous blood at us. Polanski's Murderer pauses to admire an exotic bird and shares his appreciation by smiling at its owner, Lady Macduff. In the Thalbach production, the scene was a locus of absurdity, as if two characters from Pinter, discussing the merits of fried bread, were broken in upon by agents of the holocaust or of hell itself. Macduff's memories were revealed as necessary rationalizations. All my pretty ones? Perhaps he had had hopes for the unborn child.

As might be expected, the reviews were mixed. Billington rightly argued that Thalbach's Weird Sisters, or "victorious vamps," tended to deny that "evil works . . . through the agency of human will" (1992, 21). But Billington, whatever his struggle with memories of *Macbeth* as tragedy, correctly called this manifestation emblematic of "a savage . . . force that constantly equates power with sex." And he remarks that the production "brings out, in a way British productions rarely do, . . . despotism's mixture of moral ugliness and farcical absurdity" (21). Paul Taylor recognized that "there's precious little that's tragic" about the production (1992, 30). If "tragedy" involves an "error in judgement" (*hamartia*), one must have a context against which to project the error. Here Macbeth's decision was a slightly more violent reiteration of the inherited way of doing things. Taylor found the production "bracingly iconoclastic," even if "rudely flattened into a brutal, black comic strip" (30). Malcolm Rutherford felt that the London run was too short and that "such a pyrotechnic performance . . . really ought to have been given a run of several weeks at the National or the Barbican." Thalbach tended to make *Macbeth* "a play without feeling [or] development. That's Brecht: all symbols and no individuals" (1992, 23). Attacks came from Irving Wardle and Michael Arditti. Wardle wondered "what is to be gained by reducing a moral tragedy to a brutal comic strip?" The production proved only that "the German stage [is] overfunded, director-dominated, and swimming in blood" (1992a, C-21). Arditti, again, played Thalbach against the script's ostensible genre. This production "subscribes to the post-war shibboleth that tragedy is dead. Her *Macbeth* is Ionesco's rather than Shakespeare's. [The] production is constantly played for immediate effect rather than for dramatic truth" (1992, 45). No "catharsis" occurred, no release of pity and fear as a result of our vicarious sharing of humanity with the tragic hero. Arditti applied a pre-Kottian thesis that does not account for a Central European projection of the script as a condemnation of the modern political system. The depiction of an authoritarian—or totalitarian—government through the medium of *Macbeth* satirizes our own constitutional systems. That harsh satire—as if the play were directed by Swift—is the production's "truth," and we are free to reject it. Macbeth, down left—negotiating with his conscience—found his dagger not in the air but in the auditorium. We were his alter egos, as hungry for power as he was and as willing to achieve it by any means as long as we did not have to face "judgement here."

This was existentialist drama for which this script can work. Peter Brook's bleak stage and film versions of *King Lear* drew criticism similar to Arditti's, and that is a script that supports a nihilistic vision better than *Macbeth*. Shakespeare's scripts *must* emerge from the confines of academic definition, which will perpetuate only coteries that make Shakespeare "elitist" (if that has not already happened). Shakespeare *must* escape the restrictions that Aristotle, defining tragedy on the basis of Sophocles's *Oedipus*, or Bradley, emerging from Hegel in an age of ponderous proscenium productions, might impose on the ongoing energies of a given script. It may be that the larger aesthetic dimensions are no longer available to a culture in which "tragedy" now equates to everyday events. It may be that since the egalitarian trends of the late eighteenth century a great man's fall can be only political. Certainly the need for personal appearances and the ubiquity of the television camera have broken down the distance between the common man and "greatness." The politician as "star" is now a commonplace. Where distance still applies, as in the royal family of England, there is no corresponding power, only ceremony or scandal. It is still possible for a production of one of Shakespeare's plays to educate us to its worldview, which in the case of *Macbeth* is very conservative. Nunn's *Macbeth* is an example. But it is not necessary for the worldview to be a "given," nor is it necessary for a production of a classic play to reflect older critical theories, even, if, as I have argued here, they still apply to the play as "literature." A production can be a freeing *from* literature, a replacing of literary with dramatic values. A director who has a new vision of a script—a Brook or a Warner—as opposed to the trendy surfaces with which most directors cover their *lack* of vision—can force us to look at the script anew, in light of what it has always been capable of saying but which it has not communicated until the historical circumstances and the imaginative director coincide. We suddenly discover that "our times" have been there all along, and the text in the museum's glass case breaks out one more time. Thalbach's production took several steps in the right direction, as objections to it based on "classical" approaches to Shakespeare proved. Thalbach's *Macbeth* took the play's view of the world seriously by mocking it. The caricature characterizations, the "staginess" (at times dazzling), and the editing of the script emerged from a skepticism that took none of the inherited material for granted and that was calculated to offend those who, as Noam Chomsky says, "learn about the world from the doctrinal framework that they are exposed to and . . . are expected as part of their professional obligation to propagate" (1986, 14).

The audience did respond to "bracing iconoclasm." Thalbach insisted on a reconsideration of what the Scottish Play means and of what "tragedy" means. A good production invariably challenges our preconceptions about the script, its genre, or the zeitgeist in which the production occurs. Arditti saw Thalbach as a Wizard of Oz, working with "an empty box of tricks" (1992, 45). Tricks aplenty here—and they did not add up to some unified "vision" or "single, powerful effect." But the production showed what Central Europe learned long ago and what the rest of the industrialized Western world is learning now. Regardless of the apparently affirmative closure of the play, the world around it moves in a history without *telos*. Here, no line of kings marched solemnly but surely into the seventeenth century. Instead, Macbeth awoke in a sweaty fever, aware that he was just a player in an endless sequence of murdered and murderer kings. That can be said of Macbeth. Whether it can be said of *Macbeth* is another question. Thalbach's was a *radical* interpretation, and certainly her thesis can be debated, even refuted, but her interpretation resulted in a splendid production. That is what the script is there for.

The Buttonhole version was in many ways the opposite of the Schiller, and, again, the two productions help define the spectrum across which this script can play.

Space defines what can occur within it. The Buttonhole's New End Theatre, in Hampstead, seats about 100 people. The play was modulated to a conversational level that did not clash with the World War II costuming. It takes actors of great skill to cool the language of this heated script, but the Buttonhole company did so, pulling the audience forward toward their admirably understated performances.

This was "micro-acting" modulated to the "cool medium," but, as seldom or ever happens on television, this acting created a powerful continuum of energy in the theatre, a system that is the product of our inhabiting the same space as the actors. The field of energy was particularly noticeable during the first half of the play (with the interval after the banquet scene) and during Lady Macbeth's superb sleepwalking scene.

Unlike the Schiller production, the Buttonhole stressed the development of character as opposed to the mocking of politics. This Duncan was not a pale, dirty old man, an object of ridicule because he *is* king, but an older general, in fact the only person over thirty in the production—thus in the world of the play—until the same actor (Bernard Lawrence) doubled later as Siward. Lawrence was an affectionate Duncan not sufficiently aware of the ambition of the rising generation. One powerful effect of this casting was that, once in power, the Macbeths were tentative and unsure of themselves, having knocked off their mentor and role model. More might have been made of Siward, given Malcolm's youth and Macduff's personal agenda. Siward might have reminded us of Duncan and suggested, through the filter of retrospective irony, that not all old men block the young from reaching their goals.

This was not some tragedy in which crimes smash against the face of the cosmos, but a powerful narrative of a failed relationship. Sally Mortemore's Lady Macbeth was a woman whose life and being were predicated upon her husband's career. Certainly the script supports that approach to the role. This Lady Macbeth, thin and icily reserved (her reserve a shield for her shyness), had nothing of her own and no one to share anything with—except Macbeth and his ambition. Her goal was to promote his desires even if that meant poisoning the milk of his human kindness and, in a future she could neither foresee nor consciously experience, her own.

Macbeth, however, as chillingly delivered by Ian Reddington, began to enjoy his evil career, smiling at the language he discovered as he contemplated vivid inner imagery and began to perform deeds without names. True, he got in over his head, since the ghost of Banquo—or whatever it was—went beyond even Macbeth's imaginative constructs ("Take any shape but *that*"). But Macbeth wouldn't share. Lady Macbeth asked eagerly, "What's to be done?" Let me in on it, please! But she was rebuffed, treated as a stereotypical woman, as Macduff had dealt with her earlier ("The repetition in a woman's ear"). Once more she was alone, and, in retrospect, we realized that the only moment when she achieved her goal was when Macbeth descended from the murder room and she exclaimed, "My husband!" Immediately, she had to take those daggers back into that terrible room where her alter-ego father lay in his blood. Having attempted to create a future for her husband, and thus for herself, she was thrust forever into the past, as 5.1 shows. The previous scene ends with Malcolm's "The night is long that never sees the day." Good direction like that of Chris Geelan swings us instantly into the next scene, which shows that Lady Macbeth has indeed found an endless night: "Hell is murky."

The banquet scene is notorious. It is the moment in the script where a chuckle can begin to bubble in a single bosom, grow to an undercurrent of communal amusement, and expand until people are stamping their feet and begging hand-kerchiefs of strangers in order to mop up the wild tears of their hilarity.

Here it was powerful. An offstage piano played "Strangers in the Night" so that some of the tension of the ambush scene could be siphoned off. Geelan chose not to have an apparition appear, a choice appropriate to a scaled-down modern world where the supernatural tends to be attributed to the disturbances of a single psyche. But this was a much more potent treatment than that which Alan Dessen attributes to televisual visitations from the supernatural, which are also narrowed to the psychological (1986, 1, 8). The absence of the thing in the Buttonhole production made Macbeth's sudden starts even more effective than had he been sharing them with a bleeding Banquo. Macbeth has been enjoying the dark world of his invention and has been inventing himself within it. He has forgotten what he once knew—how terrible it is to kill someone. He is now reminded—as Lady Macbeth will be from the resources of a deeper repression and a deeper understanding, from an Augustinian standpoint, of what she has done to herself. The minimalist approach of this production gave remarkable impact to the suggestion of larger powers beyond the manipulative reach of the protagonists.

Lady Macbeth mustered some final energy in the banquet scene. In a wonderful manipulation of point of view, we watched Macbeth watch Lady Macbeth "sit" on the Ghost as she said, "What? Quite unmann'd in folly?" We could almost picture the Ghost as Macbeth cried out at the terribly dangerous thing she was doing. Macbeth recovered and taught his guests to moan and shake their hands, like children pretending to be afraid of the bogeyman. They responded with sound and gesture when the Ghost reappeared and Macbeth shouted "Avaunt, and quit my sight!" Again, our point of view was nicely split—partly with Macbeth within his zone of terrible knowledge, and partly in the "natural" world of his wife and guests about which Macbeth can wonder even as he trembled at what he believed they must see too. Our own sense of humor could respond here, and we could chuckle when Macbeth, having toppled table, food, and wine onto the floor, said, "Pray you, sit still!," to his scattering guests. The scene struck a balance between our responding *as* Macbeth, as the intimate style had earlier invited us to do, but which we would have had to refuse to do as we laughed at him, and our responding *to* his wild behavior, as his movement into singularity insists that we do as the drama continues. We were asked to give a complex response here, and that response did allow for some wry laughter, but not the paroxysm that, in other productions, emerges in occasional outbursts even during Lady Macbeth's mad scene. Geelan's direction of the banquet scene was so skillful that no description of it can capture the complicated response he elicited from his audience. With the exception of Dr. Johnson and Poe, criticism is seldom as good as and never a substitute for that which is criticized. That is particularly true of live theater, which is its own unique experience occurring at a moment within the continuum between stage and spectator. Those moments can be savored later, and the recollection in tranquility *is* part of the experience, just inside the outer parenthesis that encapsulates the event of a live production of one of Shakespeare's scripts.

Other arresting moments in this production included Banquo's soliloquy ("Thou hast it now"), which was delivered under the stage's long upper platform on which Macbeth and Lady Macbeth, backs to us, acknowledged the "cheers" of the people. Banquo's fears were all the more authentic for the background of mechanically reproduced sound, which was a response to the "false face" of Macbeth's kingship. Macbeth's manipulation of the nervous and scruffy Murderers (Clive Kendall and Gerard Heys) was amusing, showing us how beautifully this sequence can work on stage. He invited them to sit in the two thrones. They put their fannies down very gingerly while Macbeth leaned his arms against the back of the thrones and chatted with them. Later, First Murderer (Kendall) was disappointed not to be invited to join Macbeth's dinner guests. He thought he had earned a knighthood within this debased dispensation. Ideology must be careful about whom it pretends to befriend. After 4.1, Macbeth found a doll abandoned by one of the Sisters. It cued his attack on Fife and, later, he touched it with his sword when he told Macduff, "My soul is too much charged / With blood of thine already." In 4.3., Macduff, having said, "No, not fit to live!" almost killed Malcolm with Malcolm's own bottle of Scotch. Malcolm's escape, it seemed, was as lucky as Fleance's.

Modernizations of Shakespeare invariably run into some problems, and this "most medieval" of Shakespeare's plays is never an exception. Two problems were not disabling but neither necessary either. First: we may not bow to kings anymore but we surely do salute generals. Neither Macbeth nor Banquo knew how to greet Duncan after battle (1.4), and the meeting was awkwardly conducted. Second: toward the end, Macbeth, buoyed by false promises, sat in Dunsinane as if it were a health club. He scrawled "FEAR NOT" on the wall and relaxed in his sweatshirt and shorts. He had put on cat's whiskers with grease paint to show that he had nine lives to go along with his three ears. One could argue that by this time Macbeth has sundered his links with humanity, having become the beast that the metaphors, including his own, make him, and that he lives within the illusory security of the allegory he has constructed of surface meanings. But the alienation devices were stylistically inconsistent with the production's earlier muted and naturalistic values and robbed us of the sense of horror that we might have shared with Macbeth—this time—at the loss of a humanity so convincingly evoked for us earlier. Those brief and barren later soliloquies are lost if the character delivering them is merely ludicrous. Eric Porter, for example, shouted, "It is a tale told by an idiot!," in the Classic Theater television production of 1974 as the camera rose judgmentally above him and the words echoed down around his ankles, indicting *him* for idiocy. But that curse of God, one of the stages in the Kubler-Ross pattern, created a complex moment in which Macbeth recognized meaninglessness but still needed something to blame for what he had done to himself. Such complexity is not easily created from behind cat's whiskers.

At the end of the Buttonhole production, Malcolm stood on the platform above the main stage. This was a young Malcolm, frail alongside his stalwart colleagues. He also favored a potation—not the tea of the Thalbach production but Johnny Walker Black. While the sounds of dubious battle were not as thunderous here as in the Thalbach version, the restoration in the Buttonhole seemed at best perfunctory and temporary, unless Malcolm proves to be a quick read. And he might. Malcolm (Steven Elder) paused on "we" in the final speech. He was speaking for the first time as "King of Scotland"—a title absorbing heredity, as the elective title, "King of Scots," would not. He thus erased the consistent "I" of his previous detractions. We were left with the hopes and fears that accompany any beginning.

The Weird Sisters, malicious schoolgirls from some nightmare of Stephen King, remained, repeating the opening scene in an undefined space soon to incorporate another play. They pulled another name from the First Sister's purse. Two and a half hours before, the paper had said "Macbeth." This time it said "Michael Bogdanov."

Bogdanov's was by far the weakest of the three 1992 productions. To explore the script as modern drama that no longer creates links with some grand cosmic design is one thing. That approach keeps the script alive for us even as Jacobean England recedes into unrecoverable "historicity." To falsify the script is something else. The cultural materialist argument collides here with what the script tells us, or, to put it another way, the critical thesis conflicts with what the characters believe to be the personal and cosmic *facts* of their world. To take the script and press it into a reexamination of politics, in which apparent virtue becomes merely a cover for malice, is one thing. Certainly the script supports that thesis on its existential level. But to impose upon the script the shallowest of recent jargon and taboos is to make for a pointless evening.

The cultural materialist approach can be very helpful with the text of *King Lear*, where whatever the cosmic facts *are* is ambiguous, or in plays where history—"the event"—is arbiter of a "truth" that is itself the murkiest of constructs. The facts in *Macbeth* are a single *fact*—unless we argue, as we can argue in the case of Richard II's murder of an uncle and seizure of a cousin's inheritance, that certain actions have sundered Scotland *permanently* from God's aegis. If that is the case, then we have to dismiss a lot of evidence to the contrary. Perhaps we consider the play's expression of its *fact* just metaphor— Lady Macbeth's madness as evidence of repression, for example, and her expression of it as merely more metaphor: "Hell is murky." The play itself is metaphor, imitation of an action, but it is metaphor that does present a moral order to us. That order must be dealt with—even if only to be scorned, as in the Thalbach production. Having said that it is not there at all, Bogdanov simply ignored it. Yet the absent "moral order" kept pestering the production that denied it. Interestingly, Graham Holderness's program note (1992) did not deal with Malcolm's elevation as "King of Scotland," a position beyond election, although Malcolm receives the necessary *collaudatio* in response to Macduff's "Hail!" Malcolm's elevation, combined with his virtue *and* political canniness, would seem to suggest that a reign has been restored, one that is destined to carry into the moment of the play's presentation before King James I. *Macbeth* is not a play that fits the cultural materialist categories, or, if it does, we need a better case than the assertions made in a program. We need the kind of challenge that Thalbach launched, a resketching of what is there into new and, as some critics complained, simplified outlines.

Modern materialist criticism is often useful in forcing reevaluations of the inherited scripts and can be helpful in going behind the pieties of Shakespeare's politicians to show the anxiety that underlies the rhetoric of a king like Henry V. But when the criticism is an accomplice to the hollowing out of a script to the meanest of contemporary metaphors, it should be condemned.

Bogdanov's version, with a world tour planned after the opening at Warwick, in February, would be the most influential. The "set," visible as the audience entered the theatre, was a huge pile of trash, which looked like the set of the Bogdanov's 1970s *The Taming of the Shrew* after Jonathan Pryce had demolished it. The dump was dominated by a huge crane. "If its purpose," said Wardle of the crane, is "to drive home some message on the evil of stage-sanctioned violence (as argued in the program), it is as ineffectual as LePage's mudbath" (1992b). The latter reference is to Robert Lepage's infamous *A Midsummer-Night's Dream*, presented at the Royal National Theatre in 1992.

Three hags entered to prey on garbage. We watched this dull and unedifying process almost interminably until a modern battle broke out. We were supposed to be shocked from the lethargy induced by the search of the dump by the hags.

Lights simulated rocket launchers, men rushed about in fatigues brandishing
modern weapons, and aircraft fired missiles. We lived again the grandeur that
was the Falklands, the glory that was Desert Storm. The actors, we were being
told, would be buried in "concept," rather than allowed to play out the ideas
that modern directors and actors still find in this early-modern encoding.

It was also clear that we would endure long and pointless pauses while stage-
hands changed sets. Pauses within scenes for emphasis or reaction? Of course.
But never *between* scenes. Shakespeare knew how to swing from one place to
another instantly. He brought a new set of actors on, had them identify themselves and tell us where they were, and did not allow the audience to lapse back
to an identity separate from that which is participating in the dramatic continuum. One of the worst examples of the many in the Bogdanov production was
the exchange of banquet for billiard table for the discussion of Lennox and Lord
(3.6). This brief scene requires no set, certainly no set change, and surely no
game of pool. Spectators talked unabashedly during the long set changes, and
some of the actors had difficulty pulling them back to the ostensible drama being
enacted. The supporting cast was weak, but it was also undercut by this unfor-
givable direction. The actors became Bogdanov's marginalized victims.

The production got some unfortunate laughs, or perhaps seeming ineptitude
was a postmodernist effort to create some intertextuality between the script and
animated cartoons. Duncan ascended the catwalk and sat on the golden throne
on top of the crane. His feet dangled ludicrously over the edge, so that his
promotion of Malcolm to Prince of Cumberland was greeted by laughter. The
pistol shots fired at a fleeing Fleance got another laugh from a startled audience,
as did the rising of the ostensible victims without benefit of blackout at the end
of the scene. There may have been a technical glitch at the beginning of the run
of this production, but it looked like another play, where ghosts rise on the
churchyard paths to glide. The end of the scene at Fife got a similar laugh for
the same reasons. This approach may have been meant to alienate us from
*over*involvement, but it forced us to reject what the script presents as factual
event. We are willing, as theatre audience, to suspend our disbelief in response
to a consistent style and tone. We got no consistency here. If the production's
purpose was to replace "tragic heroism" with the heroic efforts of actors against
an upstart machine, it did, indeed, succeed. But that is another play, and one
hates to see Shakespeare's play destroyed in the service of a far lesser one. In
caricature and political cartoons the person depicted remains in view, however
distorted, for the sake of a particular emphasis. The process will bring howls,
as did the Thalbach production. It was, however, inventive, exciting, and validly
within the School of Brecht. It showed how a postmodern vision can reignite
the script. But reignition and incineration are two different things.

Michael Pennington and Jenny Quayle fought free from the wreckage created
for them to do some superb acting, and "theirs," Wardle reported, "is a powerful and well-designed partnership" (1992b). Pennington is known as a "performer"—that is, an actor who works most effectively by himself rather than

in ensemble situations—and his soliloquies were brilliant. "If it were done" was performed in the shadows leading down from backstage right, "Is this a dagger" in the similar corridor coming from stage left, and "To be thus is nothing" from center stage, as he sat isolated on his uneasy throne. The irony of insecurity coming from the position on stage reserved for *power* was itself powerful. Quayle's first soliloquy, after she had read the letter, was partly whispered and pulled the audience forward in intense concentration. Pennington even pulled us into the banquet scene with a moving, "Blood hath been shed 'ere now." Then we were forced to watch Banquo climb to the top of the giant crane so that Macbeth could see him as Macbeth tried to toss back a needed jolt of wine. The guests did not see Banquo, of course, but they must have wondered what that crane was doing up there above the chandelier. Were they renovating battlements in anticipation of a coming siege?

As the run continued, the actors were likely to surrender to the machine, recognizing that it takes too much energy to keep pulling the audience back to the issues that Pennington and Quayle are wonderfully capable of exploring. Let the ticket buyers contemplate the trash and watch the crane, as if staring through the peepholes at a construction site. They will walk away, suitably uninspired, and think, "Well, that's Shakespeare after all, and isn't it too bad that it no longer means anything."

But it does, it does. Schiller and Buttonhole prove that even this old script retains energies that still communicate powerfully to modern audiences. But, then, it takes no ghost come from the early seventeenth century to tell us this. The problem is not just a single weak production. The problem is that such a production represents "Shakespeare" to audiences, as do bad productions in Washington, D.C., New York, and the "execrable productions of *The Taming of the Shrew* and *Romeo and Juliet* which toured [Great Britain] in the summer of 1990 with well-respected professional touring companies" that Peter Holland mentions (1991, 158). Better audiences may help drive such productions and companies off the boards, but if the audiences are told that bad productions are "good"—as they are told too often—the loser will be good productions and good companies, because, having been lied to once too often, no one will pay to see them.

The ACTER *Macbeth* of 1996, which I saw performed at Clemson University in March, demonstrated the strengths and limitations of the five-actor approach to Shakespeare's scripts.

Certain scripts work better than others with only five actors. *Much Ado*, which required the doubling of Hero and Beatrice, proved difficult. *The Tempest* was superb. A play in which magic and transformation are deeply embedded into the script allows for, even invites, the kind of agility that ACTER invariably brings to the plays. I am not sure that *Macbeth*, with its moral confusion, spiritual probing, and unfashionable emphasis on *character*, is a good script for this approach. That it is short and has no subplot did not seem to be an advantage here. The lines, though, were superbly read and, as Trewin has pointed out, "[T]he play, on an uncluttered stage, can move with the speed the Jacobeans expected" (1978, 214).

The large space—the splendid new Brook Auditorium at Clemson, which seats over 1,000—and the proscenium inhibited the transaction that ACTER demands—"the rich possibilities created by the imaginations of a participating audience" (Swander, 1996). Sam Dale, who played eight roles in this *Macbeth*, calls the ACTER process "a cross between theatre and radio" (1994). A proscenium format makes the required negotiations difficult. Ralph Cohen's Shenandoah Express had, in its three productions, abandoned the stage at moments while characters cavorted in the aisles or orated from the mezzanine. The company was exploring an inherited space and resisting its inherent limitations. *Macbeth*, as do all ACTER productions, took place within a large square inscribed on the floor of the stage.

It might be helpful if ACTER's players identified not just who they play at the outset, but also their rank or station and perhaps even mimed relationships. The speed of production can leave behind all but the most familiar with the script. Macbeth and Lady Macbeth (Gareth Armstrong and Sarah Berger), for example, appear as Old Man and Ross in 2.4 only an instant after she has been Donalbain and only a few lines after Macbeth's suggestion that they all meet in the hall. That time has passed was signaled on Shakespeare's stage not by any pause but by the appearance of a new character, the Old Man. Ross has been in the previous scene, but has no lines. Macduff enters 2.4 after twenty-six lines. Suffice it to say that it takes a moment to catch up with this kind of transition *and* to re-suspend disbelief.

The concept here was power, so that the play was about modern politics in a slightly archaic world where "heaven," "hell," and "devil" were words but not realities. Lady Macbeth was no "seductive harpy" (Trewin 1978, 213). She simply overpowered Macbeth in their debate about the murder. "That I may powre my Spirits" meant *power*, as John Andrews says in his excellent new edition of the play (1993, 28). It helped that Berger is willowy and that she wore a striking red dress, but she employed force of personality, not sexuality, against Macbeth's reluctance, suggesting a partnership that has little to do with marriage during these early parts of the play. That made her later "My Husband?" a startled recognition.

Berger recognized Macbeth's first entrance to Inverness by his footfall, waiting to really look at him on "Your Face, my Thane is as a Booke," as it is said Sarah Siddons did. Berger signaled her approaching madness by pausing between "My" and "Father," a moment of recognition that she quickly pushed down as she coped with her "Husband." "How *easy* is it then," Berger said, neatly capturing in the sound the washing off of the blood. But her faint did not tell us whether she was actually losing consciousness or, having picked up a cue from Macduff ("O gentle Lady") and one from Banquo ("Too cruell, any where") and wishing to save Macbeth from his own florid outburst when no one else can find language, she feigned her collapse. She did a half-fall into Banquo's arms and spun around to become Donalbain as Banquo and Macbeth mimed watching Lady Macbeth being carried off. This was skillfully done but did not interpret the moment. Constantly we admired the actors' technique, but often at the cost of our grasp of the dramatic issues.

Given the pace of the production and the demand for quicksilver transitions by the actors, the relationships between characters tended to be underemphasized. Not so, however, when Macbeth came to Lady Macbeth at her request (3.2.5–6). They knelt together, caring and close, but many of his words are terrible—"O, full of scorpions is my Minde, deare Wife," even if touched with a term of endearment. He tells his "dearest Chuck" that "There shall be done a deed of dreadfull note." The scene achieved what R. H. Hiecke called "an echo of that happier time when [their] mutual esteem . . . was accompanied by the delicate attentions of first love" (1846, 31), where words and actions revealed the pathos of their relationship, a moment achieved here because neither actor had to hasten into another role without missing a beat. The two-actor scenes also—and obviously—had the benefit of the advice of the other actors. At the end of the scene, Lady Macbeth refused to go with him ("So prythee goe with me"), suggesting that her alienation from him is to some extent her own choice. He, of course, turned to become the Third Murderer. It was not that Macbeth *was* the Third Murderer. This was necessary doubling that suggested Macbeth's malign ubiquity. He was also one of the murderers at Fife.

Five actors cannot achieve "thematic" doubling—Polonius and Gravedigger, Ghost and First Player, Traitors and Soldiers, for example—but at times necessity became the mother to resonance. Berger doubled Lady Macbeth and Third Sister, so that the transition that Coppelia Kahn describes was reinforced: "[T]he witches take Lady Macbeth's role as feminine powers on whom Macbeth can rely for inspiration and reassurance" (1981, 186). It was particularly apt that Lady Macbeth, who feels "The future in the instant," should be the Third Sister, who says, "that shalt be King hereafter." Lady Macbeth says, "shalt be / What thou art promis'd." The "echo effect" of this script was realized by the same voice.

At some moments—when all the actors were on stage—the need for a director was clear. The confrontation between Macbeth and Banquo and the Weird Sisters was well choreographed, each general turning as the rhythms of prophecy moved from Sister to Sister. But had Macbeth, for example, turned back to the Third Sister (Berger) on "And to be King, / Stands not within the prospect of beleefe," he would have made the instant come alive *and* forged a link between it and his coming debate with Lady Macbeth (since we would see Berger again, *as* Lady Macbeth). If Banquo makes an anapest out of "If you *can* looke into the Seedes of Time," he suggests a skepticism that contrasts with Macbeth's too eager acquisition of "truth." If Banquo emphasizes "Root" and not "insane" in "The insane Root," he tells us that the root itself is insane. That is not what the line means.

The full scene in England (4.3) was one of the best in the production, as it often is. The seldom-spoken lines about Edward the Confessor adumbrated the moral antithesis to Macbeth who supports Malcolm's crusade. The early parts of the scene were carried by Macduff's rage at Malcolm for being at once so incapable and abject. Macduff had come in search of power and, of course, got that at the end of the scene along with an almost overwhelming personal motivation.

Hecate's indictment of her subordinates (3.5.1–37) was retained here. They have gone too far. The world is out of control even in its agents of discord. Hecate's admonitions became an equivalent to those of Oberon dealing with Puck. This was an engaging moment, even if the scene is textually doubtful. In fact, the supernatural aspect of the script was well delivered; the remarkable skills of this company were nicely suited to a "magic" that we know is a trick but that convinces Macbeth. A Weird Sister mimed birth as a "child" tumbled out on "none of woman borne," and "the round / And top of Soveraignty" was made by the outstretched fingers of another Sister. That the Second Weird one was played by a man helped this production avoid the cacklingly predictable approach that can drown the lines under the calling of crows.

The full disquisition about dogs (3.1.113–22) with the murderers permitted Armstrong to show, with his eyes, that Macbeth is trapped. The scene, says John Russell Brown,

> [W]ill seem to hang fire, to lack forward drive, if the actor does not take the opportunity Shakespeare has given him to show Macbeth's half-conscious prowling within the cage of his own deed; he is restlessly insecure, doubting the murderers' resolve; he returns instinctively, as close as he may, to ideas of goodness and love. (1982, 50)

This production needed that restless irrelevance, one of Macbeth's last circling-backs to the order he has rejected and which he would fight, if only he could establish a separate stance from which to wield his lever of malignity. Armstrong also brought appropriate touches of Richard III to the scene, a role he has recently played.

Things that did not work well were the scene between Banquo and Macbeth just before the murder. Here, Fleance fell asleep. If Fleance is a focal point in the scene, however, Macbeth's contradiction of himself can make sense:

> I thinke not of them:
> Yet when we can entreat an houre to serve,
> We would spend it in some words upon that Businesse,
> If you would graunt the time.

In other words: "I don't want to talk about this with Fleance here. Can we discuss it in private?" Between the first and second lines, Macbeth assumes a royal plurality that hints of what he is about to do. That Fleance hid during the assassination of his father and witnessed it, however, was brilliantly done. The young man absorbed an indelible lesson in power. *His* revenge did not occur, but it was eerily appropriate that Sam Dale should play both Macduffs—murdered son and avenging father.

The banquet—two actors pretending to be at either end of a long table—was too paltry to simulate a "solemne Supper" or a "good meeting." But that Phillip Joseph, playing Banquo's throatless Ghost, *also* got to say, "What sights, my Lord?," and, "Good night, and better health / Attend his Majesty," lines assigned to Ross and Lennox, provided a powerful dose of what we used to call irony.

Malcolm's final lines were an invitation to us—"So thankes to all at once, and to each one, / Whom we invite, to see us Crown'd at Scone." On hearing the words, I felt that more of the script could have been directed to us: "I lay'd their Daggers ready," for example. "This house is little," complained Jenny Quayle's Regan to the audience in Adrian Noble's 1994 *King Lear*, "the old man and's people / Cannot be well bestow'd." An unsympathetic character can impale us upon a point of agreement. The Porter (Phillip Joseph) shared with us his inability to recall "th'other Devils Name." That is a role that tolerates an awareness of audience, of course, but a bit more metadrama would have helped this production.

In a spirited version presented in May 1996 on the tiny stage of the Waldo Theater in Waldoborough, Maine, directed by Jonathan Croy for Shakespeare & Company, the words were usually directed to the audience. The results were powerful. We were, in a sense, coproducers of what was happening, always being asked to agree to or at least to understand what was happening. Thus Lady Macduff's appeal was particularly potent. We were as helpless in that instance as we were when we witnessed Lady Macbeth's articulate madness. This skillfully edited script ran for a little more than an hour and a half, including one intermission.

The Nunn production of 1976–1977 created an explicitly Christian cosmos. McKellen and Dench depicted an inward spiraling exploration of evil and its consequences that became remarkably intense during the two hours and fifteen minutes of performance. The ACTER version never quite got there. The technique tended toward the brutal political cartoon, exemplified by Katherina Thalbach's 1992 German production, and at moments became an exploration of a failed relationship, as in the excellent Buttonhole production. This five-actor production created some wonderful moments, but it did not tell us what these actors believe that the play *means*, down there along its darker passages.

Works Cited

Andrews, John, ed. 1993. *Macbeth*. London: J. M. Dent.
Arditti, Michael. 1992. "Crass Absurdity." *Evening Standard* (London), 31 January, p. 45.

Barnet, Sylvan. 1987. "*Macbeth* on Stage and Screen." In *Macbeth*. New York: Penguin.

Bartholomeusz, Dennis. 1969. *'Macbeth' and the Players*. Cambridge: Cambridge University Press.

Berger, Harry, Jr. 1987. "Bodies and Texts." *Representations* 17: 23–49.

Billington, Michael. 1992. "Sexual Cauldron." *Guardian* (London), 1 February, p. 21.

Book of Common Prayer. 1605. London.

Bradley, A. C. 1904. *Shakespearean Tragedy*. London: Macmillan.

Brooke, Nicholas, ed. 1990. *Macbeth*. Oxford: Oxford University Press.

Brown, Arthur C. L., ed. 1913. *Macbeth*. New York: Macmillan.

Brown, John Russell, ed. 1963. *Macbeth*. Great Neck, N.Y.: Barron's.

————, ed. 1982. *Focus on 'Macbeth.'* London: Routledge and Kegan Paul.

Calderwood, James L. 1986. *If It Were Done: 'Macbeth' and Tragic Action*. Amherst: University of Massachusetts Press.

Carlisle, Carol J. 1983. "Helen Faucit's Lady Macbeth." *Shakespeare Studies* 16: 205–34.

Chomsky, Noam. 1986. "The Reality of 'Education,' " *New York Review of Books*. (27 June): 1, 14.

Coursen, H. R. 1995. *Reading Shakespeare on Stage*. Cranbury, N.J.: Associated University Presses.

Dale, Sam. 1994. "Performing with ACTER." *Shakespeare Bulletin* 12, no. 3 (Summer): 26.

Danson, Lawrence. 1974. *Tragic Alphabet*. New Haven, Conn.: Yale University Press.

David, Richard. 1956. "The Tragic Curve." *Shakespeare Survey* 9: 27–39.

————. 1978. *Shakespeare in the Theatre*. Cambridge: Cambridge University Press.

Davis, Derek R. 1982. "Hurt Minds." In *Focus on 'Macbeth.'* Edited by John Russell Brown. London: Routledge and Kegan Paul.

Dessen, Alan. 1986. "The Supernatural on Television." *Shakespeare on Film Newsletter* 11, no. 1 (December): 1, 8.

Downer, Alan S. 1966. *The Eminent Tragedian*. Cambridge, Mass.: Harvard University Press.

Eagleton, Terry. 1967. *Shakespeare and Society*. New York: Schocken Books.

Evans, Gareth L. 1982. "*Macbeth* in Performance." *Focus on 'Macbeth.'* Edited by John Russell Brown. London: Routledge and Kegan Paul.

Fawkner, H. W. 1990. *Deconstructing 'Macbeth': The Hyperontological View*. Cranbury, N.J.: Associated University Presses.

Frye, R. M. 1982. *Shakespeare: The Art of the Dramatist*. London: George Allen and Unwin.

Furness, Horace H., Jr., ed. 1873. Variorum *Macbeth*. Philadelphia: J. B. Lippincott.

Gibson, Andrew. 1988. "Malcolm, Macduff and the Structure of *Macbeth*." In *Macbeth*. Edited by Linda Cookson and Bryan Loughrey. London: Longman.

Gibson, Rex, ed. 1993. *Macbeth*. Cambridge: Cambridge University Press.

Girard, Rene. 1977. *Violence and the Sacred*. Translated by Patrick Gregory. Baltimore: Johns Hopkins University Press.

Goddard, Harold. 1951. *The Meaning of Shakespeare*. Vol. 2. Chicago: Chicago University Press.

Grove, Robin. 1982. " 'Multiplying Villainies of Nature.' " In *Focus on 'Macbeth.'* Edited by John Russell Brown. London: Routledge and Kegan Paul.

Harcourt, John B. 1961. " 'I Pray You, Remember the Porter.' " *Shakespeare Quarterly* 12 (Spring): 27–33.

Hiecke, R. H. 1846. *'Macbeth' erlautert und gewurdigt*. Merseberg, Germany.

Hildy, Frank. 1996. "The Globe Reconstruction." Lecture presented at Clemson University, 14 March.

Hodgdon, Barbara. 1979. "In Search of the Performance Present." In *Shakespeare: The Theatrical Dimension*. Edited by Philip C. McGuire and David A. Samuelson. New York: AMS Press.

Holderness, Graham. 1992. Note. Program for *Macbeth*. London: English Shakespeare Company.

Holland, Peter. 1991. "Shakespearean Performances in England." *Shakespeare Survey* 44: 157–90.

Holloway, John. 1961. *The Story of the Night*. Lincoln: University of Nebraska Press.

Hornblow, Arthur. 1919. *A History of the Theatre in America*. Vol. 2. Philadelphia: Lippincott.

Houseman, John. 1972. *Run-Through*. New York: Simon and Schuster.

Hunter, G. K., ed. 1994. *Macbeth*. London: Penguin.

Kahn, Coppelia. 1981. *Man's Estate: Masculine Identity in Shakespeare*. Berkeley: University of California Press.

Kennedy, Dennis. 1993. *Looking at Shakespeare: A Visual History of Twentieth-Century Performance*. Cambridge: Cambridge University Press.

Kernan, Alvin. 1974. "This Goodly Frame the Stage: The Interior Theater of the Imagination in English Renaissance Drama." *Shakespeare Quarterly* 24, no. 1 (Winter): 1–5.

Klein, Joan L. 1980. "Lady Macbeth: Infirm of Purpose." In *The Woman's Part: Feminist Criticism of Shakespeare*. Edited by Carol Ruth Swift Lenz, Gayle Greene, and Carol Thomas Neely. Urbana: University of Illinois Press.

Kliman, Bernice W. 1992. "Orson Welles's 1936 'Voodoo' *Macbeth* and Its Reincarnation on Film." In *'Macbeth': Shakespeare in Performance*. Edited by Bernice W. Kliman. Manchester, England: Manchester University Press.

———. 1995. "Welles's *Macbeth*: A Textual Parable." In *Screen Shakespeare*. Edited by Michael Skovman. Aarhus, Denmark: Aarhus University Press.

Knight, G. Wilson. 1957. *The Wheel of Fire*. New York: Meridian.

Knights, L. C. 1959. *Some Shakespearean Themes*. London: Chatto and Windus.

Long, Michael, ed. 1989. *Macbeth*. Boston: Twayne.

Mack, Maynard, Jr. 1973. *Killing the King*. New Haven, Conn.: Yale University Press.

Marcus, Leah S. 1988. *Puzzling Shakespeare: Local Reading and Its Discontents*. Berkeley: University of California Press.

Mullin, Michael. 1976. *'Macbeth' Onstage: An Annotated Facsimile of Glen Byam Shaw's 1955 Promptbook*. Columbia: University of Missouri Press.

Nevo, Ruth. 1972. *Tragic Form in Shakespeare*. Princeton, N.J.: Princeton University Press.

Orgel, Stephen. 1988. "The Authentic Shakespeare." In *Representations* 21. Edited by Stephen Greenblatt. Berkeley: University of California Press, 5–25.

Parsons, Keith, and Pamela Mason. 1995. *Shakespeare in Performance*. London: Salamander.

Rosenberg, Marvin. 1978. *The Masks of Macbeth*. Cranbury, N.J.: Associated University Presses.

———. 1982. "Macbeth and Lady Macbeth in the Eighteenth and Nineteenth Centuries." In *Focus on 'Macbeth.'* Edited by John Russell Brown. London: Routledge and Kegan Paul.

Royal Shakespeare Company Magazine. 1990. "The Eminent vs. the American." (Autumn): 3–5.

Rutherford, Malcolm. 1992. "A Brechtian *Macbeth.*" *Financial Times Weekend* (London), 1–2 February, p. 23.

Sanders, Wilbur. 1968. *The Dramatist and the Received Idea.* Cambridge: Cambridge University Press.

Scott, William O. 1986. "Macbeth's—and Our—Self-Equivocations." *Shakespeare Quarterly* 37, no. 2 (Summer): 160–74.

Sprague, Arthur C. 1953. *Shakespearean Players and Performances.* Cambridge, Mass.: Harvard University Press.

Styan, John. 1967. *Shakespeare's Stagecraft.* Cambridge: Cambridge University Press.

Swander, Homer. 1996. Letter to author, 3 January.

———. 1994. Program note. Clemson Shakespeare Festival.

Taylor, Paul. 1992. "Shakespeare Blitzkrieg." *Independent* (London), 1 February, p. 30.

Thalbach, Katrina 1992. Remarks, Goethe Institute, London, 3 February.

Thompson, Ann. 1988. *King Lear.* Atlantic Highlands, N.J.: Humanities Press International.

Trewin, J. C. 1978. *Going to Shakespeare.* London: Allen and Unwin.

Tromly, Frederic B. 1975. "Macbeth and His Porter." *Shakespeare Quarterly* 26 (Spring): 151–56.

Vollenklee, Marcus. 1992. Remarks, Goethe Institute, London, 3 February.

Waller, Gary. 1992. Review. *Shakespeare Quarterly* 42 (Spring): 103.

Wardle, Irving. 1992a. "Three First Persons Singular." *Independent on Sunday* (London), 2 February, p. C21.

———. 1992b. "A Strange Case of Swamp Fever." *Independent on Sunday* (London), 12 July, p. C23.

Watkins, Ronald. 1950. *On Producing Shakespeare.* London: M. Joseph.

Watkins, Ronald, and Jeremy Lemmon. 1964. *Macbeth.* Illustrated by Maurice Percival. Oxford: Oxford University Press.

———. 1974. *In Shakespeare's Playhouse.* Totowa, N.J.: Rowman and Littlefield.

Williams, Gordon. 1985. *'Macbeth': Text & Performance.* London: Macmillan.

Wills, Gary. 1995. *Witches and Jesuits.* Oxford: Oxford University Press.

Wilson, J. Dover, ed. 1947. *Macbeth.* Cambridge: Cambridge University Press.

Worthen, William. 1996. "Staging Shakespeare: Acting, Authority, and the Rhetoric of Performance." In *Shakespeare, Theory, and Performance.* Edited by James Bulman. London: Metheun.

Zitner, Sheldon. 1964. "*Macbeth* and the Moral Scale of Tragedy." *Journal of General Education* 16 (Fall): 23–31.

———. 1981. "Wooden O's in Plastic Boxes: Shakespeare and Television." *University of Toronto Quarterly* 51 (Fall): 1–12.

MACBETH ON FILM

Many books and articles have been written about the film versions of Shakespeare's plays. Robert Hamilton Ball's book on Shakespeare and the silent screen (1968), Roger Manvell's pioneering work (1971), Jack Jorgens's classic study (1977), Peter S. Donaldson's depth-psychology analyses (1990), and Ken-

neth Rothwell and Annabelle Melzer's filmography (1990) have become standard. Michael Mullin, Bernice W. Kliman, John Gerlach, Samuel Crowl, E.
Pearlman, Anthony Davies, and Robert Hapgood have all written eloquently on
the cinematic versions of the script. This brief note must be supplemented by
the work of others far more expert than I in the demanding but fascinating field
of Shakespeare on film.

Orson Welles's film version of *Macbeth* (1948) is "a violently sketched char-
coal drawing of a great play" (Welles in Manvell 1971, 59). He had done his
"Voodoo" version in Harlem in 1936 and another a decade later for the Utah
Shakespeare Festival. The film, an "often clumsy" effort at creating a "warped,
surreal world," according to Mullin (1973, 338), depicts "tortured grotesques
and half-mad zealots in a Black Mass or an ancient ritual" (Crowther 1950,
22). "His genius," states Rothwell, "lay in his ability to point a camera at a
subject in odd but thoroughly significant ways" (Rothwell and Melzer 1990,
151). Davies looks at it as "horror film and *film noir*" (1988, 89). In contrast
to the Schaefer film, remarks Jorgens, "Welles's film shows a world permeated
from the beginning with evil" (1977, 151). He notes the "Freudian undertones
of dripping caverns which give birth to monstrous acts" (151). Lorne M. Buchman stresses the ways in which Welles's use of multiple points of view stim-
ulates "an imaginative participation with the drama not possible before the
advent of cinema" (1988, 3). Joseph McBride says that

> The lack of any sense of the hero's moral relationship to society—intensi-
> fied by the play's supernatural aspects and by the hallucinatory, almost
> solipsistic nature of Macbeth's ambition, which is too compulsive to admit
> of rational calculation—turns the drama farther inward than in any Welles
> film until *The Immortal Story*. We are in a theater of the unconscious. (1972,
> 113)

If he discarded the voodoo, he had to move toward an external primitive religion
and inward toward an approximation of solipsism. The Macbeth head shaped at
the outset in clay by the Weird Sisters is a nod in the direction of his 1936
stage production, but it is not carried through in deeper concept in the film.
Sylvan Barnet suggests that the voodoo doll, which is being shaped of clay at
outset, is "not so much a man who made a wrong decision but a man whose
fate has been long decided" (1987, 265). Welles, Pearlman argues, "unsuc-
cessfully labours to strip *Macbeth* of its political content" (1994, 252). The
"film inadvertently generates a rudimentary political vision of its own [becom-
ing] an exploration of both dictatorship and the cult of personality" (252). At
the end of the film, "the threat of dictatorship still looms" (252). At the end,
the three Weird ones, crooks in hand, stare up at Xanadu, looking like hockey
players sitting out a long penalty.
    According to Claude Beylie,

> The cinema is only . . . the shadow of a shadow, projected upon the wall of
> a cave, the ragged garments of a clown ludicrously agitated before the light
> of a projector. Given this, [Welles's] *Macbeth* must be considered one of
> the most beautiful films ever created, in that it illustrates, with maximum
> rigor and simplicity, this definition (in no way restrictive) of our art . . . few
> films in the history of cinema . . . have come so close to what Shakespeare
> calls "life's fitful fever." (1972, 74–75)

For a fascinating account of the making of the film and of its manifestations,
see Kliman's treatment of the "three films, each highlighting different facets of
collaboration: the original release (1947), which, with several significant differences, is close to the restoration (1979), and the rerelease (1950), the response
to the film's initial poor showing" (1995, 27).

In *Joe Macbeth* (1955), directed by Ken Hughes and starring Paul Douglas
and Ruth Roman, "Duke" arrives in South Orange and stands on the porch of
the house in which he is soon to be murdered: "I like 'dis place. The air smells
good here!" Minerva Pious, the fortune-teller who replaced the Weird Sisters,
played Mrs. Nussbaum on "Allen's Alley." Douglas plays "an upstart bungler
heavily dependent on the skills of his scheming wife for success" (Willson
1982, 4). There is none of the "subtlety of the husband-wife relationship"
(1982, 4). Lily says, "Maybe it didn't happen because Rosie [the fortune-teller]
said it would but because you did what she said." The mystery of the inter-
secting of destiny and human will is nicely balanced here. It is unfortunate that
this film is not available. Students who know the play would enjoy it immensely.
In a more recent offshoot, *Men of Respect* (1991), directed by William Rielly,
with John Turturro, Katherine Borowitz, and Rod Steiger as mob-boss Charley
D'Amato (Mike) says to his wife, "Sorry I messed up your party." The film
represents "parody instead of pathos; the genre . . . cannot sustain the weight of
Shakespeare's metaphysical material" (Willson 1992, 36). "The film's finale is
a pastiche of bad, sometimes lugubrious jokes" (36). This one, unfortunately,
is available.

Bosley Crowther found Akira Kurosawa's *Throne of Blood* hilarious: "[T]he
final scene, in which the hero is shot so full of arrows that he looks like a
porcupine, is a pictorial extravagance that provides a conclusive howl" (1961,
50). But, according to Marsha Kinder, "Washizu's final *danse macabre* is the
last powerful demonstration of his superhuman energy, which defines his character; it takes hundreds of arrows to make him halt" (1977, 345). Davies points
an important contrast:

> *Macbeth* is a drama about the power of choice, and the exercise of that
> power. *Throne of Blood*, on the other hand, is a drama about inevitable
> prophetic truth. . . . Where Macbeth has choice, Washizu has only destiny,
> and the distinction between Shakespeare's play and Kurosawa's drama is
> forcibly announced at the beginning and the end of the film, by the chanting
> chorus which rings out the inevitable fate of ambitious men and proclaims

it to be a truth which transcends particular circumstances of history. (1988, 155)

> Behold within this mighty place,
> Now desolate,
> Stood a mighty fortress,
> Lived a proud warrior
> Murdered by ambition,
> His spirit walking still.
> Vain pride, then as now,
> Will lead ambition to the kill.

Donald Richie adds, "Cause and effect is the only law. Freedom does not exist" (1970, 115). Kurosawa comments, "The images of men who lived though the age [the period of civil wars in Japan for most of the sixteenth century] when the weak became a prey for the strong are highly concentrated. Human beings are described with great intensity. In this sense, I think there is something in *Macbeth* which is common to all other works of mine" (quoted in Manvell 1971, 102). "Nature in *Throne of Blood* is neither benign nor harmonious," remarks Jorgens,

> but amorphous, changing shape, sex, and tone. It is indifferent, both en-
> couraging human ambition and mocking it. The forest breeds growth, but
> also confusion and futility. The Forest Spirit seems an embodiment of an
> ironic, amoral Nature, whose even-handed law is the destruction of for-
> tresses, and the reduction of all individuals to indiscriminate heaps of bones.
> The last shots say it all: men dissolve to fog, to primal nothingness. (1983,
> 170)

"Like Shakespeare, Kurosawa renders insanity visually as endless repetition." Lady Asaji, for example, is "locked in an endless ritual of washing her hands" (Jorgens 1977, 156). "Without worrying about fidelity to the original, we can easily enjoy it for itself" (Barnet 1987, 266). We do not have to worry about a text shifted or altered for filmic purposes. We are free of the need for "crit-ical" thinking, free to enjoy the aesthetic and imaginative event of the film. That freedom is a major reason for the film's almost universal appeal.

The film incorporates much more of a political pattern than the inherited script. It is more what the materialists would make of the script—as if fate is inscribed in the only method of gaining power, as it must be, if power is the only value and goal.

> They have already discussed the possibility of killing the lord, and, more
> directly than in *Macbeth*, Asaji has argued (laconically) from a demystified
> view of feudal power relations. Washizu speaks of his loyalty in tones of

awe and respect, but Asaji points out that the lord had killed his own predecessor. (Donaldson 1990, 81)

In his brilliant chapter in *Shakespeare and the Moving Image* (1994), Robert
Hapgood asserts that Kurosawa's films "have their own integrity and can be
enjoyed on their own terms without reference to Shakespeare" (1994, 234).
While they take "liberties with the original, they are faithful . . . to some essence
in it" (234). Hapgood isolates two Japanese film genres: *jidai-geki* (period pictures, a category that includes *Throne of Blood* and *Ran*) and *gendai-mono*
(modern-story films like *The Bad Sleep Well*). The former two "are set in the
Sengoku Jidai or 'Age of the Country at War' (1392–1568). . . . *Ran* seems the
later of the two, both in weaponry . . . and decadence" (235). "Kurosawa has
explained that [the] initial inspiration [for *Ran*] came not from *King Lear* but
the Japanese warlord Montornari Mori (1497–1571) and his three sons" (236).
Hapgood deftly outlines the sources for the films: scrolls, *The Tale of the Heike*,
Noh drama, and the Buddhist hell to come, "presided over by the demon
Ashura, where warriors continue their destructive ways" (237). "Where *Ran*
sees the present moment as hell on earth, *Throne of Blood* emphasizes its persistence through the ages" (238). "*Throne of Blood* is more than anything else
a mood piece . . . [and is] one of a kind" (238, 239). "The most distinctive
hallmark of Kurosawa's general approach to Shakespeare is his constant pull
toward the graphic, the immediate, the concrete, the simple, the extreme" (242).
In *Throne of Blood*, we "come to see how the two of them [Washizu and Miki]
have been doomed to doom themselves—the film's deepest thematic resem-
blance to *Macbeth*" (247). Those who use Kurosawa's films in their teaching
will find Hapgood's essay indispensable, particularly on *Throne of Blood*.

Roman Polanski's version (1971) is "so brutal and bloody . . . that it is difficult to respond to it on an aesthetic level at all, much less think about its
relation to Shakespeare's play" (Jorgens 1977, 161); however, it is "quite a
good film" (161). According to Barnet, "What is most lacking in the film . . .
is a sense that Macbeth is a heroic figure, a man who has a moral sense—even
if he wars against it" (1987, 267). The film, clearly, is influenced by Jan Kott's
Shakespeare: Our Contemporary, as Crowl argues (1992).

Finch and Annis are "simply too young" (Mullin 1973, 333) and "too cal-
low" (Kael 1972, 76). Ambition may be a function of youth, as Kenneth Tynan
argues (1972, 27) but the desire for a *crown* is not necessarily a function of
flaming youth, as Julius Caesar may and Claudius does suggest. The Polanski
film is full of gratuitous horror—a bear to be baited is "our chiefe Guest." We
witness the murder of Duncan. The script shows a buildup *toward* observed
violence. We see Banquo ambushed, but Fleance escapes. We see Lady Macduff
trapped in her defenseless castle, and young Macduff does not escape. That
scene is well done in the Polanski film—one of the murderers pauses to admire
an exotic bird and to signal his appreciation to Lady Macduff—but we have
already supp'd full with horrors by this time. If the script is full of the language

of panic, Polanski does replicate that lexis by bringing violence before us "always a shade faster than you'd expect" (Kael 1972, 76). This is "probably the most exciting Shakespeare film ever made" (Rothwell 1973, 343). Normand Berlin points out that

> [A]lthough its form distorts Shakespeare and exploits Shakespeare's melodramatic side, [the film] is a valid modern interpretation of Shakespeare's play. Bloody, violent, unremitting in its horror, the film presents a vision of a world filled with confusions and madness, a world in which both brave Macbeth and limping Donalbain will always seek Satanic ties, a world containing only bears and dogs, a world where tomorrows are as brutal as todays. (1973, 298)

Maybe. I think that Brook's film of *King Lear* (1971) is a better example of "existential" drama emerging from a script that better supports that point of view than *Macbeth*.

At the end, however, Polanski achieves a brilliant moment. As Macduff brings his sword down on Macbeth's head, the camera makes a 90-degree jump-cut, even as Macbeth's hands grope for the crown on top of the severed head. The head falls away as the body in its armor clunks down the steps of the castle. Macduff and the soldiers are enjoying this butchery and, it seems, enjoying Malcolm's discomfort. He swallows and utters cliches: "Such a day as this is cheaply bought." The head has splatted down the wall and lies, eyes open, under a trail of blood. The crown is still in place. The opportunistic Ross removes it, wipes it with his sleeve, and presents it to Malcolm, who puts it on.

An eerie chord sounds as Macbeth's head is placed upon a pike. The camera tracks past cheering soldiers, faces blurred, mouths open but silent. Time is passing in some strange slow-motion sequence. The head bleeds, eyes still open. The camera creates a quick montage, three times to the head, twice to the soldiers' silent roar. It then takes in the crowd cheering from the courtyard's timbered balconies, which resemble the galleries of an Elizabethan theater. Macbeth's head, the object of the celebration, rises on its pole.

We have observed much of this from the point of view of the head itself—honor, love, obedience, all glimpsed through the ironic transparency of death. There *is* speculation in those eyes. But instead of being the destroyer of a ceremony of amity, as is Banquo's ghost or body, Macbeth's head is the focal point of such a festival. His audience cheers him as a "poor player" to be "heard no more" but does not realize that the final function of Macbeth's neural transmitters is to recognize what is happening.

It may be that Polanski borrows from Father Devoyod's description of an execution by guillotine:

> His head fell into the trough in front of the guillotine and the body was immediately put into the basket; but by some mistake, the basket was closed

before the head was put in. The assistant who was carrying the head had
to wait a moment until the basket was opened again; now, during this brief
space of time we could see the condemned man's eyes fixed on me with a
look of supplication, as if to ask forgiveness. Instinctively we made the sign
of the cross to bless the head, and then the lids blinked, the expression of
the eyes softened, and finally the look, that had remained full of expression,
became vague. (quoted in Camus 1951, 184–85)

For once, Polanski makes the "Macbeth leap" into almost unimaginable realms
of horror that his camera imagines for us. Mullin indicts the Polanski film: it is
"the story behind the legend, seen from the viewpoint of history . . . it does not
give us the legend as transmuted by Shakespeare because it always remains
outside the consciousness of the hero" (1973, 337). The exception I note above
shows Macbeth acceding, as perhaps he must, to the celebration of his downfall,
but doing so with the literal vision of death with which his eyes had seen the
world when he was alive. It is an extension of his words to a zone consistent
with but beyond them. Macbeth's head, raised on a pole against the timber-and-
plaster balcony of a theater interior, is a brief reminder of the traitors' heads on
poles on Tower Bridge just across the river, rotting under an umbrella of crows.

At the end, a deformed Donalbain (Richard III—get it?) shambles off to ask
the Weird Sisters to tell him his fortune. This *da capo* borrows, says Dennis
Kennedy, "a favorite dramaturgical structure from Beckett . . . the same cycle
of destruction replaying itself" (1996, 141). In her detailed and brilliant chapter
in *'Macbeth': Shakespeare in Performance*, Kliman defends Polanski's version:

> [T]he Polanski *Macbeth* reigns supreme among versions reasonably close
> to the text. . . . Polanski earns that place not merely with violence but with
> withdrawal from violence, with cinematic excellence, and with a coherent
> view shaped by the camera, by the narrative details and without relinquish-
> ing ambiguity. He creates a compelling Shakespearean drama in spite of a
> diminished Macbeth and Lady Macbeth because, like Welles and Nunn, he
> has made society the locus of his tragedy. (1992, 143)

Pearlman argues that modern film versions of *Macbeth* offer readings *counter*
to the inherited script. He makes an assertion with which the cultural materialists
disagree: "*Macbeth* unabashedly celebrates a semi-divine monarch in terms specific to the first years of Stuart absolutism. . . . The play's satisfaction with the
traditional order, though severely tested by the reign of the tyrant, is confirmed
when a second exemplary monarch succeeds his father" (1994, 250). The play
"assumes that misgovernment enters the community not because of defects in
the system of monarchy, but at the behest of agents of darkness . . . monarchy
remains the only conceivable form of government" (251). "Unlike Welles's
world, which is menacing and brooding, or Kurosawa's spare and joyless universe, Polanski's world is characterized by song, dance, and even a degree of
joy. Yet there is a sinister underside to this apparently prospering community.

It is permeated by ... gratuitous violence" (253). Polanski's "vision is even more despairing [than Welles's] ... both Christianity and monarchy are deliberately and systematically replaced by satanism" (253). "The massed ugliness of the naked witches in their cave is an imaginative expansion of the misogyny of the original play" (254). "Shakespeare's confidence in the triumph of justice has been transformed into our favourite contemporary cliche—that all events are merely accidents of an indifferent universe" (255). "In Welles's *Macbeth*, the alternative to monarchy is anarchy; in Polanski's version, the alternative is diabolism" (255). "Unlike *Macbeth*, where the witches invade a basically healthy universe, Kurosawa's universe is devoid of political virtue.... The society is characterized ... by narrow self-interest, distrust, constant fear, and the easy recourse to violence" (257). But, while "Kurosawa offers no easy answers, neither does he permit his film to succumb to authoritarian or demonic presences ... the rotten feudalism for which [Washizu] stands cannot be brought to its knees by one individual, but can be overcome by the people acting in concert" (259, 258).

Works Cited

Ball, Robert H. 1968. *Shakespeare on Silent Film*. London: George Allen and Unwin.
———. 1973. "On Shakespeare Filmography." *Literature/Film Quarterly* 1 (Fall): 299–306.
Barnet, Sylvan, ed. 1987. *Macbeth*. New York: Penguin.
Berlin, Normand. 1973. "*Macbeth*: Polanski and Shakespeare." *Literature/Film Quarterly* 1 (Fall): 291–98.
Beylie, Claude. 1972. "*Macbeth* or the Magical Depths." In *Focus on Shakespearean Films*. Edited by Charles Eckert. Englewood Cliffs, N.J.: Prentice-Hall.
Buchman, Lorne M. 1988. Paper presented to the Shakespeare Association of America, Philadelphia, Penn., March.
Camus, Albert. 1951. "Reflections on the Guillotine." In *Resistance, Rebellion, and Death*. New York: Alfred Knopf.
Crowl, Samuel. 1992. *Shakespeare Observed*. Athens: Ohio University Press.
Crowther, Bosley. 1950. "Screen: Change in Scene." *New York Times*, 28 December, p. 22.
———. 1961. "Review." *New York Times*. 23 November: 50.
Davies, Anthony. 1988. *Filming Shakespeare's Plays: The Adaptations of Laurence Olivier, Orson Welles, Peter Brook, and Akira Kurosawa*. Cambridge: Cambridge University Press.
Davies, Anthony, and Stanley Wells, eds. 1994. *Shakespeare and the Moving Image*. Cambridge: Cambridge University Press.
Donaldson, Peter. 1990. *Shakespearean Films/Shakespearean Directors*. Boston: Unwin Hyman.
Hapgood, Robert. 1994. "Kurosawa's Shakespeare Films: *Throne of Blood, The Bad Sleep Well*, and *Ran*." In *Shakespeare and the Moving Image*. Edited by Anthony Davies and Stanley Wells. Cambridge: Cambridge University Press.
Jorgens, Jack. 1977. *Shakespeare on Film*. Bloomington: Indiana University Press.
———. 1983. "Washizu and Miki." *Literature/Film Quarterly* 11, no. 3 (Summer): 167–73.

Kael, Pauline. 1972. Review of Roman Polanski's *Macbeth*. *New Yorker*, 5 February, p. 76.

Kennedy, Dennis. 1996. "Shakespeare without His Language." In *Shakespeare, Theory, and Performance*. Edited by James Bulman. London: Metheun.

Kinder, Marsha. 1977. "*Throne of Blood*: A Morality Dance." *Literature Film Quarterly* 5, no. 4 (Fall): 339–45.

Kliman, Bernice W. 1992. "Orson Welles's 1936 'Voodoo' *Macbeth* and Its Reincarnation on Film." In *'Macbeth': Shakespeare in Performance*. Edited by Bernice W. Kliman. Manchester, England: Manchester University Press.

———. 1995. "Welles's *Macbeth*: A Textual Parable." In *Screen Shakespeare*. Edited by Michael Skovmand. Aarhus, Demark: Aarhus University Press.

Kott, Jan. 1964. *Shakespeare Our Contemporary*. Garden City, N.Y.: Doubleday.

Manvell, Roger. 1971. *Shakespeare and the Film*. New York: Praeger.

McBride, Joseph. 1972. *Orson Welles*. London: Secker and Warburg.

Mullin, Michael. 1973. "*Macbeth* on Film." *Literature/Film Quarterly* 9, no. 1 (December): 332–42.

Pearlman, E. 1994. "*Macbeth* on Film: Politics." In *Shakespeare and the Moving Image*. Edited by Anthony Davies and Stanley Wells. Cambridge: Cambridge University Press.

Ritchie, Donald. 1970. *The Films of Akira Kurosawa*. Berkeley: University of California Press.

Rothwell, Kenneth S. 1973. "Hollywood and Some Versions of *Romeo and Juliet*: Toward a "Substantial Pageant." *Literature/Film Quarterly* 1 (Fall): 343–51.

Rothwell, Kenneth S., and Annabelle H. Melzer. 1990. *Shakespeare on Screen: An International Filmography and Videography*. New York: Neil-Schuman.

Tynan, Kenneth. 1972. Review of Roman Polanski's *Macbeth*. *New York Times*, 28 February, p. 27.

Willson, Robert. 1982. "The Selling of 'Joe Macbeth.' " *Shakespeare on Film* 7 (December): 1, 4.

———. 1992. "Recontextualing Shakespeare on Film." *Shakespeare Bulletin* 11, no. 3 (Summer): 34–36.

MACBETH ON TELEVISION

The shortness of the script, its relative lack of "big" scenes (the banquet scene being the exception), and probably the frequency with which it is taught in the schools have made *Macbeth* the most popular of all Shakespeare's plays for television. Its popularity, however, does not necessarily argue its success on that medium. It was not recognized early in television's commercial history, for example, that the supernatural does not translate effectively to television. Television lacks any field of depth in which special effects can occur. Television also tends to "normalize" its content, a fact accentuated by the location of the machine in our own living space. (See Dessen 1986 and Coursen 1989 on the supernatural and special effects as they are deployed on television.)

The first televised version was a fifty-minute production, broadcast in two halves in Great Britain in March 1937. In May 1949, NBC's production, with

Walter Hampden, Joyce Redmond, Leo G. Carroll, Ralph Bellamy, Walter Abel, and John Carradine, directed by Anthony Brown and Gerry Simpson, was called "trying and awkward" by *New York Times* reviewer Jack Gould (1949). "The problem is mainly technological," remarks Kenneth Rothwell, "as the blurry images on the screen take on the look of a berserk *film noir* . . . it is a little sad to see these great names from the past coming to us . . . like shadowy ghosts desperately seeking our remembrance of them as Shakespearean actors" (Rothwell and Melzer 1990, 151). Of the 22 October 1951 version with Judith Evelyn and Charlton Heston, directed by Paul Nickell, Gould commented that it called too much attention to "[t]he camera movement," that Evelyn was "superb," that Heston was "handicapped by very poor enunciation and little versatility in interpretation," and that "[t]he program's extreme reliance on . . . the stream-of-consciousness technique . . . made it hard to tell whether Mr. Heston was himself or only an automaton" (1951). Rothwell praises Betty Furness's Westinghouse commercials, but says that if "this dreary, lackluster event had anyone's name but Shakespeare's attached to it, the scenarists would have been stripped of their expense accounts and swimming pools" (1990, 152).

The first color version was George Schaefer's, with Maurice Evans and Judith Anderson. Gould called it "[s]trangely disappointing [and] regrettably often out of joint." The problem, according to Gould, was the medium:

> The compelling sweep of the unified whole appeared sacrificed to the demanding technical gods of TV . . . the underlying excitement, the sense of ambitious urgency, that drives Macbeth toward evil and doom . . . was lost. . . . On the home screen *Macbeth* was too much the story of man against man rather than man against fate. (1954)

Alice Griffin found Evans unheroic: "[H]e did not seem to convey the stature or the complexity of the character" (1955, 65). Bernice W. Kliman argues that "[t]he stagey contrivance of the set is an asset . . . because Judith Anderson's Lady Macbeth and Maurice Evans' tremolo Macbeth, both larger than life, need the artifice of a stage background to be acceptable" (1982, 144). To me, Evans's "tremolo" verges on W. C. Fields. I kept looking for the flick of a cigar ash. Evans is effective, though, as he directs his heartbroken "syllable of recorded time" speech to the woman who had cared so much for him. He remembers "such things were / That were most precious to" him.

Macbeth's second confrontation with the Weird Sisters "was changed," says Griffin, "into a dream . . . while he is lying in bed, so that his future actions lost motivation and impact" (1955, 65). The working out of the prophecies is lost here, since they had been printed only briefly on Macbeth's pillowcase. Since most of them are "sweet bodements"—the line of Banquo's issue being eliminated here—his rage at this pernicious hour upon awakening is radically unmotivated. The sequence does, however, represent an effort on Schaefer's part toward "naturalization" (Barnet 1987, 264), that is, to scale "special effects" to the medium. Griffin says that "the depiction of Banquo's presence by a disembodied head, shining with red blood and bouncing about like a tennis ball, was just short of ludicrous" (1955, 65). Gould suggests that "the restless camera work imposed lighting problems beyond color TV's grasp at the moment." The ghost, "in extreme television closeup . . . represented a lamentable slip in theatrical judgment. There is a difference between horror and the horrible" (1954, 31). Griffin says that television "turned the tragedy into a domestic rather than a cosmic one" (1955, 65), a translation not seen as absolutely inevitable in 1955.

A positive aspect of this production is the use of an overhead camera that looks down on Macbeth as he mounts the steps to murder Duncan and on Lady Macbeth as she begins to sleepwalk at the bottom of the same steps. The two moments are visually linked in this production, and the point about a "higher power" is made simply and effectively.

Anderson's performance is worth observing. Her Lady is at once bravura and detailed. Griffin notes "her concern for her husband and mounting apprehensions . . . until finally the truly terrifying sleepwalking scene" occurs (1955, 65). Anderson demonstrates the value of a stage history behind a performance. She and Evans had done the play in 1941. When I saw the remake of this production on a cinema screen in 1963, it had the feeling of a filmed play. They were popular at that time, as witness *Stalag Seventeen, The Country Girl*, and *Detective Story*. Of the film, Rothwell says that "close-ups and mid-shots tend to prevail and give it a . . . claustrophobic atmosphere" (Rothwell and Melzer 1990, 157). "The heart of Schaefer's film," asserts Jack Jorgens, "is its contrast of the moral disease of the Macbeths with a healthy, regenerative nature. . . . Schaefer's film depicts a world shaken by a murderous fever and restored to health and order" (1977, 150–51).

The BBC version of 1970, directed by John Gorrie and starred Janet Suzman and Eric Porter, was the initial offering of the Classic Theatre series in 1975, which also featured such splendid productions as *Edward II*, with Ian McKellan and James Laurenson, and *The Duchess of Malfi*, with Eileen Atkins, Michael Bryant, and Charles Kay. This *Macbeth* uses its medium well, with minimal sets, the murkiness of fog and gray skies, and an emphasis on faces and the spoken word. It practices the small economies that can work on television. After Macbeth is defeated by Macduff, for example, Macbeth's head falls into the empty bowl in the earth the Weird Sisters had used to make their charming stew. At this time in her career, the great Janet Suzman was essaying the finest Cleopatra of modern times both in her 1972 Royal Shakespeare Company stage production and in the splendid remounting for television, both directed by Trevor Nunn. Suzman brings a vivid sexual vitality to her Lady, simply overwhelming Porter's dull thane. But we recognize later that much of her strength had been a frenzy she did not understand but that comes to understand her in a harrowing mad scene. Porter does not articulate Macbeth's early tug-of-war ambivalence, but, like many Macbeths, improves as the play develops. He shouts his "Tale / Told by an idiot" at a camera rising judgmentally above him. The nihilism echoes around his own feet, indicting him, not some idiot in the sky. When he threatens the Weird Sisters with "an eternall Curse," they cower in fear, recognizing that their reluctant pupil has become their master. The scene in England is excellent. John Alderton's Malcolm experiences a psychic struggle as he deals with his lack of "The King-becoming Graces," so that the scene functions as a disjunctive analogue to Macbeth's earlier debate with himself. Malcolm *expels* the temptations flesh is heir to. This excellent production deserves to be made commercially available.

Stephen Siddall raises some excellent questions regarding the choices productions make with this script, and thus for its audience: "Should one try," Siddall asks, "to judge what Shakespeare 'intended'—and inform that judgement with scholarship about his plays and audiences? Or is it better to acknowledge that the play lives only at the time of its performance, and to focus on those aspects which seem relevant to each particular decade?" (1988, 82). The great RSC production of the late 1970s, produced for television in 1979, remarks Siddall, "did not assume that people can feel and understand only what is close to their own lives" (83). It educated its audience to issues, as opposed to catering only to what they know. One of the more ridiculous premises of multiculturalism is that we can consume only our own culture. Banquo and Macbeth, Siddall continues, "have stepped from the brink of chaos back into the social order" (83), as in Hemingway's "Soldier's Home." Siddall adds that "it is dimly evident that such violence could exist outside the common good" (84). That was particularly true in McKellen's uneasy Macbeth—his uncertain, even suspicious eyes, and the trouble he had bringing his language forward from a throat that kept constricting. At the end of the banquet, Siddall notes, "It was the prospect of a long succession of these unfelt gestures that made [Lady Macbeth] shriek these final lines at them ['Stand not upon the order of your going, / But go at once']" (87).

The television production of the RSC *Macbeth* is a chiaroscuro version, in which, as Sean Day Lewis notes, "[t]he lines and faces are enough" (1979). The production "on stage was already in psychological close up," says Dennis Kennedy.

> The video director, Philip Casson, had simply to accent its imbedded mode of performance and bring the camera in close. . . . Television is . . . —by convention, if not inherently—suited to a drama of psychologizing, a characteristic that works well in the domestic environment where we normally see it. Since we are in a space resonant with the ordinary, we are less likely to accept representations of the extraordinary on the screen. (1994, 9)

This reduction to the psychological is inherent in the medium and has become conventional, as television directors have realized that the limited depth of the television screen erases a conceptual space that can accommodate the supernatural or elaborate special effects. Kennedy argues that the television production's final image—"Macduff's hands . . . holding two . . . daggers still smeared with the tyrant's blood . . . made the final moment darker and considerably more pessimistic than on stage" (10). Perhaps, but the stage version's final moments, in which an exhausted Malcolm (Roger Rees) could barely utter the obligatory syllables of thanks and reward, suggested that a great energy had left the world and that the energy consumed in defeating Macbeth had erased much hope of a new beginning. The stage version ended like *King Lear* and could hardly be called optimistic.

According to Herbert Kretzmet,

> *Macbeth* could have been written for television. . . . It is a play of close-up and shadow. Philip Casson's miraculous production . . . recognizes and exploits the claustrophobic nature of a play composed exclusively of nightmare and darkness. There are no sets to speak of, few props, no blasted heaths or battlefields. Sudden squares of light indicate doors opening elsewhere, unseen. Soliloquies and suspicions are confided directly into cameras which keep moving into unblinking, alarming mouth-to-eyebrow enlargements of the human face. . . . Television is honored by this *Macbeth*. (1979, 23)

One reason for the production's power is, Rothwell says, that it "disdains to conceal the uglier side of this ambitious couple" (1990, 165).

In a close-up production like this one, the acting has to be superb. It is so here, but no television production can capture the *immediacy* of a stage production, particularly one as intense and demanding as this greatest of recent *Macbeth*s.

The Sarah Caldwell production of 1981, with Maureen Anderman and Phil Anglim, is a good one. It is a televised version of a live performance and, like others of that genre, establishes some sense of the participation that being within the space the actors inhabit can evoke.

The feeling of a "theatrical event" is uneven, however. Unlike the Papp and Sherin *King Lear* of 1974, in which the audience becomes part of the texture of the production, this one shows the audience only, it seems, when a long shot must include the first few rows of the auditorium. Stage and television are uneasy with each other here. The television production uses titles between scenes, a "silent screen" technique that further confuses the generic issue and slows the pell-mell pace of this script.

But, as often with *Macbeth*, this one gets better as it goes along. Anglim is unconvincing at first, having studied his lines but not having settled on an acting style appropriate for stage or for television. The lines have no subtextual energy or intention working through them. Instead, as Maurice Charney and Arthur Ganz remark, Anglim is guilty of "thick, monotonous vocalizing. We were deprived of both the monster and the poet" (1982, 22). Jo McMurtry asserts that he is "dazed and ponderous" (1994, 124). But Anglim comes alive as he descends from his coronation for his chilling catechism of Banquo. Macbeth's final question is cued by Fleance's appearance. "Goes *Fleance* with you?" Macbeth's "Tomorrow" speech is a moving expression of grief, accented by a tear. At the end, he tosses his shield aside, crosses himself, and accepts Macduff's sword. He sighs "enough" after the fatal thrust. This Macbeth becomes more sympathetic as he becomes the victim of the dark world he chooses to explore.

Anderman's Lady is cold and commanding at the outset, but not overpowering. She does not pull the silly sexual stunts of the Ladys of Jane Lapotaire in the BBC production or Piper Laurie in the Bard version, who attempted to compensate for starveling scrawniness in the first instance and thick rotundity in the second. Anderman becomes more sensuous as the production develops, kissing Macbeth at the banquet, for example. Her mad scene, hair down around a chalky face, one hand stretched upward, is grippingly good. Since Macbeth seems a paltry object for her affections and ambitions, her early scenes with him are flat; however, the murder scene is splendid. Anderman shows that this is Lady Macbeth's scene—for all of his frenzy—by nerving herself up for the long journey back to Duncan's chamber, along an overhead catwalk, and by returning with almost hysterical good humor. "*I* have done it!" she seems to be saying. She convinces us that she had been in that room, as she did much later in her mad scene. The sense of failed relationship comes through strongly here, and remarkably, since Anglim and Anderman have not established a relationship at the outset, as Dench and McKellen do so vividly in the Thames version.

Of several good moments in this production, a few are worth noting: Fleance playing at soldier with his father's sword; Macbeth's sudden and reluctant knee as Duncan names Malcolm Prince of Cumberland; Lady Macbeth's *not* sitting at the banquet table, but "keep[ing] her state," as the line says she does; Macbeth's exit from the upstage banquet for Duncan and Lady Macbeth's pursuit a moment later; their return in resolution to kill their happy guest; Banquo's first appearance as a silver-gray ghost along the catwalk that rides over the stage; the later line of spectral kings along the same slender bridge, a frame of the future that absorbs and dominates mere Macbeth; the Weird Sisters' delight at Macbeth's threat to curse them eternally. "The curse is on *you!*" they imply.

The scene in England is splendid, the point being that Scotland, represented by Macduff, does not know Malcolm. Nor is Malcolm certain that Scotland *wants* "the King-becoming Graces." He will not return until Macduff confirms the kingdom's need for the spiritual opposite of Macbeth. Like Macduff, we must learn who this prince and future king is if we are to believe in the crusade he leads. Malcolm's final speech is potently rendered from the commanding position of the catwalk, now a bridge to the future.

I question the production on a point or two. The Weird Sisters are two women and a soldier. They have no beards, but Banquo's line is there. What do directors think the line means?—that Banquo is hallucinating? While the Sisters and their brother sing some of their opening, this Verdian effect is not carried through by Caldwell, whose genre is opera. Why did she cut the ingredients of the Sisters' stew later? *That* would have made for a little night music! Macbeth "wakes up" at the banquet after the Ghost's second visitation and finds himself standing on his own festive board. He jumps off and gets a laugh from the outer audience, even as the inner observers remain appalled. It is a silly piece of business. The Porter's soliloquy is cut. One wonders why. It would have gotten some laughs, of course, from a New York audience, but it might also have been a haunting reminder of ultimate issues on this huge, dark stage. Otherwise, this remains a solid production.

The Bard production of 1981, directed by A. Allan Seidelman, with Jeremy Brett and Piper Laurie, is not worth the waste of a twig of Birnam Wood. (See Coursen 1992, 210–12, and Schlueter, who calls it "indefensible on all accounts" [1988, 4].)

The BBC production of 1982, directed by Jack Gold, with Nicol Williamson and Jane Lapotaire received mixed reviews. David Richards regards it as "one of the strongest offerings in this series to date. . . . Both lead performances have a lot of the panting beast in them" (1983, 23). Arthur Ungar notes that it "may be one of the . . . greatest versions of *Macbeth*. It would be hard to imagine a more savage and driven, a more naive and self-deceived, a more conscience-stricken and nearly understandable Macbeth than . . . Williamson's" (1983, 17). Michael Mullin finds it "superbly acted." Williamson "searches his way through lines, wringing from them new readings in every speech. To complain that his speech is sometimes slurred and often far from musical is to fault an actor who seems to be actually experiencing the struggles that the words convey." Lapotaire's "snug gown and feline grace make her seductive power over Macbeth easily credible. . . . Her lack of foresight and feeling make a strong contrast to Macbeth's overwrought personality, and, as he hardens himself to evil, her collapse suggests his greater strength." The production "will reward viewing again and again" (1984, 2). Kenneth Rothwell commends the leads for their "sheer dynamism and energy" (1990, 167).

According to Peter Ackroyd, however, "The closer the camera came to the Macbeths the more murky and formless they become" (1983). This is to contrast the production with the Thames version. G. M. Pearce asserts that "Williamson assumed a strangled voice interspersed with rasping breathing which may have conveyed Macbeth's anguish effectively, but murdered most of the poetry" (1984, 26). McMurtry calls Williamson "agonized and often incoherent" (1994, 124). Peter Kemp agrees:

> Williamson employs two different vocal registers . . . a ringing, resonant tone for public utterance, and a hoarse, introverted mutter for private disturbance. Increasingly exaggerated, this split-level approach eventually breaks up the character, as well as the sense of numerous lines. In particular,

Macbeth's final scenes—all ogreish howls and rapid simian gibber—are drastically reduced to sound and fury, signifying nothing.

Lapotaire is

> most suited to mannered comedy [and] gives a fatally lightweight performance. . . . Macbeth's prediction that his letter "will make joyful my wife's hearing" can seldom have received more striking vindication. Clutching the exciting scrap of parchment to her on a couch, panting, writhing, splay-legged and kneading her "woman's breasts," Lapotaire gasps out "Unsex me here" in the throes of an orgasm. Only in the sleep-walking scene does she turn her ingenuity to bringing out what's in the play instead of super-imposing things alien to it: in a neatly chilling touch, she uses the conventional out-stretched-arms posture of the sleep-walker to portray Lady Macbeth pushing her rigid, tainted hands as far from her as possible. (1983, 683)

I find the production barely adequate. Williamson's voice, varying from a timorous tadpole of a whisper to a bullfrog croak, as if he had contacted croup in the murk of the studio, was not that of someone *experiencing* the words for the first time but of an actor determined to read the lines as they had never been read before. The lines certainly offer variations in emphasis for an actor to discover and exploit, but they do have a rhythm, and that rhythm supports their sense. To say, "There would have been time for such a word tomorrow" makes sense, I suppose, if Macbeth is saying that he would have had time to mourn *after* the battle, but it makes nonsense of the rest of the line of which the first "Tomorrow" is also the first word. Why Lapotaire is cast in roles requiring a field of sexual energy—Cleopatra and Lady Macbeth—is beyond me.

The apparitions are products of Macbeth's fevered imagination, but it takes stronger acting than Williamson's to convince us that the numina are there. It may be, however, that Williamson's performance is so overwrought that we wonder why he is not hallucinating constantly.

At the end, Fleance comes in from somewhere to stare at Malcolm and the Thanes Malcolm has just promoted and who has just given him a *collaudatio* as "King of Scotland." Why? This confusing ambiguity is not in the script. This production had not prepared us for it. The medium cannot accommodate it. Television insists on normalization.

The murder of Lady Macduff and her children is chillingly powerful in this production. That scene as rendered here is worth careful study in contrast to other versions on film and television.

A second, very pedestrian Thames television version of 1988 starred Barbara Leigh Hunt and Michael Jayston. It is an unpretentious, low-budget affair, not nearly as absorbing or as disturbing as the production of 1979. McMurtry describes Jayston's Macbeth as "withdrawn and cold," while Leigh Hunt's Lady "has a careworn, fragile face with large eyes. . . . Her sleepwalking scene is absorbing'' as she alternates between ''the voices she has used throughout the play'' (1994, 128).

The animated version (1992), abridged by Leon Garfield and illustrated by Nicolai Serebriakov, is melodramatic and simplistic, as any half-hour adaptation would tend to be, but at times moving. The script resists reduction to a cartoon. This production benefits from the vivid readings of Brian Cox and Zoe Wana- maker in the lead roles. A lot of the language *is* there, though one misses Macbeth's echo of the Weird Sisters and their ''A deed without a name.'' The Porter is gone—he does not fit into the chiaroscuro style. The line of kings is also deleted. Unfortunately, the production ends with Macbeth's being blinded by a vision of Lady Macduff and her children—whom he had *not* seen, having murdered them by proxy—and thus being beheaded by Macduff, and then with the Old Man's wishing ''God's benison'' upon us. The illustrated text that ac- companies the cassette ends more conventionally, with Macbeth's ''hold enough!'' and a description of his head on Macduff's sword. This combination of tape and booklet provides a valid introduction to the story, but only for students who will then read the play or see more complete productions of it.

A solid amateur version, produced in 1994, was made from the Bob Jones University stage production of late 1993 in the giant Rodehever Auditorium in Greenville, South Carolina, directed by Janie and William McCauley, and fea- turing Beneth Jones and her husband, Bob Jones III. See my review of the stage production (Coursen 1994, 17–18).

Works Cited

Ackroyd, Peter. 1983. Review of BBC-TV *Macbeth*. *Times* 7 November, p. 38.

Barnet, Sylvan, ed. 1987. *Macbeth*. New York: Signet.

Charney, Maurice, and Arthur Ganz. 1982. ''Shakespeare in New York City.'' *Shake- speare Quarterly* 33, no. 2 (Summer): 218–21.

Coursen, H. R. 1989. ''Special Effects on Television.'' *Shakespeare on Film* 14, no. 1 (Winter): 8.

———. 1992. *Performance as Interpretation*. Cranbury, N.J.: Associated University Presses.

———. 1994. ''The Bob Jones *Macbeth*.'' *Shakespeare Bulletin* 12 (Spring): 17.

———. 1995. *Reading Shakespeare on Stage*. Cranbury, N.J.: Associated University Presses.

Dessen, Alan. 1986. ''The Supernatural on Television.'' *Shakespeare on Film* 11, no. 1 (December): 1, 8.

Gould, Jack. 1949. Review of *Macbeth*. *New York Times*, 22 May, p. 30.

———. 1951. Review of *Macbeth*. *New York Times*, 24 October, p. 27.

———. 1954. Review of ''Adaptation of 'Macbeth' Shown on N.B.C.'' *New York Times*, 29 November, p. 31.

Griffin, Alice. 1955. ''Shakespeare on Screen.'' *Shakespeare Quarterly* 6 (Winter): 63– 72.

Jorgens, Jack. 1977. *Shakespeare on Film*. Bloomington: Indiana University Press.

Kemp, Peter. 1983. "Schizoid Schemers." *Times Literary Supplement* (18 November): 683.

Kennedy, Dennis. 1994. "Shakespeare Played Small." *Shakespeare Survey* 47: 1–14.

Kliman, Bernice W. 1982. "The Setting in Early Television: Maurice Evans's Television Productions." In *Shakespeare and the Arts*. Edited by Cecile W. Cary and Henry S. Limouze. Lanham, Md.: University Press of America.

Kretznet, Herbert. 1979. Review of Nunn *Macbeth. Daily Mail* (London), 5 January, p. 23.

Lewis, Sean D. 1979. Review of Nunn *Macbeth. Daily Telegraph* (London), 6 January, p. 29.

McMurtry, Jo. 1994. *Shakespeare Films in the Classroom*. Hamden, Conn.: Archon.

Mullin, Michael. 1984. "The BBC-TV *Macbeth*." *Shakespeare on Film* 9, no. 1 (December): 1–6.

Pearce, G. M. 1984. Review. *Cahiers Elisabethains* 26 (April): 26.

Richards, David. 1983. Review of BBC-TV *Macbeth. Washington Post*, 17 October, p. 23.

Rothwell, Kenneth, and Annabelle H. Melzer. 1990. *Shakespeare on Screen: An International Filmography and Videography*. New York: Neil-Schuman.

Schlueter, June. 1988. "Bad Shakespeare in the Classroom." *Shakespeare on Film* 13, no. 1 (December): 4–8.

Siddall, Stephen. 1988. "Ceremony in *Macbeth*." In *Macbeth*. Edited by Linda Cookson and Bryan Loughrey. London: Longman.

Ungar, Arthur. 1983. "The BBC-TV *Macbeth*." *Christian Science Monitor*, 17 October, p. 17.

SELECTED BIBLIOGRAPHY

Adelman, Janet. 1987. " 'Born of Woman': Fantasies of Maternal Power in *Macbeth*."
In *Cannibals, Witches, and Divorce: Estranging the Renaissance*. Edited by Marjorie Garber. Baltimore: Johns Hopkins University Press.

Andrews, John, ed. 1993. *Macbeth*. London: J. M. Dent.

Bartholomeusz, Dennis. 1969. *'Macbeth' and the Players*. Cambridge: Cambridge University Press.

Battenhouse, Roy W., ed. 1994. *Shakespeare's Christian Dimension: An Anthology of Commentary*. Bloomington: Indiana University Press.

Bayley, John. 1981. *Shakespeare and Tragedy*. London: Routledge and Kegan Paul.

Benham, William, ed. 1911. *The Prayer Book of Queen Elizabeth: 1599*. Edinburgh: John Grant.

Berger, Harry, Jr. 1980. "The Early Scenes of *Macbeth*: A Preface to a New Interpretation." *English Literary History* 47 (Spring): 49–57.

Bergeron, David. 1993. "The King James Version of *Macbeth*." In *Shakespeare Set Free*. Edited by Peggy O'Brien. New York: Washington Square Press.

Berry, Lloyd, ed. 1969. *The Geneva Bible*. Madison: University of Wisconsin Press.

Booth, Stephen. 1983. *'King Lear,' 'Macbeth,' Indefinition and Tragedy*. New Haven, Conn.: Yale University Press.

Bradley, A. C. 1904. *Shakespearean Tragedy*. London: Macmillan.

Brooke, Nicholas, ed. 1990. *Macbeth*. Oxford: Oxford University Press.

Brooks, Cleanth. 1947. "The Naked Babe and the Cloak of Manliness." In *The Well Wrought Urn*. New York: Harcourt, Brace.

Brown, Arthur C. L., ed. 1913. *Macbeth*. New York: Macmillan.

Brown, John Russell, ed. 1963. *Macbeth*. Great Neck, N.Y.: Barron's.

———, ed. 1982. *Focus on 'Macbeth.'* London: Routledge and Kegan Paul.

———, ed. 1996. *Macbeth*. New York: Applause Books.

Bullough, Geoffrey. 1973. *Narrative and Dramatic Sources of Shakespeare*. Vol. 7. London: Routledge and Kegan Paul.

Bulman, James, and H. R. Coursen, eds. 1988. *Shakespeare on Television*. Hanover, N.H.: University of New England Press.

Coleridge, S. T. 1960. *Shakespearean Criticism.* Edited by Thomas M. Raysor. New York: E. P. Dutton.

Cookson, Linda, and Bryan Loughrey, eds. *Macbeth.* London: Longman.

Coursen, H. R. 1967. "In Deepest Consequence: *Macbeth.*" *Shakespeare Quarterly* 18, no. 4 (Autumn): 375–88.

————. 1976. *Christian Ritual and the World of Shakespeare's Tragedies.* Cranbury, N.J.: Associated University Presses.

————. 1979. "Agreeing with Dr. Johnson." *Ariel* 10, no. 2 (April): 33–42.

————. 1986. *The Compensatory Psyche: A Jungian Approach to Shakespeare.* Lanham, Md.: University Press of America.

————. 1988. " 'Morphic Resonance' in Shakespeare's Plays." *Shakespeare Bulletin* 6, no. 2 (March/April): 5–8.

————. 1995. *Reading Shakespeare on Stage.* Cranbury, N.J.: Associated University Presses.

Curry, Walter C. 1937. *Shakespeare's Philosophical Patterns.* Baton Rouge: Louisiana University Press.

David, Richard. 1978. *Shakespeare in the Theatre.* Cambridge: Cambridge University Press.

Davies, Anthony. 1988. *Filming Shakespeare's Plays: The Adaptations of Laurence Olivier, Orson Welles, Peter Brook, and Akira Kurosawa.* Cambridge: Cambridge University Press.

Davies, Anthony, and Stanley Wells, eds. 1994. *Shakespeare and the Moving Image.* Cambridge: Cambridge University Press.

Dawson, Anthony. 1996. "Performance and Participation: Desdemona, Foucault, and the Actor's Body." In *Shakespeare, Theory, and Performance.* Edited by James Bulman. London: Metheun.

Dean, Leonard F., ed. 1967. *Shakespeare: Modern Essays in Criticism.* New York: Oxford Galaxy.

De Quincey, Thomas. 1823. "On the Knocking at the Gate in 'Macbeth.' " *London Magazine* (October). Reprinted in Paul N. Siegel, ed. 1964. *His Infinite Variety.* Philadelphia: J. B. Lippincott, 322–27.

Diehl, Huston. 1983. "Horrid Image, Sorry Sight, Fatal Vision: The Visual Rhetoric of *Macbeth.*" *Shakespeare Studies* 16: 191–204.

Donaldson, Peter. 1990. *Shakespearean Films/Shakespearean Directors.* Boston: Unwin Hyman.

Doran, Madeleine. 1983. "The *Macbeth* Music." *Shakespeare Studies* 16: 153–74.

Dowden, Edward. 1872. *Shakespeare: A Critical Study of His Mind and Art.* Reprint. New York: Capricorn, 1962.

Eagleton, Terry. 1967. *Shakespeare and Society.* New York: Schocken Books.

Farnham, Willard. 1973. *Shakespeare's Tragic Frontier: The World of His Final Tragedies.* Oxford: Basil Blackwell and Mott.

Fawkner, H. W. 1990. *Deconstructing 'Macbeth': The Hyperontological View.* Cranbury, N.J.: Associated University Presses.

Foakes, R. A., ed. 1995. *Macbeth.* New York: Applause Books.

Foucault, Michel. 1971. *L'Order du discours.* Paris: Etudes XX Siecle.

Frye, Northrop. 1961. "The Argument of Comedy." In *Shakespeare: Modern Essays in Criticism.* Edited by Leonard F. Dean. New York: Oxford Galaxy.

Frye, R. M. 1963. *Shakespeare and Christian Doctrine*. Princeton, N.J.: Princeton University Press.

———. 1982. *Shakespeare: The Art of the Dramatist*. London: George Allen and Unwin.

Furness, Horace H., Jr., ed. 1873. Variorum *Macbeth*. 1904 edition. Philadelphia: J. B. Lippincott. Reprint. New York: Dover, 1963.

Garber, Marjorie. 1987. *Shakespeare's Ghost Writers: Literature as Uncanny Casuality*. London: Metheun.

Gardner, Helen. 1959. *The Business of Criticism*. Oxford: Oxford University Press.

Granville-Barker, Harley. 1995. *Preface to "Macbeth."* Portsmouth, N.H.: Heineman.

Harbage, Alfred. 1963. *William Shakespeare: A Reader's Guide*. New York: Noonday.

———. 1964. *Shakespeare: The Tragedies*. Englewood Cliffs: N.J.: Prentice-Hall Spectrum.

Hawkes, Terrence, ed. 1977. *Twentieth Century Interpretations of 'Macbeth.'* Englewood Cliffs, N.J.: Prentice-Hall.

Hazlitt, William. 1930. *Complete Works*. Vol. 4. Edited by P. P. Howe. London: Chatto & Windus.

Holloway, John. 1961. *The Story of the Night*. Lincoln: University of Nebraska Press.

Houseman, John. 1972. *Run-Through*. New York: Simon and Schuster.

Johnson, Samuel. 1960. *Samuel Johnson on Shakespeare*. Edited by W. K. Wimsatt. New York: Hill and Wang.

Jorgens, Jack. 1977. *Shakespeare on Film*. Bloomington: Indiana University Press.

Jorgensen, Paul A. 1971. *Our Naked Frailties*. Berkeley: University of California Press.

Kahn, Coppelia. 1981. *Man's Estate: Masculine Identity in Shakespeare*. Berkeley: University of California Press.

Kennedy, Dennis. 1993. *Looking at Shakespeare: A Visual History of Twentieth-Century Performance*. Cambridge: Cambridge University Press.

Kernan, Alvin. 1970. *Modern Shakespearean Criticism*. New York: Harcourt, Brace, and World.

———. 1974. "This Goodly Frame the Stage: The Interior Theater of the Imagination in English Renaissance Drama." *Shakespeare Quarterly* 24, no. 1 (Winter): 1–15.

Kettle, Arnold, ed. *Shakespeare in a Changing World*. New York: New World.

Kimbrough, Robert. 1983. "Macbeth as Prisoner of Gender." *Shakespeare Studies* 16: 175–90. A revised version of this article appears as Chapter 9, "Myth and Countermyth in *Macbeth*" in *Shakespeare and the Art of Human Kindness*. Atlantic Highlands, N.J.: Humanities Press International, 1990.

Kittredge, G. L. 1929. *Witchcraft in Old and New England*. Cambridge, Mass.: Harvard University Press.

———, ed. 1939. *Macbeth*. Boston: Ginn and Company.

Klein, Joan Larsen. 1980. "Lady Macbeth: 'Infirm of Purpose.' " In *The Woman's Part: Feminist Criticism of Shakespeare*. Edited by Carol Ruth Swift Lenz, Gayle Greene, and Carol Thomas Neely. Urbana: University of Illinois Press.

Kliman, Bernice W., ed. 1992. *'Macbeth': Shakespeare in Performance*. Manchester, England: Manchester University Press.

Knight, G. Wilson. 1931. *The Imperial Theme*. Oxford: Oxford University Press.

———. 1953. *The Shakespearean Tempest*. London: Metheun.

———. 1957. *The Wheel of Fire*. New York: Meridian.

Knights, L. C. 1947. *Explorations*. London: Chatto and Windus.

———. 1959. *Some Shakespearean Themes*. London: Chatto and Windus.

Leech, Clifford, ed. 1965. *Shakespeare: The Tragedies*. Chicago: University of Chicago Press.

Long, Michael, ed. 1989. *Macbeth*. Boston: Twayne.

Milward, Peter. 1987. *Biblical Influences in Shakespeare's Tragedies*. Bloomington: Indiana University Press.

Moelwyn, Merchant W. 1966. "His Fiend-Like Queen." *Shakespeare Survey* 19: 75–81.

Muir, Kenneth, ed. 1964. *Macbeth*. London: Metheun.

———. 1977. *The Sources of Shakespeare's Plays*. Vol. 2. London: Methuen.

Mullin, Michael. 1973. "*Macbeth* on Film." *Literature/Film Quarterly* 9, no. 1 (December): 2.

———. 1976. *'Macbeth' Onstage: An Annotated Facsimile of Glen Byam Shaw's 1955 Promptbook*. Columbia: University of Missouri Press.

Murry, J. M. 1936. *Shakespeare*. London: Society of Authors.

Nevo, Ruth. 1972. *Tragic Form in Shakespeare*. Princeton, N.J.: Princeton University Press.

O'Rourke, James L. 1993. "The Subversive Metaphysics of *Macbeth*." *Shakespeare Studies* 21: 213–27.

Parsons, Keith, and Pamela Mason. 1995. *Shakespeare in Performance*. London: Salamander.

Paul, Henry N. 1950. *The Royal Play of Macbeth*. New York: Macmillan.

Rabkin, Norman. 1981. *Shakespeare and the Problem of Meaning*. Chicago: University of Chicago Press.

Rickey, Mary Ellen, and Thomas B. Stroup, eds. 1966. *Certaine Sermons and Homilies*. 1623 ed. Gainesville Fla.: Scholar's Facsimiles.

Rosenberg, Marvin. 1978. *The Masks of Macbeth*. Cranbury, N.J.: Associated University Presses.

———. 1982. "Macbeth and Lady Macbeth in the Eighteenth and Nineteenth Centuries." In *Focus on 'Macbeth.'* Edited by John Russell Brown. London: Routledge and Kegan Paul.

Rothwell, Kenneth, and Annabelle H. Melzer. 1990. *Shakespeare on Screen: An International Filmography and Videography*. New York: Neal-Schuman.

Sanders, Wilbur. 1968. *The Dramatist and the Received Idea*. Cambridge: Cambridge University Press.

Schoenbaum, Samuel, ed. 1991. *'Macbeth': Critical Essays*. New York: Garland.

Scott, William O. 1986. "Macbeth's—and Our—Self-Equivocations." *Shakespeare Quarterly* 37, no. 2 (Summer): 160–74.

Shaheen, Naseeb. 1987. *Biblical References in Shakespeare's Tragedies*. Newark: Delaware University Press.

Sinfield, Alan. 1986. "*Macbeth*: History, Ideology and Intellectuals." *Critical Quarterly* 28 (Spring): 63–77.

Skovmand, Michael, ed. 1995. *Screen Shakespeare*. Aarhus, Denmark: Aarhus University Press.

Smith, D. Nichol. 1936. *Shakespeare Criticism*. Oxford: Oxford University Press.

Snyder, Susan. 1992. "*Macbeth*: A Modern Perspective." In *Macbeth*. Edited by Barbara Mowat and Paul Werstein. New York: Washington Square Press.

Spencer, Theodore. 1961. *Shakespeare and the Nature of Man*. New York: Macmillan.

Sprague, Arthur C. 1953. *Shakespearean Players and Performances*. Cambridge, Mass.: Harvard University Press.

Stewart, J.I.M. 1949. "Steep Tragic Contrast in *Macbeth*." In *Character and Motive in Shakespeare: Some Recent Appraisals*. London: Longman, Green.

Stoll, E. E. 1933. *Art and Artifice in Shakespeare*. Cambridge: Cambridge University Press.

Styan, John. 1967. *Shakespeare's Stagecraft*. Cambridge: Cambridge University Press.

Traversi, Derek. 1956. *An Approach to Shakespeare*. Garden City, N.Y.: Doubleday Anchor.

Trewin, J. C. 1978. *Going to Shakespeare*. London: Allen and Unwin.

Turner, John, ed. 1992. *Macbeth*. Buckingham: Open University Press.

Veeser, H. Aram, ed. 1989. *The New Historicism*. London: Routledge.

Vickers, Brian. 1993. *Appropriating Shakespeare*. New Haven, Conn.: Yale University Press.

Waith, Eugene. 1950. "Manhood and Valor in Two Shakespearean Tragedies." *English Literary History* 17 (Fall): 265–68.

Waller, Gary. 1988. "Decentering the Bard: The BBC-TV Shakespeare and Some Implications for Teaching." In *Shakespeare on Television*. Edited by James Bulman and H. R. Coursen. Hanover, N.H.: University of New England Press.

Watkins, Ronald. 1950. *On Producing Shakespeare*. London: M. Joseph.

Watkins, Ronald, and Jeremy Lemmon. 1964. *Macbeth*. Illustrated by Maurice Percival. Oxford: Oxford University Press.

———. 1974. *In Shakespeare's Playhouse*. Totowa, N.J.: Rowman and Littlefield.

Webster, Margaret. 1957. *Shakespeare without Tears*. New York: Fawcett Premier.

West, Robert. 1968. *Shakespeare and the Outer Mystery*. Lexington: University of Kentucky Press.

Whitmore, C. E. 1915. *The Supernatural in Tragedy*. Cambridge: Cambridge University Press.

Williams, Gordon. 1985. *'Macbeth': Text & Performance*. London: Macmillan.

Wills, Gary. 1995. *Witches and Jesuits*. Oxford: Oxford University Press.

Wilson, J. Dover, ed. 1947. *Macbeth*. Cambridge: Cambridge University Press.

Worthen, William. 1996. "Staging Shakespeare: Acting, Authority, and the Rhetoric of Performance." In *Shakespeare, Theory, and Performance*. Edited by James Bulman. London: Metheun.

Zitner, Sheldon. 1981. "Wooden O's in Plastic Boxes: Shakespeare and Television." *University of Toronto Quarterly* 51 (Fall): 1–12.

INDEX

Abel, Walter, 189
Abercrombie, Lascelles, 3
Ackroyd, Peter, 194
ACTER (A Center for Theater Research), 1, 143, 173–77
Adams, J. Q., 3, 4–5, 42–43
Adelman, Janet, 106–7
Adler, Alfred, 100
Alderton, John, 190
Alger, W. A., 36
Anderman, Maureen, 192, 193
Anderson, Judith, 189
Anderson, Tommy, 157
Andrewes, Lancelot, 14
Andrews, John, 7–9, 37, 62, 63, 68, 83, 174
Anglim, Phil, 192–93
Annis, Francesca, 184
Antony and Cleopatra, 2, 11–14, 23, 35, 47, 83, 109, 190, 195
Archimedes, 56
Arditti, Michael, 165, 166
Arendt, Hannah, 51
Aristotle, 65, 135, 166
Arminianism, 53
Armstrong, Gareth, 174, 176
As You Like It, 114
Astor Place Opera House, 156
Atkins, Eileen, 190

Auden, W. H., 79
Augustine, Saint, 68, 101, 129

Bainter, Fay, 5
Ball, Robert H., 180
Barnet, Sylvan, 4, 142, 143, 145, 147, 150, 154, 155, 181, 183, 184, 189
Barroll, J. L., 2
Barron, David, B., 108–9
Bartholomeusz, Dennis, 145, 150
Barton, John, 43
Battenhouse, Roy W., 67
Bayley, John, 123
Beaumont, Francis, 143
Bellamy, Ralph, 189
Beowulf, 134
Berger, Harry, Jr., 107, 143
Berger, Sarah, 174–75
Bergeron, David, 22
Berlin, Normand, 185
Bernard, Saint, 47, 56, 65, 101, 129
Bernardete, José, 112
Berry, Lloyd, 53
Bethel, S. L., 90
Beylie, Claude, 181–82
Billington, Michael, 161, 164, 165
Birenbaum, Harvey, 102
Bob Jones University, 196
Bodenstedt, H., 36

About the Author

H. R. COURSEN teaches at the University of Maine (Augusta). He is the author of more than forty books, and his many articles have appeared in journals such as *Studies in English Literature*, *Studies in Philology*, *Shakespeare Quarterly*, *Shakespeare Studies*, and *Shakespeare Bulletin*.

Greenwood Guides to Shakespeare

Henry V: A Guide to the Play
Joan Lord Hall

ISBN 0-313-30047-X

EAN

9 780313 300479

HARDCOVER BAR CODE

90000>